By Noon Prayer

By Noon Prayer

The Rhythm of Islam

Fadwa El Guindi

BERG
Oxford • New York

First published in 2008 by
Berg
Editorial offices:
1st Floor, Angel Court, 81 St Clements Street, Oxford, OX4 1AW, UK
175 Fifth Avenue, New York, NY 10010, USA

Berg is the imprint of Oxford International Publishers Ltd.

Library of Congress Cataloguing-in-Publication Data
El Guindi, Fadwa.
By noon prayer : the rhythm of Islam / Fadwa El Guindi.
p. cm.
Includes bibliographical references (p.) and index.
ISBN-13: 978-1-84520-096-1 (cloth)
ISBN-10: 1-84520-096-9 (cloth)
ISBN-13: 978-1-84520-097-8 (pbk.)
ISBN-10: 1-84520-097-7 (pbk.)
1. Islam—Essence, genius, nature. 2. Rhythm—Religious aspects—Islam. 3. Time—Religious aspects—Islam. 4. Prayer—Islam. 5. Anthropology of religion—Islamic countries. I. Title.

BP163.E44 2008
297.3'6—dc22 2008023633

British Library Cataloguing-in-Publication Data
A catalogue record for this book is available from the British Library.

ISBN 978 1 84520 096 1 (Cloth)

ISBN 978 1 84520 097 8 (Paper)

Typeset by Avocet Typeset, Chilton, Aylesbury, Bucks
Printed in the United Kingdom by Biddles Ltd, King's Lynn

www.bergpublishers.com

Dedication

I dedicate this book to the memory of my late parents, my father and mother, who died in Cairo, Egypt, while I was in the United States. My father died on January 16, 2001, the month of and hours after the time of birth in the United States (California) of my son Khalid in 1974. My mother died a little over a year later on March 5, 2002, the month in which my daughter Magda was born in 1970 also in the United States (Texas). Perhaps there are metaphysical connections of life and death, this world and other worlds, living space and sacred space, homeland of birth and adopted home of choice?

My father's death and my deeply felt desire to have been at his side and at his burial inspired the title of this work, *By Noon Prayer*. After receiving the news by telephone of my father's death, I pleaded with the family for a delay of his burial until my arrival. The response was firm: "this is Islamic burial; prayer for the dead has to be by noon prayer. You cannot possibly make it in time even by a Concorde." The body was to be cleansed, shrouded, and in the mosque for the prayer of the dead by noon prayer in preparation for burial in the family's burial grounds before sundown.

When my mother passed away and I was again informed by a long distance call from Cairo, my pain persuaded family members to postpone burial twenty-four hours to allow for my immediate travel to Cairo. I was grateful that I was able to be at my mother's burial after warmly and affectionately cleansing her body myself according to Islamic precepts, and shrouding her in preparation for Islamic burial. I also performed the noon prayer for the dead in the coffin's presence in the mosque, surrounded by family and friends, then painfully bid her the last farewell as her body was placed alongside my father's at the family burial grounds. I still feel the sensation of gliding the warm sudsy loofah over her entire body and braiding her long hair as I sobbed and kissed her on her cold cheek, slightly warmed by the cleansing water and the intensity of emotion.

In anthropological terms, the expression "by noon prayer" stands for a core aspect of a unique rhythm that is characteristically Islamic – a rhythm that expresses and shapes the temporal and spatial worlds, interweaving private and public, secular and religious, ordinary and sacred, life and death. The rhythm never leaves the homeland.

Los Angeles, California
July 23, 2002

Contents

Figures and Tables

Figures

Tables

Preface

This book promises a new understanding of the dynamics of Islam – its conceptual fundamentals, roots and origins, doctrine and regenerative revitalization. Restating the Five Pillars is a recurrent reminder of the cornerstones of Islam: *shahada* (declaration of faith), *salat* (prayer), *sawm* (fasting), *zakat* (almsgiving and charity), and *hajj* (pilgrimage), but stopping there reduces a rich, multilayered, and nuanced cultural system into clinical prescriptions and rites. A new analysis can reveal its richness and counter some falsehoods woven by propaganda machinery (now called public diplomacy).

Provocations against Muslims come from many directions. Recently, the Danish newspaper *Jyllands-Posten* published a series of notorious cartoons defaming the Prophet of Islam;[1] followed by the defamation of Islam itself in the Pope's remarks; and these events were preceded by state action banning headscarves in France (see discussion on this in Chapters 3 and 6) followed by other European nations – all defended in the name of freedom of expression, secularism, democracy, or intellectual and moral humanism. The irony of such argument is in the parallel Western promises of freedom and democracy while simultaneously engaging in immoral brutalities, exploitation of resources, and shameful torture dramas inflicted in public view on Arabs/Muslims. Massacres are sadistically committed against Palestinians. Such violence fuels stronger resistance to occupation in Palestine, Afghanistan, Lebanon, and Iraq, and a more steadfast Islamic resistance gone global and diffuse.[2] In that confrontational context, Islam is expediently broken into a good Islam "without fangs" and a bad Islam "with horns," and a reification of division into Shi'a and Sunni.

Instead of atomizing, dichotomizing, or fragmenting Islam, this monograph looks analytically at "a one Islam,"[3] an integrative whole and a unified and coherent phenomenon that is creative, generative, flexible, and dynamic. To explore this majestic phenomenon, a study cannot remain confined within the canons of one discipline. It has to draw upon multiple sources and cross-disciplinary bodies of knowledge. Building on insights deriving from the author's primary field research and original anthropological observations over decades, this analysis integrates many sources and methodologies: cross-cultural comparisons, ethnographic descriptions, fieldwork-derived data, and an analytic perspective that would be applied to historical information, visual materials, Arabic poetry, Islamic textual knowledge from the Qur'an to the Hadith to qur'anic exegesis, and segments from biblical, Egyptological, and Egyptian papyrus texts. This methodological approach[4] is similar to the one developed in my earlier broadly conceived work: *Veil: Modesty, Privacy and Resistance*. Throughout such a research project, anthropology remains the methodological and theoretical anchor holding together different elements. This multiplicity of data sources and bodies of knowledge generates data, context, and perspective for understanding time and space in Islamic life.

By Noon Prayer is about innovation, the innovation of Islam, by Islam and in Islam. In its emergence, Islam brought into its fold individuals and groups from the margins of power and wealth, embracing multiple faiths and transcending tribal identity. These elements cohesively enter the construction of a sociocultural, multicultural community founded on an already existing sociopolitical base, but with a distinct morality. This distinct morality is founded on an idea that was revealed in the local geography of the seventh-century, marked by identities of tribe and a developed system of international trade which it strove to reform and transform. But, as in all innovations, as it widened its horizons, refined its meanings, and broadened its scope, it still had to build on some existing patterns. Inherent in it is a timeless universality of philosophy that integrates culture with the natural universe, a morality that insists on reform of thought and action. Its appeal is shown to be unbounded by borders.

A current shift in analysis to a framework called complexity, which is now widely used in the life and cognitive sciences, combines qualities of holism, emergence, and nonlinearity. This informs the development of a new paradigm presented in Chapter 6, which aims to illuminate aspects of innovation leading to and underlying Islam. As theoretical physicist Fritjof Capra explains, "[t]he view of living system as self-organizing networks whose components are all interconnected and interdependent has been expressed repeatedly, in one way or another, throughout the history of philosophy and science. However, detailed models of self-organizing systems could be formulated only very recently when new mathematical tools became available that allowed scientists to model the nonlinear interconnectedness characteristic of networks" (1996: 112). Capra stresses how discovery of this new "mathematics of complexity" is "increasingly being recognized as one of the most important events in twentieth-century science" (112).

Within this framework, analysis shifts from "objects to relationships, from quantity to quality, from substance to patterns" (113). This is the new direction in social science as well. Notions of pattern and ecology traced to Gregory Bateson (Bateson 1972, 1979) are revalidated by Capra, who draws on "deep ecology" for a deeper and broader perspective, in which life is conceptualized as a web of nested interconnections and embeddedness. Following premises of "deep ecology," a theory of Islamic rhythm is developed that incorporates the three cultural qualities of *qudsiyya* (sacred), *khususiyya* (privacy), *jama'iyya* (collectivity).

By synthesizing these three elements into one unified theory the analysis can reveal the rhythm of Islam.

The subject of this book is Islam and its particular rhythm, which manifests itself in social life consistently with cultural notions of time and space. The challenge for any study of Islam is to capture its "feel" or its "pulse" as it were, and the fluidity and interweaving qualities that together form a process that deeply provides its adherents with simultaneous serenity, vitality, and strength. The comparative base extends the analysis to other cultural systems and social groups whenever such studies adequately weave a wider and more colorful tapestry of visions, religions, ideologies, and cultures against which Islam is better understood.

By Noon Prayer: The Rhythm of Islam, the title of this book, refers to a special quality of Islam that interweaves space and time in a specific rhythm embedded in the very essence of the culture. To understand this rhythm, my analysis follows a nonlinearized path identifying relational qualities of life as they intersect with notions of space and time, manifesting their transformationality onto nature and culture. Revealing this quality takes us straight to the heart of Islam's rhythm – a rhythm that Muslim people, perhaps uniquely I might add, feel, experience, live by, think with, and internalize.

The book is organized around three parts. Part I, Chapter 1, is entitled "Conceptual Overview," and lays theoretical foundations leading to the analysis throughout the book, and is followed, by "The Anthropology of Time and Space" (Chapter 2) which covers a background survey and overview of studies of time and space. Part II, "Cosmos and Calendar," consists of an original analysis of Egyptian cosmology that weaves a creative synthesis of a multifaceted universe. Analysis of Egyptian cosmology reveals a meaningful coherence, a holistic worldview, seeing the world as an integrated whole rather than a dissociated collection of parts. It is an example of a deep ecological view since the Egyptians created a universe that brings together humans, animals and gods, nature and culture, society and gender in nonlinearized complexity. Deep ecological awareness recognizes the fundamental interdependence of all phenomena.[5] The analysis of Egyptian cosmology is preceded by a presentation of the narrative of biblical creation which is a linearized vision of creation that is anthropocentric, or human-centered, with humans seen as above nature and animals and the source of all value and worth. The biblical version elevates human-centeredness to divine levels.

Capra brings up a distinction made in the 1970s between shallow and deep ecology. The difference can apply to the difference between the Egyptian vision of a universe and the biblical vision of creation. Visions of deep ecology stress interconnectedness and interdependence among phenomena – a cosmos of the whole, as the Egyptian cosmology analyzed in Chapter 3 might be called. Manifestations of continuity and discontinuity are revealed in such exploration bringing into focus insights about the intersection of nature and culture and specifically the centrality of sun and moon in the cyclicity of life. This feeds into understanding Islam's vision, which also integrates nature and culture as it generates a rhythm that underlies the lives of Muslims today. Laying out the biblical narrative in contrast with the universe of the Egyptians demonstrates different worldviews and provides perspective for understanding contemporary Christian reactions and dominant structures of time and space.

Part III provides an original synthesis of Arabo-Islamic temporality and spatiality – the week, the month, the year, the calendar and developments anchored in the Aramaic Semitic ancestral language, still in use today, in formal and spoken spheres, and subsequent transformations from Arabic to Islamic. This is laid out in Chapter 5. More than synthesis, this involved an original ordering of scattered data in the form of tables. Chapter 6 introduces a new theory of rhythm, which pulls together threads of time and space grounding them in anthropological theory and conceptual Islamic constructions, to reveal the rhythm that is manifested in the lives of Muslims, a rhythm that is live, fluid, and interweaving between "ordinary" and "sacred" times and spaces. Cultural notions of the sacred, collectivity, and privacy are integrated into one paradigm that presents a model of life that might be an alternative to the dominant globalized model offered by the West and presumed universal. The Islamic model is shown to be successful, often taking center stage, in today's economically and politically globalized world.

Acknowledgments

As in any research exploration, ideas, threads, connections, and influences come from many directions. I am indebted to this anonymous contribution to the crystallization of this project. I thank Berg Publishers' team for believing in my idea of this book from the start and for their unwavering support and patience through the long gestation phases due to personal losses, disturbing world events, and dramatic career moves. I thank peer reviewers of the draft manuscript whose criticism assisted in making improvements. I thank two partners in thinking as we engaged in extended inspiring conversations: my son Khalid (regarding European history) and long time friend engineer Fawwaz Zedan (regarding Arab history) for locating historical materials and hidden connections. I also thank Ms. Janet McMahon, Managing Editor of *Washington Report on Middle East Affairs*, for assisting in tracking down copyright owners of two media photos, and Agence France-Presse for granting permission to use them. Dwight Read, husband and colleague, gives unconditional support at all levels. In addition, his assistance in fine-tuning graphics and in rescuing the manuscript from recurrent "master document" glitches was indispensable. My daughter Magda was emotionally and poetically engaged with the formulation of the dedication of this work to her Egyptian grandparents.

The idea of the "rhythm" and the theory built to explain Islam's time and space formed in my head over a long time and through many field research projects. Seeds of the idea were already scattered in the book *Veil*. *By Noon Prayer* was already in progress (since 2003) when I moved to Doha to join the faculty of Qatar University (in 2006). More inspiration confirming ideas behind the analysis came from life in Qatar. Qatar is a living example of a successful globalized system that maintains its own cultural rhythm. It presents a present-day model of the central idea of the book. I appreciate the extra time I was granted by Qatar University between semesters (February–March 2007), to complete the draft of this book that was sent out for peer review.

Los Angeles, California
August 2007

Part I
Spatiality and Temporality

–1–

Conceptual Overview

Time is sheer succession of epochal durations: it goes on and on.
Alfred North Whitehead (1927: 158)

The Idea of Time

Time, after all, is an idea. It gets reified as fact. It gets spent, wasted, saved, killed, kept, and lost. There is leisure time, quality time, bad time, good time, no time, much time, etc. The phrase *tempus fugit* (time flies) is attributed to the Romans who equated time with weather. Time is divided into years, months, weeks, days, hours, minutes, and seconds. Classical archaeology takes time back in time, giving it chronological depth. Marshak (1972) argues that early "calendars" dated back more than 20,000 years to the last ice age. While his evidence and interpretation remain controversial, one can accept an interpretation of engraved marks on bones and rocks found in Africa and Europe as rudimentary forms of time-reckoning.

Aveni (1989) asks if these marks represent notations used to mark the counting of days of a periodic cycle. The fact, according to Marshak, that these notations were arranged in groupings corresponding to the interval between the first sighting of the waxing crescent moon in the west after sunset and the full moon, or between full moon and the last sighting of the waning crescent in the west, points to how old bones and stones may be time's earliest concrete evidence of the "ingenious attempts of early humans to keep track of celestial rhythmicity through a written medium" (Aveni 1989: 67).

Time is about regularity and order. As it is, the world in which we live is in fact a very chaotic place. Humans are always trying to make sense of it. Nature, on the other hand, is regulated. Physical laws regulate the movement of physical bodies and biological laws regulate the functioning of organisms. This natural order cannot easily be perceived in its totality by individual persons even though they recognize recurrent patterns of moon rising and moon waning, sun rising and sun setting. But the human mind can put all the elements, domains, and spaces together coherently and transmit it as visions that remain alive for generations and millennia. A structuring is imposed on the apparent chaos to create a coherent order that relates various elements from the natural, the social, and the animal worlds into a meaningful whole. Structuration, whether by cosmologies, calendars, mythical narratives, or formal systems, imposes order on disparate elements giving them coherence and unity. Rhythmicity is imposed on nature and society, and people experience their world as if inherently structured.

When people consider their world structured and orderly they are already filtering their view through overarching doctrines or systems of meaning. Overarching "systems,"[1] such as secular constitutions, religious commandments, cosmologies, calendars, green or red books, descent structures, or Protestant ethic, function to provide ordinary folk with perceived coherence and unity. In some situations and for the same people and within one culture several such doctrines may compete or alternatively coexist by design or coercion in new hybrid form. Time can also be deified. As Whitrow points out, "[w]hen, in 1916, Summer Time was first introduced in the United Kingdom by advancing the clock one hour, there were many who objected to interfering with what the popular novelist Marie Corelli called 'God's own time'" (1989: 3).

Time is a fundamental quality of human experience; it has not suddenly appeared with modernity. We can safely assert that, outside fictional narratives, there are no humans without time. We do not know how humans would manage without time. An extraordinarily rich literature has been written on the notion of time,[2] approaching it from rather divergent theoretical backgrounds using different sources and analyzing them differently. Two fundamental questions preoccupy and puzzle humans in general and scholars and scientists in particular. They are: *What is time?* and *What Time Is It?* The first asks about the nature of time and the second refers to its intervalization. Neither question is simple or has easy answers. Does time go on and on as mathematician and philosopher Alfred North Whitehead (1861–1947) stated in 1927 in the above quote? Do people living their daily lives experience time as sheer succession? Or do people of different cultural backgrounds experience time differently? Is "time" fixed, linear, cyclical, incremental, or universal?

The second question was the context of a recent encounter surrounding the interval called "noon," which most Americans would take for granted as being at 12.00 midday. At a conference in Jordan recently some colleagues were arranging to meet and it was suggested that all should gather at the hotel lobby at noon. But then a Muslim colleague asked "whose noon"? A precise hour was then established. This intervention made me reflect. Is the American noon not a universal "noon"?

At that time I had already conceptualized this book, and called it *By Noon Prayer*, and was intensely immersed in working on it. *Whose noon?* is an insightful intervention. One might locate cross-linguistic equivalents for noon, but cross-cultural knowledge already casts doubt on its universality as it has on time's universal linearity. What is noon in Muslim life and how is it tied to Muslim prayer? What is time and how is it tied to space in Arabo-Islamic life? As a way to answer these questions we first think about how to think about time. This necessitates putting temporality in a comparative framework, by providing cross-cultural background, by addressing the variability in the language of time and time's linguistic and gestural referents, and by placing the notion of temporality within a conceptual framework. Anthropologists use diverse bodies of data. They are not bound by primary data production of an ethnographic nature. True, they do make valuable contributions from cross-cultural field-based ethnographic knowledge about any subject. But they also contribute a particular way of analyzing familiar materials from any field or discipline. The key to a distinct kind of analysis is how such materials are approached, how such bodies of data are incorporated and analyzed. We begin in the next section with a discussion of cross-cultural temporalities, followed by the language of time.

Cross-Cultural Temporalities

Time for Difference

Long before the Western notion of academic disciplines shaped academic curricular plans, and before anthropology had become a discipline in Europe and North America, Arab scholars during the golden years of Islam in Baghdad, Damascus, Cairo, and Andalusia had already contributed foundational thoughts on the notion of culture *(al-'umran)* with a developmental theory of human community based on conceptual formulations of society and culture (Ibn Khaldun), basic formulations about visual technology (ibn al-Haytham), contributions of cross-cultural ethnographies (see al-Biruni and others), and fundamentals that led to the Renaissance (Ibn Rushd). During the nineteenth century, accounts of different worlds and customs kindled the fire of imagination among the elite publics of the West. Some imageries were interpreted as noble, others as barbaric – rarely as real, sophisticated, and complex people and systems. Naïve and elitist at first, anthropologists were "cocking horn-rimmed spectacles at . . . [local customs] . . . before they saw much of its real nature" (Howells 1948 [1962]: 1) and the significance of discovering and properly communicating worlds beyond Europe and Western Christianity.

Scientists have come to see different cross-cultural social and religious practices not as disorderly, inferior, or simply superstitious customs, but rather as different models shaping worlds, a framework of developmentally connected institutions, held on to for reasons of comfort and feelings of security. The same applies to Americans in suburbia of the United States or Europeans in rural provinces as elsewhere in the world. No difference. This observation was considered early on in anthropology to be "profoundly true of religion as it is of government and law; religious ideas help in the struggle for existence as verily as a bow and arrow, or a fish trap" (Howells 1948 [1962]: 1). These simple sociological observations from the 1940s sound almost naïve in this day of postmodern polemics and public diplomacy publications on the US political agenda. Underlying public diplomacy are tools to manufacture a supportive public discourse and a consensus.[3]

All along, anthropologists recognized the value of the perspective acquired from cross-cultural knowledge. The cross-cultural perspective is not simply about diversity. It is about both commonality and difference. Stressing difference alone ultimately leads to hierarchy. Combining the commonality of the human species and the difference of uniqueness maintains the balance. Difference is not an alternative to universality. There is a single humankind, sharing capacity for creativity, production and reproduction, cognition and intelligence. Difference in cultural manifestations is about uniqueness. Uniqueness and universality make up two sides of a rich humanity. It is interesting to note that the qur'anic Sura al-An'am, 60:21,[4] states that "among God's signs for the learned are: the creation of the heavens, the earth, and the diversity of human languages and colors" (my translation and paraphrasing). Ironically, globalism and dominant globalist politics find difference inconvenient for commercial corporate consumerist behaviors. They are engaged in a dangerous process of homogenization. One ideological model coercively imposed requires radical changes at the cultural, religious, social, and political levels of other peoples' systems. There are ideological impositions against family, society, and culture; missionary coercion to change religion; and feminist intervention to force American-style middle-class constructions on other womanhoods. There is a coercive drive for uniformity (using hegemonic means of pacification). Civilizational nations show strong resistance to such coercions, as they have thousands of years of civilizational heritage and contribution to knowledge, including the religions of the region.

Language of Time

> al-Jazeera mobile – because time does not wait (in *Arabic: li'anna 1-waqt la yantathir*)
> Ongoing Commercial in Al-Jazeera Arabic Satellite TV since 2006
> (my translation from Arabic)

Can time, as the al-Jazeera commercial says in its effective advertising campaign for its mobile news-carrying telephone, wait or not wait, or stop, or go, or run? Metaphoric and anthropomorphized expressions using time are plentiful. But some people in fact do perceive time in those terms. Rosen describes two ways of looking at time that he considers to be persistent dichotomies, perhaps the most persistent across many pre-modern societies: cyclical time and teleological time. He sums them up this way: "[O]ne considers the inevitable progression of a human life from birth to death and concludes that time marches inexorably forward toward a *telos*, or goal. At the same time, this apparently linear progression of a human life span is situated within the temporal markers of nature that seem repetitive, cyclical, and fundamentally stable through time." (2004: 6)

The late anthropologist Edmund Leach, in two classic short essays[5] on the symbolic representation of time (1961b: 124–32, 132–6),[6] observes that the notion of time implied in the earlier quote by Whitehead represents time only in Western culture. People from other cultures do not necessarily experience time in linear mode as "a succession of epochal durations" with a sense of "going on and on in the same direction . . . a coordinate straight line stretching from an infinite past to an infinite future" (126). Nor, according to Leach, would they see it in "the other English way," the cyclical, as "round and round the same wheel" (126), which he considers to be tied too much to "the formulations of the astronomers" (126). Envisioning repetition in time as a circle or a cycle, Leach observes, is a "purely geometrical metaphor which only mathematicians" (126) are ordinarily inclined to think of in that way – an aspect of motion in a circle. When sequences of agricultural activities or ritual exchanges of a series of interlinked marriages are described as "cyclic," Leach remarks, we impose a geometrical notation that may be entirely absent in the thinking of the people concerned.

Anthropological field studies produced many ethnographic accounts showing different ways across cultures by which populations experienced time. The phrase "time-reckoning" was widely used to describe activities by different groups used to mark time or associated with marking time. In his study of the Trobrianders, Malinowski (see Malinowski 1927) describes in remarkable detail their gardening activities (on this, see Munn 1992). Another phrase introduced in cross-cultural studies of time was "oecological time." Evans-Pritchard (1939) used it in describing the Nuer concept of time. He derived this notion through his examination of Nuer time-reckoning activities. Munn, in a critical overview of cross-cultural notions of time, sees "oecological time" as different from that in which time is "experienced through immersion in the activities" (1992: 96).

The classic example that has often been cited is that of the Hopi of Arizona, whose language was studied in great detail by Benjamin Lee Whorf, who concluded that the Hopi language contains no words, grammatical forms, constructions, or expressions that refer to time or any of its aspects. Yet Whitrow (1989: 9) considers the contention by Whorf that the Hopi language "contains no reference to 'time,' either explicit or implicit" to be too sweeping. The Hopi have a sense of time, although it seems to be different from the one that has evolved in Europe. Whitrow (1989), citing McCluskey (1977), points out that the Hopi "have successfully developed in agricultural and ceremonial calendar, based on astronomical lore, that is sufficiently precise for particular festivals" (9).

It is common to begin one's investigation with a familiar notion from one's culture. Leach began his inquiry with English time and ritual then proceeded to discover that the Kachin of Highland Burma did not have one single referent in their language that could be considered by itself equivalent to the English word "time." Evans-Pritchard in his study in the Sudan of both the Azande (1937: 347) and the Nuer (1940: 103), found no equivalent of our word time. "Though I have spoken of time and units of time," Evans-Pritchard notes, "it must be pointed out that, strictly speaking, the Nuer have no concept of time and, consequently, no developed abstract system of time-reckoning" (1939: 208). Having no concept of time is questionable, I think. Theirs has to be different, however. He goes on to distinguish between structural time and ecological time, emphasizing that genealogical time is in fact structural not historical time (213).

The Nuer, he claimed, have no units of time such as hours or minutes, for they do not measure time but think only in terms of successions of activities – many of which concern cattle. Evans-Pritchard called it "cattle-clock." He distinguishes different times and different levels of time-reckoning. "Time is not always the same to Nuer at different seasons, the dry season appearing to represent "slow" time, the wet season "fast" time; and, second, there appear to be different "levels" of time-reckoning among the Nuer, physical, ecological, and social, each of which has its own "rhythm" (1939: 192).

Whitrow considers this approach to investigating cross-cultural linguistic equivalents to be ethnocentric and erroneous since it presents the Nuer perception of time as no more than the movement of groups through the social structure and therefore does not yield true temporal distances like that produced by our techniques of dating (Whitrow 1989: 14, 15). He goes on to observe that humans have methods of time-recording and time-reckoning based either on the phases of nature – that is, temporal variations of climate, plant, and animal life – or on celestial phenomena revealed by elementary astronomical observations.

Time-reckoning is the continuous counting of time-units. It was preceded by time-indications provided by particular occurrences, such as readily recognizable recurrent phenomena. An example of a recurrent phenomenon used by many groups is the moon. It has been used to produce a temporal unit between the year and the day. The beginning of the month would be determined by observing the new moon and the month would be based on lunations. It is, however, inconvenient for measuring time, since the movement of the sun determines seasons and the rhythm of life associated with them. The moon's waxing and waning provide a continuous means of time-reckoning. As such "the moon can be regarded as the first chronometer" since its continually changing appearance drew attention to the durational aspect of time (Whitrow 1989: 16, 17).

Rigby (1995: 206) differentiates the use of time-reckoning itself. He points out that Beidelman's analysis of Kaguru time-reckoning differs from that of Evans-Pritchard in two important respects: first, in suggesting that Kaguru time-reckoning does not show a dramatic relationship between these concepts and Kaguru social structure and economy; and second, in establishing that the Kaguru have not only one but two terms for the abstract notion of time (Beidelman 1963: 10–11). Beidelman, Rigby notes, thus "ignores genealogical time and focuses almost exclusively upon conceptual and categorical ideas" (1995: 207). Also, Rigby points out how Beidelman himself found that the Kaguru do not have "chronology as we know it" (208).

Rigby continues with his critique of time-reckoning studies. He considers Bohannon's study of Tiv time concepts as being along the same lines, except for his observations about "conjuncture" (Bohannon 1967: 316) between future and past. The Tiv of Nigeria do not associate their fairly deep genealogical reckoning with "myths and legends." They do associate genealogical progression with population trends and territorial expansion (326). Rigby adds that therefore "there is quite clearly among the Tiv an awareness of constant historical change, linking together ecological, demographic, and social factors, despite their different temporal 'rhythms' into one coherent process" (Rigby 1995: 208).

H. R. Barnes (1995) shifts the grounds of dispute. He observes that our Western sense of time depends upon our instruments of measurement, and that what those instruments measure results from our need to know different things than those Indonesian societies need to know. Barnes presents a village community whose "daily life" is at once influenced by "mythical or legendary events" yet critically and literately aware that legend is a pragmatic "index of the insecurity of inherited arrangements." He insists that, however nuanced a society's figuring of time may be, "the underlying experience of duration is irreversible." That implies that the spatial analogy is limited and finally inadequate (Barnes 1995: 3). Barnes also concludes, as a further limitation to spatial analogies, that his findings do not allow any neat association of the linear, historical, and "modern" as opposed to the cyclic, legendary, and indigenous.

In "The Cultural Anthropology of Time," Munn (1992) wrote a critical review of the anthropological treatment of the notion of time, a phenomenon she describes as "diffuse, endlessly multiplying studies of sociocultural time" (1992: 93). She notes that time has always been studied in the shadow of other subjects, such as social organization, ritual, history, etc., which fragmented the topic into other anthropological dimensions. So she sketches a tentative notion of "temporalization" that views time as "a symbolic process continually being produced in everyday practices" (116). There is contradiction in the composite of ideas conceptualized by Munn and that are interspersed throughout her comprehensive coverage of the topic (92–123). She is critical of studies on "sociocultural time." But, I add, when she writes of "time as symbolic process" and "time being continually constructed by actors" is there not an ambiguity of contradictory approaches?

Whitrow observes that "[m]ost people, however primitive have some method of time-recording and time-reckoning based on either on the phases of nature indicated by temporal variations of climate and of plant and animal life or on celestial phenomena revealed by elementary astronomical observations" (1989: 14). As seen from the discussion so far there is much anthropological work (see, for example, Gell 1992; Munn 1992; James and Mills 2005) that is concerned with the nature and the cross-cultural notions of time.

Whatever critique is made of anthropological studies it is recognized that it has made valuable contributions in bringing to knowledge diverse cross-cultural manifestations of time and time-reckoning. Anthropologists themselves are self-critical about leaving out the historical factor. James and Mills write in the introduction to their edited volume: "[a]nthropological writings on time tend to be ahistorical in their approach. They have often been explicitly concerned to emphasize cultural conventions of measurement and the symbolic structuring and representation of time" (2005: 1). They go on to say that anthropologists tended to link social time with social practice and that when the historical factor was considered it was mainly as projection of representations of the present and now.

Alfred Gell (1992) saw the role of anthropology as one focusing on real action by real people in real time. Wendy James and David Mills are critical of Gell, not only in his approach to time as articulated in *The Anthropology of Time* (1992) but also in his later work *Art and Agency* (1998). To them Gell's emphasis on "what is done" by people in real time, rather than the way people represent phenomena is insufficient (James and Mills 2005: 2). They advocate both action and representation as necessary and especially in historical perspective.

Others stress time as culturally embedded or as socially derived. Durkheim saw time as deriving from the regularity of social experience manifested in festivals, gatherings, and social solidarities. In a seminal essay by Henri Hubert in 1905 and in collaboration with Marcel Mauss, a sophisticated conceptualization of time emerged that built on Durkheimian insights but departs significantly from Durkheim's complete focus on society. When Hubert introduced his refined conceptualization of time and a few years later in 1909 Arnold van Gennep produced his classic universal model marking stages in the life cycle of individuals and groups cross-culturally manifested, the conceptual foundation for the study of time was laid. They constituted a major influence on subsequent explorations, and specifically the project carried out by Edmund Leach.

Whitrow distinguishes time-reckoning from the earlier practice of time-indications. Time-indications are marked by particular occurrences. According to Whitrow, early methods of counting time were based on "some readily recognizable recurrent phenomenon" (1989: 14), whereas time-reckoning is the continuous counting of time-units. During the period between the 1920s through the 1970s many anthropologists were involved in ethnographically recording how different groups mark time. These mainly descriptive ethnographic accounts became known as time-reckoning studies. Numerous scholars used time-reckoning as orientation (including Nilsson 1920; Malinowski 1927; Austen 1939; Evans-Pritchard 1939; Bohannon 1967; Pocock 1967; Maltz 1968; Eickelman 1977).

Edmund Leach was particularly critical in "Primitive Calendars" (1950) of Malinowski's time-reckoning study among the Trobriands. His objective was to go beyond describing cross-cultural variations in time-reckoning to ask a more general question about time. "How," he asks, "do we come to have such a verbal category as *time* at all? How does it link up with our everyday experiences?" (1961: 125; italics in original). He is, of course, referring to English people and

English time. To answer his own query, Leach proceeds to examine cross-cultural materials from ethnography on the Kachin in Burma. Peter Rigby (1995: 209) considers Leach's work penetrating but offers a critique. He agrees with Leach's proposition by which he correctly states that "there is nothing intrinsically geometrical (i.e. linear, cyclical, circular) about time as we actually experience it: (1961: 124–6). But Rigby (1995: 132) notices how Leach observes that although we experience time we do not do so with our senses. Rigby describes Leach's query as "reminiscent of Lenin's remark, following Mark and Engels,[7] that bourgeois philosophers, having set up the abstract idea of reified 'objective' time, then want to feel, taste, and see it, that is, *actually*, experience it!" (italics in original).

To begin an exploration using a familiar term or idea from one's own culture, as Leach does when he begins with English calendrical rituals and moves to Kachin vocabulary, is as legitimate as beginning anywhere; in itself it is not a faulty beginning. This is how Leach's curiosity was aroused about time in the first place. He asked a question about how the English perceive and use time. Scientific curiosity can come from any direction. The question becomes: does understanding remain anchored in one's own culture (in Leach's case, English culture) or does it lead beyond the original question toward something of more general import? Leach's stated goal was the latter.

One near-universal way to mark calendars is by festivals and public celebrations. Leach proclaims that people universally mark out their calendars by means of festivals (1961: 134). "We ourselves," Leach writes, "start each week with a Sunday and each year with a fancy dress party" (132).[8] Clearly, other status and ethnic groups, in England itself, do not necessarily start each week with a Sunday and each year with fancy dress party. The week is not homogeneously defined nor is a year. But Leach is focusing on the English upper crust.

Linguists looking at time and space stress the importance of speech patterns, suggesting that, on the basis of strong evidence, patterns of linguistic usage correspond to patterns of categorization and conceptualization, which in turn shape cognitive patterns of speakers, referred to by linguists Núñez and Sweetser as "thinking for speaking" (2006: 402). It is significant that Núñez and Sweetser go beyond linguistic evidence, which "only gives a certain amount of insight into what these cognitive patterns are" (402), to examine real-time gestural production, which they propose as an equally important source of relevant data, particularly in cases where the data are ethnographic rather than experimental. "Gesture is always there, and visibly present in the videotaped data" (403).

Studying gestures is not new to anthropologists or sociolinguists. Adam Kendon (1982, 1983, 1990a, 1990b, 2000, 2004; Kendon and Ferber 1973) has systematically shown the value of empirically studying gestures, and few anthropologists today would argue against this methodological stance. Visual anthropologists in particular would concur with Núñez and Sweetser (see El Guindi 1998; on the value of gestures not only in filming culture but also in editing film on culture, 2004).

Through speech and gesture they explore time and link it with space. Núñez and Sweetser tell us that "[w]e have good cross-cultural evidence for a range of experientially based ways of thinking for speaking about time" (2006: 442). Specifically, on the basis of an empirical study of Aymara speech and gestural data, linguistic and visual analysis of Aymara spatial construals of time show how "fundamental abstract everyday concepts such as time . . . ultimately grounded in the same universal human bodily experience of the world, can get shaped in specific ways to generate cultural variability" (442). In other words, their study shows that time can be both universal and specific.

According to Núñez and Sweetser,

> [i]t is widely recognized that time is conceptualized spatially in a broad range of languages and cultures – indeed, that all languages so far examined take their vocabulary of time primarily from that of space. Specifically, a few basic metaphoric mappings from the spatial domain to the temporal one recur in language after language. Models involving (a) the temporal experiencer as mover in space . . . and (b) times as entities moving with respect to a static experiencer . . . have been noticed as cross-linguistically dominant over and over again. (2006: 401–2).

Lakoff and Johnson (1999) are described in Núñez and Sweetser (2006) as having "hypothesized that experiential bases for spatial construals of time lie in shared bodily experience of space and its correlation with temporal experience, thus suggesting a universal basis for spatiotemporal metaphors" (402). Another well-documented view is that of diversity in cultural conceptualizations of time.

Interestingly, Núñez and Sweetser accept both views. Since humans "often have more than one construal of a given complex domain, even in mathematics," they assert, "it would be perfectly possible for there to be both some very culture-specific and some universal models of time" (2006: 402). It seems like the two views reflect different levels of abstraction. In that sense there would be diversity at one level, the experiential, and universality at the abstract conceptual level. I am not sure that this particular point is what Núñez and Sweetser mean in their 2006 journal article.

Leach faulted early collections of facts explaining them as survivals of primitive thought and practice. He was particularly critical of Sir James Frazer (1906) for explaining behaviors connected with birthdays and New Year's Eve by "treating them as survivals of primitive magic." "Frazer may be right," writes Leach, "but he is inadequate" (1961: 132). The reason why Leach considered Frazer inadequate was that "[I]t is not good enough to explain a world-wide phenomenon [ritual behaviors] in terms of particular, localized, archaic beliefs." So one is tempted to ask: Is it more adequate to explain particular localized practices, such as in his case those of the upper-class Christian English, in terms of universal principles or patterns? That is, can Leach reach an understanding about the nature of time by focusing on English time? To address this, one needs to examine the methodology of taking a term or concept from Western culture and looking for it or its equivalent in another culture and where this exercise might lead. This is discussed next in Veil of Time.

Veil of Time

Despite the title, this section is about time and more significantly about method. It was noted earlier that the method of inquiry used by Edmund Leach in "Primitive Calendars" (1950) and his other works on the subject began by asking: "How do *we* [italic added] come to have such a verbal category as *time* [italic in original] at all? How does it link up with *our* [italic added] everyday experiences?" (Leach 1961: 125). He starts with "time" as a word in the English language,[9] then seeks equivalents in the language of the Kachin people of North Burma but finds none: "[T]he language of the Kachin people of North Burma seems to contain *no single word* which corresponds at all closely to English *time*" (Leach 1961: 124). In his search for words in the Kachin language equivalent to the English word time, Leach encountered many different Kachin expressions that refer to various kinds and uses of time (for some of these, see Leach 1961: 124). There is a parallel to this methodological sequence in my exploration of veil (see El Guindi 2003 [1999]). There was no single equivalent referent in the Arabic language. But in this case there were hundreds of terms that can connote veil – body covers, face covers, head covers, etc. This brings up the non-trivial question of the connection between verbal categories and cross-cultural translations.

A set of issues emerges:[10] Can we take a linguistic referent from Western culture for concrete or abstract phenomena, such as time, veil, and privacy, words with meanings that make sense in Western conceptualizations, and look for their linguistic or conceptual equivalents in other cultures? The paradox seems to lie in the question of whether it is possible simply to translate a term found in one culture then search for the translated term in another? To illustrate what this question means in the case of "veil," we identify a phenomenon in Arab culture that will be the subject of study, take its translation in English (veiling) and explore this translated concept in Arab culture. Another related question is: Can there be a conceptualization revealed in analysis as central to a particular culture, but which has no corresponding term in the language of that culture? Both issues emerged during my earlier study on veil and veiling. The first concerns the notion veil and the second concerns the notion privacy. A brief discussion of each case follows next.

Veil It became evident that when the single English term "veil" is applied to the phenomenon as it is manifested in Arab culture, this methodological technique used for convenience will tend to oversimplify, distort, and obscure what otherwise is a complex phenomenon with multiple referents and layers of meaning. The real problem is not in searching for an equivalent of the term "veil" in the Arabic language and encountering numerous terms and diverse usages, different kinds of veils and different usages of the practice of veiling, but in what this observation connotes. A linguistic term carries with it cultural significations. The Western word often cannot adequately deal with such complexity. The inherent differentiation in the concept is itself the gate to the exploration. Research tools must be appropriate for dealing with complexity. This led to a reconceptualization of research approach and of veil as concept and practice. In the process, there was a discovery of significant ethnographic facts.

One of these is that veiling, as a religious practice, was predominantly a Christian habit of secluded cloisters, long before Muslim women adopted such covers as ordinary or Islamic dress. However, while bodies and heads are covered by women in both Christianity and Islam, the meaning is different for the two practices.[11] The difference lies at the fundamentals of the two faiths and their respective relationship to notions of celibacy, sexuality, and purity (El Guindi 2003 [1999]: 19–22). Material resemblance of form among objects is not sufficient to assume shared meaning. Meaning does not easily extend across contexts nor carry over with term use.

Another challenging fact was that Arab and Muslim men veiled too. None of the studies on Muslim veiling brought this up nor seem to have seen a connection. The flaw was in methodology. Any understanding of the phenomenon of the veil is lacking without taking this fact into consideration and searching for the embedded meanings in men's veiling as well. Reconsidering the phenomenon with this fact in mind necessitated a broadening of the entire conceptualization.

At the conceptual level, examining women's veil in the Arab world led to a related cultural conceptualization of privacy, which also has no exact or adequate single or, in this case, multiple reference. We go back to the question raised above: Can there be a conceptualization revealed in analysis as central to a particular culture, but which has no corresponding term in the language of that culture? Privacy, which proved to be a core concept in Arab culture, which is related to veil, and in this study to time and space, had to be explored.

Privacy Like time, privacy is a non-material intangible abstract notion. Though not concretely visible, with analysis it becomes observable. The interest in privacy came about during the investigation that led to seeking cultural correlates for the practice of Arab women's veiling. Most studies on Arab social life tended to frame gendered life within the assumed division of space into public and private. During the course of the study, this division was shown to be ethnographically and conceptually inapplicable in the Arab case. The construct "privacy" was being re-examined.

The dilemma in resorting to privacy, an English-language term-concept, was the fact that like any cultural term it carries with it a complex of cultural connotations.

The common English usage "privacy" refers to conditions of seclusion and freedom from unsanctioned intrusion, ultimately relating to Western notions of individualism and individual rights to property. The Western notion of privacy ranged in meaning from secrecy to seclusion to individuated space to aloneness – not at all the connotations of such a construct in Arabic. Looking for Arabo-Islamic privacy required locating local constructs that are meaningful in the two core spheres in Arab life in which privacy is most relevant. Arab privacy does not connote the "personal," the "secret," or the "individuated space." It is applicable to particular core spheres in Arab sociocultural systems, namely those of family and women. It is specifically in those two spheres that privacy is considered sacred and is collectively guarded. Instead of focusing the search on seeking simple equivalent linguistic referents, particularly in light of the absence of such straightforward equivalents, the objective was to reveal central ideas or a complex of constructs that connote privacy in a culturally meaningful way. The complex comprises *sanctity–reserve–respect* (in Arabic *hurma, hishma, tahashshum, haya', sutra,* etc.). These related components together form a code that underlies a cultural notion of privacy,[12] which in this study combines with another two constructs, the sacred and the collective, to form a cluster of interrelated cultural constructs central to understanding temporality and spatiality in Islam. Arabo-Islamic notions of time and space (the focus of Part III, Chapter 6) are intertwined with these three cultural notions.

Next as we broaden our terrain to more complex visions of time, we briefly discuss temporalities and notions of time that defy simplified linearities and circularities. China and India provide examples of such temporalities – more nuanced and complex.[13]

Complexity of Time

> Since mankind is one entity within nature . . . heavenly timeliness and earthly advantages . . . [must be basis for laws]. When man and heaven are in accord, only then can the perfection of heaven and earth come into being.
>
> Comment attributed to chief minister of the first Hegemon, Duke Huan of the state of Qi, in the seventh century BCE (Hsiao 1979)

"Complexity" has become a fashionable word in science and scholarship. Scholars from the fields of the humanities and area studies are jumping on the complexity bandwagon and are also beginning to use it,[14] but in this case it is employed as a word meaning "not simple." Most studies using area studies approaches are taxonomic or causally oriented descriptions. In science, complexity has a more theoretical and scientific connotation, not simply meaning "not simple." Complexity has been emerging in the fields of mathematics, the life sciences, and cognitive science. Its objective is to uncover the complex ways in which interdependencies are formed. Later its use was extended to the social sciences as a paradigm that would more adequately characterize complexities of sociocultural systems the nesting of interrelatedness.

Examples of Chinese and Indian temporality serve to question the assumed linearity of temporal systems and to question conceptions of time as cyclical. They show how concepts of time can be much more complex than assumed, thus serving to introduce in this section the development of the notion of complexity. In a separate chapter (Part II, Chapter 3), an original analysis of Egyptian cosmology reveals a layered and complex Egyptian vision about a universe of mapped spaces within spaces and interconnections of nature, culture, life and death, birth and rebirth, male and female, etc. It is analyzed in detail in this work because of its relevance as a good instance within regional development of ideas and thought that would provide developmental context to Islamic vision. In this section a brief discussion is presented of Chinese temporality. Ralph M. Rosen (2004: 7) sums up a discussion by David W. Pankenier (2004: 129–46) pointing to the existence of debate in the field of scholarship on ancient China that challenges Western scholars who make sweeping statements regarding the conception of time in ancient China being basically linear and irreversible. He states that Western notions of temporality and postures of ethnocentrism often impede a deeper understanding of how the ancient Chinese conceptualized time and temporality. There is an early idea in Chinese culture of "connectedness" and "correspondence" among events that cannot be reduced to an oversimplified Western notion of linear temporality or causation.

A textual analysis of hexagrams from *The Book of Changes* (Wilhelm 1981), a work by the influential Han dynasty philosopher and Confucian thinker Dong Zhongshu (*c.*179–104 BCE) uncovers "a metaphorical conceptualization of time and history drawn from weaving, where the warp and weft of a fabric proceed in a direction simultaneously linear and recursive" (for full discussion, see Pankenier 2004: 129–46). The overall pattern, far from being simply linear, shows concrete and spatial aspects and also abstract and symbolic properties. To grasp the Chinese worldview on temporality, Pankenier suggests we "eschew conventional ideas of causality" (136). He invokes Needham's alternative idea of "acausal orderedness," that things are connected rather than caused (Needham and Ling 1956; Needham 1969).

Classical India provides another field of investigation, and its conception of time has been the object of interest for many scholars. The eleventh-century Arab Muslim scholar, al-Biruni, devoted twelve chapters of his famous cross-cultural "ethnographic" work *Tarikh al-Hind*[15] (al-Biruni 1964: 327–88; al-Biruni 1914, cited in Rocher 2004: 91) to the analysis of Indian conceptualization of time and temporality. Rocher describes Hindu cyclical time as

> four world ages, called yugas, succeed each other with no interruption . . . Throughout these four periods everything goes diminuendo – time itself, people's life spans, their

intelligence, and their morals and standards of behavior (*dharma*). At the end of the fourth and worst period Vishnu descends on earth in the form of his tenth *avatàra* . . . and reinstates the new "golden age." (2004: 93, emphasis in original)

Mechanism to Holism

Discovering the fundamental blocks of life was, without question, a major achievement of molecular biologists. Now it is realized, as theoretical physicists remind us, that this success in determining the basic elements that constitute life is not sufficient to help us understand the complexity characterizing and underlying the dynamics of life. There is something to learn from this in approaching Islam. Approaches that still dominate studies of Islam tend to be componential and mechanistic. Reducing Islam only to the Five Pillars or to media-created single subjects like veil, women's piety movement, jihad, Islamism, among a few others, or breaking it into Shi'a versus Sunni, good or bad Islam, rewrites Islam in static, simplistic, and dichotomous terms. This superficial exercise is not sufficient even descriptively to capture a multilayered living phenomenon like Islam.

Complexity has been emerging as a new paradigm in the fields of mathematics, the life sciences, and cognitive science. It was defined in a way best suited to deal with non-sociological phenomena. Sociology and sociocultural life has always been a challenge to the life sciences. Few could appreciate the observability of a less material, less physical world of behaviors, beliefs, and actions. There is no obvious parallel application, although in the case of "complexity" there is less difficulty than other methods and paradigms. It seeks to uncover the complex ways in which interdependencies are formed and this can be extended to apply to sociocultural systems.

After being immersed in more rigid componential approaches, science successfully moved from mechanism toward holism. Holism is one of three components of the complexity paradigm, the other being emergence. I add embeddedness as the third. Thinking in terms of complexity and holism is a positive development that needs to go further. Theoretical physicist Fritjof Capra elegantly elucidated the shift in paradigm from mechanism (parts and components) to holism (complex whole).

While not new in the history of science, it is now more obvious that a tension exists between mechanism and holism. It is an inevitable dichotomy between substance (matter, structure, quantity) and form (pattern, order, quality). Sociocultural phenomena are more than shape, more than a static configuration of parts in a whole. There is continual flux of energy through a living system, there is development, there is evolution. The Western model that has dominated thinking entails deeply engrained ideas and values – among them, Capra mentions, the view of a universe as a mechanical system composed of elementary building blocks, the view of the human body as a machine, the view of life in society as a competitive struggle for existence, the belief in unlimited material progress. All these assumptions are being challenged by recent events. This paradigm is now receding, causing a shift in the paradigmatic environment and thus allows for new approaches. This book on Islam goes beyond rigid approaches that either dissolve Islam altogether or alternatively, albeit inadvertently, ossify it as a static, lifeless, divided, dichotomized phenomenon – in need of fixing, adjusting, reforming, or fine tuning.

The dynamics of Islam from its conceptual fundamentals, to its roots and origins, its doctrine and regenerative revitalization movements, is the subject of focus. It is a rich story of a broad subject, which is not merely about a religion, belief, or body of rituals. It invokes large-scale innovative changes and major transformations in thought and practice, in traditions and patterns of life. Islam began as a geographically local idea that inherently contained a universality of thought, action, and community. It is a new energy, an innovative idea that worked. The idea was revealed in the midst of an existing sociocultural system that has been developing over millennia, and which it sought to reform and transform, but yet, like all innovations before and after it, it had to build on some existing patterns as it widened its horizons, refined its meanings, and broadened its scope.

The study of Islam, and all other sociocultural phenomena, can benefit from what molecular biologists learned, namely that a new language was needed to deal with the new approach to life. Instead of components of a system, we look at nesting linkages and complexity. It was realized that to fully comprehend systems, be they life systems or sociocultural systems, a new paradigm can shed better light on entwining interdependencies. However, I contend that in order to examine sociocultural systems, there is still more to be taken into account than the existing paradigm of complexity allows. In cultural domains that are primarily those of connections, interconnections, social networks, correlations among social systems, then tools of complexity might be adequate. While adequate these tools remain insufficient, since culture remains missing. There is more to culture than holism, emergence, and embeddedness; there is "interactive dance," as it were.

Pattern as Interactive Dance

> We have been trained to think of patterns, with the exception of those of music, as fixed affairs. It is easier and lazier that way but, of course, all nonsense. In truth, the right way to begin to think about the pattern which connects is to think of it as primarily . . . a dance of interacting parts . . .
>
> Gregory Bateson, *Mind and Nature* (1979: 13)

How do we include properties of culture in a paradigm that has the features of holism, emergence, and embeddedness? This question raises the issue of thinking about phenomena of a sociocultural nature in a different way. It is not enough to focus on patterns if patterns are fixed and static. Thinking of phenomena as fixed patterns is easy and lazy science. Gregory Bateson is absolutely right. I concur that while the shift in focus to relationality caused by the "complexity" paradigm constitutes a major step forward, relationality is not sufficient a methodological shift to make analysis robust. Examining networks is not new to anthropology. Paradigms are finally catching up with what anthropology has been doing for centuries, although identifying links between nodes is not going far enough because such linkages are static and reveal patterns that remain fixed.

Written for anybody and everybody, this work uses an anthropological approach to comprehend Islamic temporality and spatiality. How does one begin this quest? Edmund Leach, anthropologist, looked at New Year festivities in London and asked what time is. He sought answers by looking at the Kachin of Burma. Aveni, a historian, began his exploration of time in the 1980s, by looking for the term "time" in dictionaries and found in Webster's 1956 unabridged dictionary that time gets more space than space itself. Aveni considers space to be time's archetypal counterpart. He finds that time is more extensively covered than "nouns as general as *thing* and *god*, and more than basic adjectives like *good* and *evil,* much more space than *space*, its archetypal counterpart." (Aveni 1989: 5, emphasis in original) He is hard-pressed "to find a word that has more descriptions or conflicting and confusing meanings than this innocuous member of the family of four-letter words" (5).

Capra acknowledges Bateson's contribution to major scientific thinking but, in my opinion, misses the essence of Bateson's creative thought. The key to Bateson's creative thinking about life lies in the idea behind the word "dance," not simply in the concept of pattern. The above quote by Bateson about a "dance of interacting parts" (Bateson 1979: 13) is what scientific observation should reveal – a dance of interaction not interactional relations. This is particularly so if the universe we are concerned with is not only a physical universe, not only a social world, but the whole of life, central to which is human culture. Dance is foundational for understanding culture but is not easily observable by the limited tool kit of science. Visual anthropology added the camera to the scientific methodological tool kit, but unfortunately its significance in uncovering "movement" has not yet caught on. The camera has to be held by the scientific observer for it to become a crucial tool of observation (for extended discussion, see El Guindi 2004). Dance of interacting parts becomes a necessary quality of anything human and everything about culture.

Three examples discovered in my own field observation can perhaps somewhat illustrate what "dance" means in this context. The first example derives from the study of the veil. The exciting discovery during my earlier exploration of the phenomenon the "veil" and practice of "veiling" (El Guindi 2003 [1999]) was when it was revealed in analysis that face veiling by women and men is best understood when a systematic observation is made about how and when persons wearing it move face or head covers up, down, or around their face in specific circumstances. This fluid manipulation of head or face cover told us much about the veil's different functions, usages, and meanings in different social settings.

The second situation described in an earlier work (El Guindi 2004) concerns gestural culture. A movement of the hand pointing with one finger to the eye in silent response to a verbal question spoke volumes, not only about cultural nuances but also about how culture is manifested on the ground. Mastering verbal language is necessary but not sufficient for understanding another culture. Culture is spoken in verbal and nonverbal ways. The final situation concerns the subject of this book – time and space.

One cannot understand Muslim life without understanding, not Islam's structure, but Islam's rhythm – how Muslims weave in and out, from ordinary space and time to sacred space and time, throughout the day, every month, throughout the year for a lifetime. This is the thrust of this study. It is not simply a relation between parts, but a dance of interacting parts – nonverbal gestures, fluid manipulation of dress, interweaving patterns – that reveals the culture. If we don't reveal the dance, we are reducing culture to matter. To deal with rhythm requires an element of art. It is the art in the science that makes science scientific. It is also what time and space are about. It is my argument in this study that the fluid nature of space and time, the dance of parts as it were, constitutes the foundational understanding of Arabo-Islamic culture.

Rather than a mere adoption of new vocabularies, this book introduces a new language altogether, one that brings about a new understanding and promises an innovative conceptualization – one that reveals the essence underlying Islam's true inner vitality and its real wide and growing appeal. This, hopefully, sets forth a new and deeper understanding of Islam. Whitrow (1989: 14–17) discusses how humans measured time on the basis of nature (climate, plant and animal life) and according to celestial movement based on astronomical observations. The moon, Whitrow tells us, in its waxing and waning, has always been used to produce a temporal unit between the day and the year. The beginning of the month is determined by the new moon, the month would be based on lunations, while the sun determines seasons and the related rhythm of life. It is indeed in the interweaving of moon and sun that the Arabo-Islamic rhythm choreographs the dance of its parts.

Toward understanding Islam's spatiality and temporality this study examines cross-disciplinary contributions on the general subject, ancient cosmologies, cross-cultural ethnography, calendar development, lunar and solar cycles, Arabic language, culture and market. To undertake exploring this majestic phenomenon one cannot be confined by borders drawn by disciplines or interdisciplines. My approach consists of drawing upon multiple sources and bodies of knowledge, as I have shown in my previous broadly conceived work (*Veil: Modesty, Privacy and*

Resistance). Anthropology is the anchor to the whole study. It provides perspective, methodology, and theory, including cross-cultural comparisons, ethnographic descriptions, systematic fieldwork-derived data, and an analytic perspective that would be applied to historical information, visual materials, Islamic textual knowledge from the Qur'an (in Arabic) to the Hadith to qur'anic exegesis. It covers society and culture and it deals with function, structure, and process.

Complexity in analysis makes nonlinear connections, deals with emergence, and covers holism. No claim is made here that contemporary ideas and practices originated out of one single point. Influences are neither simplified nor linearized. Hybridity of and among ideas develops out of a long and dynamic process. The claim postulated here is that a cultural region with millennia of processual development in contiguous civilizational traditions, such as today's Arabic-speaking region, produces and shares ideas that are variably manifested in different forms and through practices that are ever changing. The Arabic-speaking region today is a culture area that shares core material, cultural and expressive traditions developing in continuity over millennia and which are continually reinforced by the continuation and increased sharing of popular and formal culture and through intensified communication in a shared language of shared roots.

Out of the analysis of Egyptian cosmology, pre-Islamic Arabia, biblical traditions, and calendars in historical context emerges the process of an emergent theory, described in Part III, which is rooted in Henri Hubert's conceptualizations of time and space – a theory of rhythm. This theory is the framework within which Islam's rhythm unfolds. The book title *By Noon Prayer: The Rhythm of Islam* refers to a quality of Islam that interweaves space and time in a specific rhythm embedded in the very essence of the culture – a rhythm that Muslim people feel, experience, live by, think with, and internalize. It is about the feel of Islam to Muslims and the pulse of Muslims in Islamic communities. I contend that complexity is still not sufficient, as it does not convey life's movement. In order fully to comprehend Islam as it is lived by Muslims, we need a new language and a new synthesis not only to go beyond the mechanistic identification of components, but also to move beyond complexity straight to the heart of Islam.

In this chapter, a conceptual overview uses ethnographic, philosophical, and historical materials to explore the diverse ways by which a language of time develops, laying out its cross-cultural manifestations, linguistic referents, and gestural correlates. In the next chapter, an analytic social science overview of time and space continues what began in this chapter. The exploration of conceptualization of time through English False Noses (masquerades and calendrical celebrations), a study by Edmund Leach, and Henri Hubert's theory are fully examined in the next chapter, "The Anthropology of Time and Space."

–2–

The Anthropology of Time and Space

The Pendulum of Greek Mythology

The anthropologist Edmund Leach turned to classical Greek language and mythology and used symbolic logic to explain time.[1] He derives his insights on the meaning of Greek mythology from Greek philosophy, pointing out how in the classical period the idea of time had become an oscillation of vitality between two contrasted poles. To Leach "the 'beginning of time' occurred at that instant when, out of an initial unity, was created not only polar opposition but also the sexual vitality that oscillates between one and the other – not only God and the Virgin but the Holy Spirit as well" (Cornford 1926: 129, cited in Leach 1961: 129). Here we find Christian ideas transposed onto Greek mythology and notions of time.

In the Greek myth, Cronus separates Sky from Earth in which, unlike the Egyptian narrative of beginnings, Greek gender associations are reversed – Sky is male and Earth is female. Leach explores the myth of Cronus and its transformations over time, in philosophy, literature, and religion. Basing his analysis on observations made by Fränkel (1955), Leach notes how early Greek ideas about time underwent considerable change. "In Homer *chronos* refers to periods of empty time and is distinguished from periods of activity which are thought of as days (*ephemeros*)" (Leach 1961: 129; italics in original). Leach goes on to say that by the time of Pindar this verbal distinction had disappeared. But, he writes how "a tendency to think of time as an 'alternation between contraries' active and inactive, good and bad, persisted" (Leach 1961: 129) becomes explicit in Archilochus (seventh century BC).

Aveni asks: "What is it about Kronos that makes him an appropriate symbol for time?" (1989: 62). He goes on to say that what Kronos represents is depicted by a series of actions that go back and forth between extremes: one action seems to be the reverse of the other, in contrast to our modern notion of time as an endless chain of events. Today, Aveni notes, "Kronos" is still the Father of Time and is still associated with the new year.

In the separation of Sky from Earth, Leach sees not only that male is distinguished from female but that a third element that is mobile and vital oscillates between the two (1961: 129). In Greek thought, according to Leach, this third element was represented in explicit, concrete form as "crude pictorial representations" (130) of semen and phallus, the presence or absence of which marks the distinction between male from female. On this Leach concludes that "[t]he myth is a creation myth, not a story of the beginning of the world, but a story of the beginning of time, of the beginning of becoming" (131). "The beginning," Leach says, "would be the creation of contraries" (131). Accordingly he goes on, "[M]y thesis has been that the Greeks tended to conceptualize the time process as a zig-zag" (131).

It is likely that Leach borrowed the idea of oscillations from Fränkel (1955: 251–2), and recast it, mostly diagrammatically, in structural form as an alternative way of thinking about time to the more commonly used linear or cyclical modes. Leach's conclusions about the social aspects of time expressed in the oscillatory nature of the themes of myths seem to have resonated with Aveni, who applies the idea of reversal used by Leach to a ritual associated with Kronos that resembled a new year's celebration in which masters and slaves reversed roles (Aveni 1989: 62).

Boldly[2] Leach declares that in "primitive" society "time is experienced as something discontinuous, a repetition of repeated reversal, a sequence of oscillations between polar opposites: night and day, winter and summer, drought and flood, age and youth, life and death . . . scheme [in which past is] simply the opposite of now" (Leach 1961: 126).

False Noses

The idea of oscillation proposed as a property of time fascinated Aveni. Moreover, we already know there are universal behaviors associated with calendrical rituals and rites of individual passage through phases of development. Van Gennep's study of this class of rituals (rites of passage) showed they are universal in form (1960 [1909]), a classic reference curiously left out of the page of references in Leach (1961: 137–43). Leach, writes Stanley Tambiah, "attempts to solve the puzzle of why people all over the world mark out their calendars by means of holidays and holy days, feasts and fasts, festivities and rites of passage" (2002: 351). Leach wanted to examine how the English experience time stripped of technological instruments of measurement. He distinguished two different kinds of experience: repetition, "that certain phenomena of nature repeat themselves," and non-repetition, "that life change is irreversible" (1961: 125). He then expanded on these two and added a third way humans experience time: the rate at which time passes (132). In terms of repetition he mentions time-intervals and durations such as a "pulse beat, a clock strike, New Year's Day." For non-repetition he mentions irreversible aging and entropy, how "[A]ll living things are born, grow old and die" (Leach 1961: 132).

Linearity of time is not universal. Many think of time as going back and forth. The pictorial metaphor of pendulum is, argues Leach, "the essence of the [pendulum view of time] is not the pendulum but the alternation" (134). "I would maintain," Leach concludes, "that the notion that time is a 'discontinuity of repeated contrasts' is probably the most elementary and primitive of all ways of regarding time" (134). Leach, in other words, views time, not as the sequential markings on a tape measure, but as repeated opposites (133–4).

Basing his premise on the classic Van Gennepian formulation of *rites de passage*, Leach then transposes processual pattern onto the Durkheimian formulation of the sacred and profane, then with a twist of imagination, he brings in "the funny hats" and "false noses" of *bals masqués* and festivals. He characterizes this phenomenon as moving between the contrasting opposites of "formality" and "masquerade" with "role reversal" as the symbolic means to transfer from one opposite to the other: secular to sacred, death to birth, etc. (136). With this Leach wove a journey from English time, to Greek mythology, to Kachin language, to Van Gennepian rites, to Durkheim's society, applying the pendulum metaphor from Greek philosophy to ritual as a human activity that puts order in social life. It is about time.

By invoking Van Gennep's *rites de passage* (1960 [1909]) Leach brings ritual into the discussion on time (his debt to Hubert is obvious and should have been acknowledged). He links the formulation of passage from "a symbolic death, a period of ritual seclusion, a symbolic rebirth" to time. For this conceptualization to be "logically plausible," Leach finds it necessary to link rites of passage to a specific view of time, namely that of a pendulum, instead of a view of time as "going on and on" or "going round and round" (Leach 1961: 133). "Why," he asks, "should we demarcate time in this way?" (132) Going back to England (and European customs) he adds: "Why should it seem appropriate to wear top hats at funerals, and false noses [hence the title of the article: "Time and False Noses"] on birthdays and New Year's Eve?"

On Time

> I know African time, I know Polynesian time, I know Native American time, and of course there is Draconian time. The difference is not about being late. Not about calendars. It is about social relations and personal interactions. It is a qualitative difference.
>
> Tom Blakely, October 2004

The quote above is from a telephone conversation with a colleague in the United States, visual anthropologist Tom Blakely. Tom prefers African time – a metaphor for a more relaxed notion of time than that adopted as the ideal in the West. That is how he conducts the Visual Research Conference, a successful project he innovated close to two decades ago for the Society of Visual Anthropology. Almost annually the Society tries to put pressure on Tom to conduct it differently – to follow deadlines, stick to time limits for presentations, etc. Tom strongly clings to his mode of operation, which he sums up as African time, using his long-term ethnographic experience in Africa as a guide for a workable alternative to the North American notion of time and space. He challenges the absoluteness and imagined universality of one notion of time and the very idea of "being on time."

It is not only in Africa that African time is employed. Among the Valley Zapotec, during my fieldwork in San Francisco Lachigoló,[3] villagers were telling me about the one man whom they felt should be collectively punished through the village council because, they said, he "doesn't waste time." Asked to clarify, they explained how since his conversion by evangelists from Roman Catholicism to the Protestant Baptist church (quite rare in this part of Mexico at the time in the 1970s) his overall behavior changed dramatically. He stopped drinking, which of course affected his participation in local rituals (for extended discussion on this topic, see Selby 1974), and rarely socialized with the people in the community. He began to equate time with money, to be accumulated and not wasted, thus going always on the road (he was itinerary peddler) leaving his village, home, family, and children behind. Rumors circulated around the village of marital disloyalty and children out of wedlock on his "peddling" route. Villagers considered his behavior antisocial and his conduct a form of dysfunctionality. "Wasting time" is highly valued. It is the basis for social relations, the glue that binds villagers together in a community, and the way to share information and responsibility. He was not being a good "citizen."

There have been organized attempts to globalize time. They failed. Aveni tells the story about America's recent attempts to imperialize time: "Like those merchants of old who sought to design the elusive perpetual motion machine, the dream . . . [was] . . . a perpetual calendar, which would self-adjust the irregular months, equalize the quarterly divisions of the years, and fix the sequence of weekdays and month dates so that they would be identical from year to year" (Aveni 1989: 160–1). This plan by the United States for a world calendar was seriously considered by the United Nations – "a scientific system of time measurement without sectional, racial or sectarian influence." It is the kind of thinking similar to post World War II universalism including such propositions as a common language (Esperanto) and "one world calendar for one world." The rationale was the same that drove the old medieval mercantile class: "time is money."

Gary Stix remarks about American calendrical celebrations as follows:

> Recalling where we fit in the order of things determines who we are. So ultimately, it doesn't matter whether time, in cosmological terms, retains an underlying physical truth. If is a fantasy, it is one we cling to steadfastly. The reverence we hold for the fourth dimension, the complement of the three spatial ones, has much to do with a deep psychic need to embrace meaningful temporal milestones that we can all share: birthdays, Christmas, The Fourth of July. (2006: 5).

That may be true, but there are Americans who do not "recognize" Christmas or celebrate the Fourth of July. But, for those who do, Stix goes on to write that "[D]oing so seems to be the only way of imposing hierarchy and structure on a world in which instant messaging, one-hour photo, express checkout and same-day delivery threaten to rob us of any sense of permanence" (5).

Edmund Leach (1961) was trying to demonstrate the cross-cultural variation in the translation of time as a backdrop to understanding the English notion of time. Chronus whom he invoked in his analysis, as Aveni observes, is "not a sun god, or even the god of the heavens; he is the god of the circle of the year, the personified expression of the calendar" (1989: 120). Time, Leach writes, "is an essential part of our lives" (1961: 125). It is a given factor in the English case, where the technology of clocks and radios and astronomical observations abound. Whitrow observed that people have become time-conscious in contemporary modern society. "The moment we rouse ourselves from sleep we usually wonder what time it is. During our daily routine we are continually concerned about time and are forever consulting our clocks and watches" (1989: 17; and, for more on the advent of the mechanical clock, see Whitrow 1989: 99–114).

Zerubavel (1981: 32–44), using the work by Harold A. Innis, among others, traces the pervasiveness of daily rhythm to Benedictine monasteries.[4] Mumford (1963: 16), Zerubavel claims, argues that "orderly punctual life in the West first took shape in the monasteries" and then asserts that "the temporal rigidity of monastic life definitely presupposed *punctuality*" (1981: 35). Zerubavel sees a connection between the first mechanical clock and religious services. "It is not surprising," he concludes, "that the earliest wheel-and weight-driven clocks . . . were all introduced to the West through the monasteries (1981: 38).[5] He supports his idea by citing Reinhard Bendix (1962: 315–18) in depicting the monk as "the first 'professional' of Western civilization" (Zerubavel 1981: 32), and by invoking the folk characterization of the monk in the French song "Frère Jacques, Frère Jacques." We know, however, that the origin of calendar, clocks, and time measurement goes much earlier than that.

Not all studies trace modern obsessions with time to bells keeping time in monasteries. Landes proposes that "[i]t is the mechanical clock that made possible, for better or worse, a civilization attentive to the passage of time, hence to productivity and performance" (quoted by Stix 2006: 4). "Time is more accurately measured than any other physical entity . . . elapsed time is marshaled to size up spatial dimensions" (4). To Weber it is the ethic and morality. He writes: "The introduction of clocks and time-pieces in factories became an early tool for imposing the new work discipline. This imposition was reinforced by a moral endorsement from the Protestant ethic, while other notions of time were condemned. 'Waste of time is thus the first and in principle the deadliest of sins,' declared Richard Baxter's Christian Dictionary" (Weber 1984 [1904]: 157).

In one sense, time can be envisioned as a quality of modern life. Stix observes how "[M]ore then 200 years ago Benjamin Franklin coined the now famous dictum that equated passing minutes and hours with shillings and pounds" (2006: 3). Here is where time becomes measured by money and is counted and perceived in numbered units. Obsessive or "draconian," as some put it, punctuality and the linking of time with income or production are core to the ideals of the Protestant ethic, now the ethos underlying life in the United States.

Focusing on time as technology, Stix notes that "time is a continuum in which one event follows another from the past through to the future. Today the number of occurrences packed inside a given interval, whether it be a year or a nanosecond, increases unendingly . . . a tripartite oddity that parses into past . . . present and future" (2006: 3). With the advent of the Internet there is simultaneity. "In Internet time, everything happens everywhere at once – connected computer users can witness an update to a Webpage at an identical moment in New York or Dakar." The wired world is one without borders, one that erases barriers. "Time has, in essence, triumphed over space." He goes on to say that

> over the eons, the capacity to gauge duration has correlated directly with increasing control over the environment that we inhabit. Beginning in the thirteenth century the mechanical clock initiated a revolution equivalent to the one engendered by the later invention by Gutenberg of the printing press. Time no longer flowed as it did literally in a water clock. Rather it was marked off by a mechanism that could track the beats of an oscillator. When refined, the device let time's passage be counted to fractions of a second. (2006: 4)

He further points out how "[A]tomic clocks . . . play a role in judging location" (4) and that "[T]he Global Positioning System (GPS) satellites continuously broadcast their exact whereabouts as well as the time maintained by onboard atomic clocks. A receiving device processes this information from at least four satellites into exact terrestrial coordinates for the pilot or the hiker, whether in Patagonia or Lapland" (4). The measurement of time is becoming all the more accurate. "A team from France and the Netherlands set a new speed record for subdividing the second, reporting in 2001 that a laser strobe light had emitted pulses lasting 250 attoseconds – that is 250 billionths of a billionth of a second." (5). "The modern era has also registered gains in assessing big intervals. Radiometric dating methods, measuring rods of 'deep time,' indicate how old the earth really is" (5). This ability "to transcend time and space effortlessly – whether on the Internet or piloting a GPS-guided airliner – lets us do things faster." (5). Marking time with increasing precision began early, as the next chapters demonstrate. While, as Aveni notes, with the combined influences of religion, commerce, the rise of towns, and the bureaucracy that accompanied them in the twelfth and thirteenth centuries "the 'work clock' slowly began to dominate life in the thickly settled European urban communities" (Aveni 1989: 93). Long before the increasingly expanding and interlocking market economy pushing invention toward more precision, synchronicity and simultaneity time had already become money.

Arab Roots of Modern Theory and Technology

Medieval Arab science made some contributions to the notion of time and space. In general, Arab and Muslim scholarship from the tenth to the fifteenth century was seminal to the development of science and technology, making significant contributions in the history of thought and science about the development of society and culture. In my earlier study on Arabo-Islamic dress (El Guindi 2003 [1999]: 341) unexpected but interesting ideas about dress were found buried in works not focused on the "dress," such as that by fourteenth-century scholar Ibn Khaldun. Then in my subsequent study on visual anthropology it was discovered that a historical track of visual anthropology can be constructed beginning with eleventh-century scholar/scientist Ibn al-Haytham (965–1041)[6] for his inventions and theories about vision and optics (El Guindi 2004), and in this present project on space and time eleventh-century Muslim scholar Abul-Rayhan al-Biruni (d. AH 440/AD 1048, considered the first ethnographer) made seminal observations on early calendars in the region (see Chapter 5) and so on.

The prominent social thinker, Ibn Khaldun (full name, Abu-Zayd Abdul Rahman bin Khaldun al-Hadrami, AD 1332/AH 732 – 1406/808) innovated a theory of sociocultural change that centers on a particular Arabic notion of solidarity (*'asabiyya,* a term derived from *'a-s-b*, which means nerve center) to formulate a dynamic paradigm of changing patterns of ecological/political adaptation. His model of dynamic change is empirically derived from the civilizational world events of his time, that is to say the Arabo-Islamic universe that was the center of progress, science, and thought.[7] What is interesting about Ibn Khaldun's theory of culture is that it included religion as a factor in his developmental scientific paradigm in which it is considered pivotal in carrying forward the social bond in the course of development of society from elementary to more complex social forms. 'Asabiyya, in Ibn Khaldun's theory, functions as the glue that binds society together. It weakens when kinship bonds weaken (Ibn Khaldun 1961; Jami'at al-Duwal 1980). Religion becomes the locus of moral fabric considered the glue to sustain 'asabiyya, as the social group grows larger and as its institutions become increasingly more complex. This theory of culture change was formulated by Ibn Khaldun in the fourteenth century. It is a sophisticated theory that is not uncomfortable with people's faith or with centering religion[8] in its framework[9] and predates the French school on collective representation by four centuries.

Whitrow mentions an important contribution by Arab scientists to temporal concepts leading to the music in Europe. Early medieval church music was all plain-chant, in which time values were fluid. Mensural music, in which the durations of the notes had an exact ratio among themselves, was a direct contribution of the Arabs through their inventions and discovery. The idea was introduced into Europe about the twelfth century, after which there appeared in Europe the system of notation in which the exact time-value of a note is indicated by a lozenge on a pole. As regards the theoretical and philosophical analysis of time, the most important and original contribution of medieval Islamic thinkers was their theory of discontinuous or atomistic time. A proponent of this theory is the twelfth-century Arab philosopher Musa ibn Maimun ibn Abdullah al-Qortobi,[10] whose original main work in Arabic, handwritten in AD 1190, was *Dalalat al-Ha'erin* (English translation entitled, *A Guide for the Perplexed*). In the *Guide*, he writes: "Time is composed of time-atoms, i.e. of many parts, which on account of their short duration cannot be divided . . . An hour is, e.g. divided into sixty minutes, the second into sixty parts and so on; at last after ten or more successive divisions by sixty, time-elements are obtained which are not subjected to division, and in fact are indivisible" (1885: 314, 315). This atomistic view of time was associated with a drastically contingent and acausal[11] concept of the world, its existence at one instant not implying its existence at any subsequent instant.[12] This approach predates mechanistic approaches in European science by several centuries. Time was considered in terms of constituent components.

The climate of learning in the Muslim world ignited interest in scientific subjects and aroused curiosity and inquiry in scholarly pursuits.[13] The scientific library and institute set up in Baghdad was the regional magnet for research and discovery. Islam did not pose barriers to scientific pursuits. *Bayt al-Hikma* (House of Wisdom), as the institute was called, attained its highest reputation during the caliphate of al-Ma'mun (813–33), son of Harun al-Rashid (known for *The Arabian Nights*), himself an astronomer. There was original thinking and there was translation of earlier scholarship.

By the end of the ninth century, many Hellenistic scientific and technological works had been translated into Arabic, including Ptolemy's great astronomical book *Syntaxis*, which is usually known today by its Arabic title *The Almagest*. Knowledge of Greek science and technology, combined with Arab original discovery and scholarship merging with Asian (particularly Indian) traditions, enhanced scientific studies and led to inventions, spreading throughout the entire Islamic world, including Sicily, southern Italy, al-Andalus (Islamic Spain), where by the twelfth century there were centers of learning in Cordoba, Toledo, Damascus, Cairo, and Baghdad.

All parts of the Islamic world needed mathematically educated experts who would be able to determine the astronomically defined times of prayer and the direction of Makka. Many portable instruments for the determination of time were required, including the chief instrument used by Arab astronomers, the astrolabe. The form of astrolabe used in medieval Europe was derived from the Muslim type found in southern Spain.[14] The astrolabe, which Whitrow describes as an early form of analog computer, was primarily designed to solve problems of spherical trigonometry to shorten astronomical calculations. From the scales engraved on it, it was possible to determine the positions of the so-called "fixed stars" in relation to the horizon and of the sun, moon, and the planets in relation to the stars. Designed for the latitude of a particular place, its most important use was to determine the precise time of day or night from an observation of the altitude of the sun or one of the stars mapped on the rete (a pierced plate on an astrolabe), having projections whose points correspond to the fixed stars. By modern standards, the result was not very accurate. Moreover, although the astrolabe enabled long calculations to be avoided, the computing of planetary positions, for example, for casting a horoscope, still involved a considerable amount of work.

There were other time-measurement instruments, such as water-clocks. Extensive remains of two monumental Islamic water-clocks still survive at Fez in Morocco.[15] Whitrow (1989: 79) mentions a book in Arabic on The Construction of Water-clocks, possibly composed after AD 1150, which preserves the idea of the invention of the basic machinery of a water-clock by Archimedes, together with later ingenious additions to the mechanism made by Muslim inventors and craftsmen.[16]

Western industrialization and the long struggle to impose a mechanized time benefited from the earlier discoveries and inventions introduced from civilizational regions (Egypt and Babylonia), which thousands of years earlier had already mastered conceptualizing the cosmology of heaven and earth, the science of time for agrarian and religious purposes and, with the Arab golden age under Islam, constructed the technologies of time-reckoning and measurement.

Finally, we move from science and scholarship to where abstract principles meet life, as in Islamic architecture throughout Andalusian Spain, we see a remarkable contribution of art and science exquisitely merged in the architectures of Cordoba, Seville, and Granada that interweaves living and worship spaces with nature and culture, garden fragrances (orange blossoms and fruit trees) and soothing sounds of water (from fountains), moonlight and sunlight, inside and outside, scholarship and life, science and religion. This symphony of interwoven elements was Islam's highest moment. This is where rhythm became life.

Sacralized and Desacralized Temporal-Spatiality

As shown in Chapter 1, the British and American traditions of anthropology produced many cross-cultural ethnographic accounts about how different people marked time or temporally measure their daily and agricultural activities, leaving a large repertoire of comparative data on different cultural conceptualizations of time. While much social science work on time is interesting and the analysis by

Edmund Leach brought a level of analytic excitement to the subject when he linked time to English calendrical celebrations, it was not until the nineteenth-century French sociological/anthropological school that a conceptual leap forward was made. This French school brought space into the picture and complexity in its theory. It not only reunited space with time, it brought forth fresh conceptualizations[17] about structure and process, society and culture. I consider the theoretical ideas formulated by Henri Hubert in particular on the subject of space and time to be of special significance in enhancing analysis. His conceptualization provides valuable insights for my analysis in this book of Islam's temporality and spatiality.

Collective Representations

> Time is an object of collective representations in the same way as space.
>
> Henri Hubert, 1902, *L'Année Sociologique*, IV, 234.[18]

To view time and space as entwined with sociological collectivity pushes the understanding of these phenomena to a sophisticated level. This observation is best understood in the context of the larger school out of which it arose. *L'Année Sociologique* is the name of a sociology journal founded in 1898 by Émile Durkheim who served as its editor. It was published annually until 1925, then revived as a publication with a new name, *Annales Sociologiques*, from 1934 to 1942. After World War II it resumed publication and has continued under the same name to the present day. Durkheim had a new sociological paradigm and needed a forum for publishing his work and that of his students. *Annales Sociologiques* then came to refer to the distinctive approach associated with this school of thought during the first two decades of the twentieth century. Besides Émile Durkheim, the major names of this school are Marcel Mauss, Robert Hertz, and Henri Hubert. This French ethnology made outstanding contributions to the conceptualization of society.

Émile Durkheim (1858–1917) was the founder of this whole tradition. Marcel Mauss (1872–1950), maternal nephew and student of Émile Durkheim, is another social scientist considered by many to be a father of French ethnology who had profound influence on the development of the French social and human sciences, particularly after Durkheim's death, carrying on in collaboration with Hubert (1909) the Durkeimian school and *l'Année Sociologique*. Evans-Pritchard writes that "[S]ome of the most stimulating and original contributions to its earlier numbers were written . . . in collaboration with Durkheim and Hubert" (Evans-Pritchard 1967: v). The first major work by Marcel Mauss was conceptualized and written in collaboration with Henri Hubert (1872–1927) on the phenomenon of sacrifice (1899, *Essai sur la nature et la function du sacrifice*). Marcel Mauss is best known for his seminal work *Essai sur le don* (*The Gift*) (1967 [1925], 1990), on the phenomenon of exchange and the role of "the gift" in building systems of exchange. This study is considered a classic in the social sciences.

In his concluding remarks to the restored translated work by Marcel Mauss, *La Prière*, translated as *On Prayer* (Mauss 2003 [1909, French]), Howard Morphy wrote:

> The works of Durkheim and others associated with the *Année sociologique* were central to theoretical developments in both sociology and anthropology. These shifted any explanation away from a simple base fixed on evolutionary models and towards an understanding of phenomena in the context of the societies in which they occurred. Simultaneously a revolution was taking place in ethnographic method. Until the late nineteenth century, missionaries, traders and government officials had collected, in a piecemeal way, facts about other cultures that provided the basis for the construction of theories. (Morphy 2003: 139)

Temporal Equality versus Time Equivalence

Henri Bergson (1859–1941), an influential French philosopher of the late nineteenth and early twentieth century, proposed four properties of space (1896, 1904). They are: quality rather than quantity, discontinuity rather than continuity, indivisibility rather than the capability of infinite subdivision, interpenetration rather than exteriority. Hubert accepted these characterizations and added further distinctions: the difference between quantity and quality, between equality and equivalence. Equality, in his view, is about a quantity, and is determined by measurement, whereas equivalence is about a quality and is based on similarity. It is not to be understood simply in terms of structural or mathematical correspondences, since it can and does "establish a communication between the various parts of this time, in its mythical part and its ritual part," In his view, there are "sympathetic associations" between moments of time in rites and in myths which connect sacred objects to each other. Hubert considers equivalence to be the foundation of repetition in myth and in rite. He makes no distinction between the two domains. Both are situated in what he calls "a time-environment" (1905). In religious time "the same dates bring back the same events" (Hubert 1909, 1999 [1905]: 205, 206). This extends to formal calendars, in which symmetrical parts of time occupy the same position. They get identified and marked on calendars. Durations of different length become units of time, such as week, month, year, season, and are presented as similar (1905, 1909: 204–5). This, to Hubert, is equivalence. He accepts Bergson's equation that religious time is to secular time as mathematical time is to duration (Bergson 1896, 1904), which put in equation form would be:

Religious Time : Secular Time :: Mathematical Time : Duration

In elucidating Hubert's conceptualization, François-André Isambert mentions that "[s]eparate moments in secular time can coincide in religious time" (1999: 72). Hubert (1905, 1909) finds continuity between secular and religious time, such that "[w]hether moments or durations, their qualities are defined only by the facts with which they are necessarily and constantly in a positive or negative relation" (211). He does not view time in essentially quantitative terms, but rather in qualitative terms "composed of discontinuous parts, heterogeneous and ceaselessly revolving" (229). Hubert distinguishes two distinct qualities of time: "time as the fulcrum of intervals and time as a set of reference points enabling an event to be positioned" (Isambert 1999: 19), or time in myth and ritual and, mathematical time. He considers time to be a symbolic structure and thus broadens understanding beyond social time – it is a genus that encompasses the preceding species and makes up the qualitative time that pervades our social life. On the one hand, time markers are located in astronomical phenomena and through numbers serving as reference points, and on the other, Hubert recognizes, events, ceremonies, and rites exist in all their qualitative richness. Time appears at the meeting point of the two.

Rhythm of Collectivity

Alfred Gell (1992: 3–4) traces the anthropology of time to a well-known passage in the introductory chapter of Durkheim's *The Elementary Forms of the Religious Life* (1961 [1912]: 9–11). In the passage Durkheim writes that "religious representations are collective representations which express collective realities . . . The divisions into days, weeks, months, years, etc. correspond to the periodical recurrence of feasts and public ceremonies. A calendar expresses the rhythm of collective activities . . . to assure their regularity . . . what the category time expresses is the time common to the group, a social time, so to speak." Gell considers this forthright theoretical statement as crucial. It places the problem of the sociology of time in an explicit philosophical framework and it brings out the circularity inherent in interpretative sociology of the kind Durkheim initiated: "that collective representations (of time, space, etc.) are both *derived from* society and also *dictate to* society" (Gell 1992: 4, emphasis in original).

This centered the notion of collective representations in studies of society. There is circularity in this kind of thinking. Collectivity derives from society and at the same time shapes society. But Gell sees in this circularity the beginning of a distinctive phase in the history of thought, one of sociological interpretation and sociological explanation. Nevertheless, Gell finds a powerful allure in Durkheim's doctrine of the social origin of "time" as a category of the mind that has inspired many notable ethnographic analyses of social time and refinement of theoretical work. Gell brings up "Durkheim's notable anthropological successors . . . Evans-Pritchard, Lévi-Strauss and Leach who made excessive metaphysical claims for the Durkheimian approach to time – but notably none of them could have arrived at his perfectly valid insights without Durkheim's example" (1992: 14).

The crucial step forward, according to Gell, is that Durkheim "rejects the 'naïve realist' assumption that time just is what it is, and that time-reckoning concepts enable people to 'grasp' time as it if were one more external fact of nature among many" (1992: 4). Here the possibility is raised that "collective representations of time do not passively reflect time, but actually *create* time as a phenomenon apprehended by sentient human beings" (Gell 1992: 4). It is only at this point, Gell points out, that the "*time*" problem becomes interesting at all.

The Sacred

François-André Isambert sees it differently. The interesting problem lies elsewhere. He considers the classic *Essay On Time* (1905, 1909, 1999 [1905]) by Henri Hubert to be the theoretical work with the deepest impact. In it, Hubert's thinking went beyond Durkheim's ideas. In the Introduction to the English translation of the *Essay On Time*,[19] Isambert (1979, 1999) describes Hubert's "*Etude sommaire . . .*" as a penetrating work at the intersection of "where the sociology of religion and the sociology of knowledge meet" (3). Within the French school of ethnology, Isambert considers Hubert's work to be the most crucial as it moved the notion of the sacred to the center of Durkheim's approach to religion. He cites Henri Hubert (1979) himself when he wrote about his collaboration with Marcel Mauss and their shared thought, stating that they together "singled out the idea of the sacred: . . . as a category of the mental operations implied by religious facts" (1976, 1999: 7).

Emergent Theory: Interweaving Time, Fluid Space

Emerging from the various theories advanced by the French School of Ethnology are elements which, when combined with primary empirical observations on Islam, cross-cultural insights, and cross-disciplinary knowledge, become foundational in the development of the theory in this study on time and space in Islam.[20] Let us now follow the progression of conceptual developments coming out of the French school. Émile Durkheim, the founder and father of the school, located time and space squarely in society. In his thinking the rhythm of social life is the basis of the category of time and the space. Society provides the material for the category of space (Durkheim 1912: 628).

This explicit Durkheimian position on time, space, and society is not accepted by Isambert, who describes this Durkheimian school overall as "an enterprise of sociologising categories . . . collective empiricism which consists in somehow reproducing categories in the social organization presented as a basic datum"

(Isambert 1976: 30). Moving with time and space in a different direction, Henri Hubert focused on the notion of the sacred and centered it in the sociology of religion. According to Isambert, Hubert was instrumental in centering the notion of the sacred in the Durkheimian school of the sociology of religion (1976: 37, n.7). He insightfully distinguishes between sacred as attribute and sacred as category. By doing so, it is noted, he departs from the strictly Durkheimian premise that assumes a social genesis of time. This becomes a significant development and a major shift. Hubert developed the idea of the sacred in a way that was seminal to the development of a definition of religion at that time.

According to Hubert, "[r]eligion is the administration of the sacred" (1904: xlvii). Sacred acts impose "conditions on experience and on reasoning" (Hubert 1904: xlvii, cited in Isambert 1999: 11). Thus in this conceptualization the sacred, which in practice acts as a general constraint on ritual behavior, becomes at once a general constraint "operating on religious thought" (11). Isambert expands on Hubert's idea by describing the sacred as an "environment . . . which one enters into and emerges from" (11) and whose nature regulates the operations taking place within it. In this sense the sacred is considered a category.

François-André Isambert points out that Henri Hubert did not consider time simply to mean change in the face of the immutable sacred, but more importantly that it is "plastic, variously representable like space" (19). What Hubert calls the "category of the sacred" is relevant here, since the sacred, in this view, penetrates time. Isambert sees the essential point being that time itself becomes sacred. Hubert and Mauss (1904) correlate the sociology of time with the sociology of space. According to Isambert, Hubert formulates a theory of social time that uses the idea of social rhythms in a far more sophisticated way than a simple record of social rhythms. To Hubert, time is a symbolic structure provided with rules – an "operating system" (31), as it were. And even though Hubert shares with Durkheim the notion that time is instituted by society, to him it does not reproduce aspects of society. Isambert rightly finds the idea of time by Hubert to be most original, and one in which the origin of the idea of time is transcended. This conceptualization, which provides seeds of a paradigm that places rhythm in the sacred, and the sacred in time and space, leads to the original analysis of time and space in Islam. This theory is discussed in detail in Part III, Chapter 6.

We have seen how Leach turned to Greek mythology to explain English time. To explain Islamic time and space, this work goes back in time and space to analyze the Egyptian cosmos in comparison with spatio-temporality of biblical origins. And, as André Leroi-Gourhan points out,

> [h]uman time is and remains an ambiguous measure because natural rhythms are shared by all living matter. The measurement of lived time refers to phenomena unrelated to measurement as such . . . in all agricultural-pastoral civilizations, the complex movements of the stars have engendered astronomic reference systems that tend,

> whether it be among the Maya, the Chinese, the Egyptians, or the Romans, to order the passage of the seasons geometrically within a grid established by the periodically recurrent position in space of some of the main celestial bodies. Endeavors to ensure regularity of the calendrical grid are inseparable from advances in computing space and quantities. (1993: 316)

Analysis of the Egyptian cosmology follows a presentation of the narrative of biblical creation next in Part II, Chapter 3. Then Chapter 4 discusses the development of spatio-temporality as it leads into the institution of formal calendars.

Part II
Cosmos and Calendar

–3–

Order and Creative Beginning

Astrological Gaze

A thousand years ago there was a sudden appearance in the sky of a "new star" that outshone all the other stars, twice as bright as Venus. Like the moon, this entity cast shadows onto the city of Cairo (the English distortion of the Arabic word *al-Qahira*, meaning Victorious). An eighteen-year-old Egyptian man called Ali ibn Radwan was intently watching the sky from the open courtyard of al-Azhar.

Al-Azhar

Al-Azhar al-Sharif[1] (the Noble Azhar) means "the most flourished and shining," possibly named either for being the shining beacon of learning or for being surrounded by the lights and glitter of great monuments in Islamic Cairo. It is an old Egyptian institution of higher learning, world-renowned for its position as a center for Islamic education and scholarship, and for being the oldest continually (to this day) operating university in the world. It was built by the Shi'a Fatimid Dynasty (909–1171), which established Cairo as its capital. The university was always connected to Al-Azhar Mosque in Old Cairo. The name is also associated with Sayyida Fatima al-Zahra', daughter of the Prophet Muhammad.

The foundation for al-Azhar was laid in AD 969 and the mosque was built two years afterward. Studies began in al-Azhar in Ramadan, in October 975. A school of theology (*Madrasah*[2]), attached to the mosque, was founded in 988. Teaching first began in al-Azhar when Chief Justice Abul Hasan Ali ibn al-No'man started to teach the book "al-Ikhtisar," which focused on Shi'ite jurisprudence. Later, toward the end of the Middle Ages, the focus shifted to Sunni jurisprudence, which remains the focus of scholarship in al-Azhar to this day. Today al-Azhar is considered the most prestigious school of Islamic learning, producing the most reputable scholars in the Muslim world.

A millennium after ibn-Radwan observed the sky from al-Azhar we learn that the new star he was intently looking at was the supernova of 1006, simply known today as SN1006. At the time of its appearance in the sky, on the evening of April 30, 1006, Ibn Radwan had begun to study medicine while he earned a livelihood by working as astrologer. Ibn Radwan considered astrology of value for understanding the past and predicting the future, but nevertheless an imprecise art without mathematical and geometrical calculations. In his autobiography, which he wrote at the age of fifty-eight, forty years after his penetrating observations as a young man, he described himself as astronomer. His self-identity, shifting from astrologer to astronomer, is parallel to a change in Egypt at that time in the climate of learning, scholarship, and science.

Dar al-'Ilm, Bayt al-Hikma

At the time of the appearance of the supernova, Egypt was under Fatimid rule. There was much emphasis on education and learning. During the rule of Caliph Al-Hakim, in AD 1004 to be specific, *Dar al-'Ilm* (House of Science and Knowledge) was founded in Cairo. Another name for it was *Dar al-Hikmah* (House of Wisdom), a phrase that had precedence in the region.

Before Egypt's house of learning, the Abbasid dynasty, which had replaced the Umayyad dynasty with its center in Damascus, began leading the Islamic empire in AD 750. In AD 762 the caliph al-Mansur (754–75) built Baghdad and made it the capital. More than two centuries before the one in Cairo, he founded a center for learning, research, and translation called *Bayt al-Hikma* (House of Wisdom). It attained its highest reputation during the caliphate of al-Ma'mun (813–33), himself an astronomer and son of Harun al-Rashid, becoming a venue where scholars from the surrounding region met, debated, researched, translated, discovered, and invented. By the end of the ninth century many great works were accessible, including Ptolemy's astronomical book *Syntaxis*, better known by its Arabic title *The Almagest.* No wonder that, whereas papermaking was a Chinese invention (papyrus and parchment which were already in use much earlier were considered fragile), the first paper mill was established in Baghdad. This facilitated the reproduction of books and collections. Works on astrology, mathematics, agriculture, medicine, philosophy, and geography were translated into Arabic from Aramaic (which some scholars equate with Syriac, which was a Hellenic renaming of Aramaic, and consider it an earlier form out of which Arabic developed),[3] Farsi, Indian, and Greek. *Bayt al-Hikma* expanded in mathematics, astrology, and science. Scientific knowledge spread throughout the Islamic world, including Sicily, southern Italy, and especially Andalusia.

The Arabs in three faiths within the fold of Islamic culture and rule in various dynastic regimes from al-Andalus to Damascus to Baghdad to Cairo were absorbed by learning, knowledge, and scientific research that blended into poetic architectural feats and monuments of grandeur and beauty. At the peak of *Bayt al-Hikma*, Baghdad was indeed the center of intellectual gravity in the world.[4] Islamic interest in science and scholarship continued to grow and flourish. By the twelfth century the main centers of learning in Spain were in Cordoba and Toledo. Cairo's *Dar il-'ilm*[5] was a prominent public institution that served as a house of learning (university) and a center for research (scholarship). The Fatimid ruler in Cairo pushed for science,[6] encouraging astronomy over astrology, and banishing astrologers. He encouraged *'ilm* (scientific knowledge) over the use of stars for personal imaginings. An astronomical observatory was being constructed at the time that the young man, Ibn Radwan, was observing the sky with his naked eye on the evening of April 30, 1006. By age thirty, Ibn Radwan had published major works ranging from a commentary on *Tetrabiblos*, a contribution by the second-century astronomer and mathematician Ptolemy, to medical treatises. By the time he died in 1067 or 1068 he had written more than 100 works.

From Ibn Radwan's observational data on the supernova a team of English and Australian astrophysicists was able to narrow down the area of sky in which the supernova would have occurred. It was also Ibn Radwan's account that led to determining its degree of brightness. His observational account was the only one to compare the supernova's brightness with that of both Venus and the moon, observations that served as benchmarks to the team of scientists for estimating its brightness (for a fuller account see Donsbach 2006).[7] Space, the focus since ancient times for building science and constructing cosmology, the subject of observation since the Greeks and subsequently the Arabs, is also a domain of modern social scientific conceptualization.

Biblical Creation

> I never could accept the first step of the Genesis story: "In the beginning the earth was without form and void." That primary tabula rasa would have set a formidable problem in thermodynamics for the next billion years. Perhaps the earth never was any more a tabula rasa than is a human zygote – a fertilized egg.
>
> Gregory Bateson, *Mind and Nature* (1979: 5)

Gregory Bateson knew there is a scientific basis for the beginning of life and for creationist processes. The earth had been spinning for millions of years prior to the appearance of living matter and, much later, the emergence of humankind. Julius Thomas Fraser puts it this way: "The earth had been spinning on its axis for some 1,000 million years before living matter appeared, and for another 3,000 million years before man emerged. There is no period in the story of life when the cyclic process of day and night and that of the seasons did not operate" (1975: 45). The Bible presents a specific script describing how it all began and in this version of the story there is a denial of form and motion to the universe.

Bateson clearly rejects the biblical rendering of the beginnings, which is described in terms of a *void* and *formless universe*. It is a void and formlessness that awaits the biblical God's command and divine intervention to inject life into the universe, creating earth and heavens, seas and plants, animal beings and human beings, all in six days. In order to better understand Bateson's objection, I break his remarks in the above quote into two parts. The first part concerns the void as envisioned in Judaic-biblical beginnings. The second concerns Bateson's interesting analogy between earth and egg. With regard to the first part, segments from the biblical text (Genesis) are presented next and analyzed.

According to the Judaic-biblical version of creation as it is laid out in Genesis at the very beginning of the Bible (the Old Testament), the universe was created by God's command and in a linear sequence of events, each task or set of tasks marking a day, itself divided into morning and evening. Using the Revised Standard Version of the Bible, the relevant verses are presented below as originally rendered, except that they are organized according to a chronology of days, i.e. Day One, Day Two, etc. The image in Figure 3.1 is that of the dedication page in the copy used in this analysis.[8]

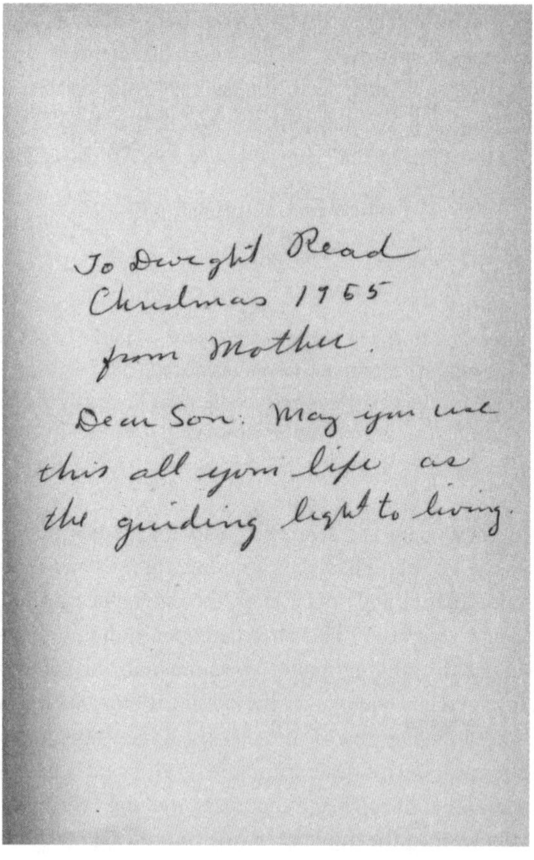

Figure 3.1 King James Bible "the guiding light to living." © El Nil Research

Biblical Text Segments

Genesis [or The First Book of Moses] 1

Day One

(1) In the beginning God created [or: when God began to create] the heavens and the earth.
(2) *The earth was without form, and void,* and darkness was upon the face of the deep, and the Spirit [or: wind] of God moved upon the face of the waters (emphasis added).
(3) And God said, "Let there be light," and there was light.
(4) And God saw that the light was good, and God separated the light from the darkness.
(5) God called the light Day, and the darkness he called Night. And there was evening and there was morning, one day.

Day Two

(6) And God said, "Let there be a firmament in the midst of the waters, and let it divide the waters from the waters."
(7) And God made the firmament, and separated the waters which were under the firmament from the waters which were above the firmament. And it was so.
(8) And God called the firmament Heaven. And there was evening and there was morning, a second day.

Day Three

(9) And God said, "Let the waters under the heavens be gathered together into one place, and let the dry land appear." And it was so.
(10) God called the dry land Earth; and the waters that were gathered together he called the Seas. And God saw that it was good.
(11) And God said, "Let the earth put forth vegetation, plants yielding seed, and fruit trees bearing fruit in which is there seed each according to its kind, upon the earth." And it was so.
(12) The earth brought forth vegetation, plants yielding seed according to their own kinds, and trees bearing fruit in which is their seed, each according to its kind. And God saw that it was good.
(13) And there was evening and there was morning, a third day.

Day Four

(14) And God said, "Let there be lights in the firmament of the heavens to separate the day from the night; and let them be for signs and for seasons and for days and years,
(15) and let there be lights in the firmament of the heavens to give light upon the earth." And it was so.

(16) And God made the two great lights; the greater light to rule the day, and the lesser light to rule the night: he made the stars also.
(17) And God set them in the firmament of the heavens to give light upon the earth,
(18) to rule over the day and over the night, and to separate the light from the darkness. And God saw that it was good.
(19) And there was evening and there was morning, a fourth day.

Day Five

(20) And God said, "Let the waters bring forth swarms of living creatures, and let birds fly above the earth across the firmament of the heavens."
(21) So God created the great sea monsters and every living creature that moves, with which the waters swarm, according to their kinds, and every winged bird according to its kind. And God saw that it was good.
(22) And God blessed them, saying, "Be fruitful and multiply and fill the waters in the seas, and let birds multiply on the earth."
(23) And there was evening and there was morning, the fifth day.

Day Six

(24) And God said, "Let the earth bring forth the living creatures according to their kinds: cattle, and creeping things, and beasts of the earth according to their kinds." And it was so.
(25) And God made the beasts of the earth according to their kinds and the cattle according to their kinds, and everything that creeps upon the ground according to its. And God saw that it was good.
(26) *Then God said, "Let us make man in our image, after our likeness; and let them have dominion* over the fish of the sea, and over the birds of the air, and over the cattle, and over all the earth, and over every creeping thing that creeps upon the earth." (emphasis added)
(27) So *God created man in his own image*, in the image of God he created him; male and female he created them. (emphasis added)
(28) And God blessed them, *and God said to them, "Be fruitful, and multiply, and fill the earth and subdue it; and have dominion* over the fish of the sea, and over the birds of the air, and over every living thing that moves upon the earth. (emphasis added)
(29) And God said, "Behold, I have given you every plant yielding seed which is upon the face of all the earth, and every tree with seed in its fruit; you shall have them for food.
(30) And to every beast of the earth, and to every bird of the air, and to every thing that creeps on the earth, everything that has the breath of life, I have given every green plant for food." And it was so.
(31) And God saw every thing that he had made, and behold, it was very good. And there was evening and there was morning, a sixth day.

Genesis 2

Day Seven

(1) Thus the heavens and the earth were finished, and all the host of them.
(2) And on the *seventh day God finished his work* which he had done, *and he rested* on the seventh day from all his work which he had done. (emphasis added)
(3) So *God blessed the seventh day and hallowed it*, because on it God rested from all his work which he had done in creation. (emphasis added)[9]

In content and tone, this set of linear developments leaves no room for the operation of natural forces and processes. Taken literally, in chronological and lincar mode, heavens and earth, waters and light, beasts and man are created and blessed by God in single commands. In the process, the seven days of the week are defined in Genesis 2, verses 2 and 3 – six for work and the seventh as the day of rest. In this formulation, God works like humans and rests like urban Western humans – certainly this schedule is not that of peasants or laborers anywhere in the world. God anthropomorphized, rests after the hard work of creation. This divine behavior becomes exemplary for humans. They too – at least urban middle-class Europeans and Americans – end the working week with "the weekend," a day (or some hours) of which is dedicated to collective worship. There is, of course, circularity – God is like humans, works and rests from work, which in turn makes rest sacred and drives humans to follow the sacred path carved by God. Otherwise there is nothing sacred about the *Sabbath*, originally an Aramaic[10] term referring to "seventh" – in contemporary Arabic seventh is *sābi'*.[11] Then there is the critical premise, in verses 26 and 27 above, which states that humans are made in the image of God. Anthropologist Edmund Leach (1967 [1962]) considers biblical stories to be "myths for the devout Christian, whether they correspond to historical fact or not . . . [with their] . . . non-rationality . . . [as their] . . . very essence, for religion requires a demonstration of faith by the suspension of critical doubt" (1).[12]

In the theater of the imagination, let us look at the commandments presented above as a scenario dramatized as a theatrical play. The curtain rises on an opening scene of emptiness, darkness, void, and nothingness. God appears or his voice is heard, masculine and larger than life, giving commands. He orders the void be filled. The void is filled with earth and the heavens. By command he splits the waters and creates heaven in between waters above and waters below. He orders light. He creates all beings with humans last, and gives humans his likeness and dominion over all life. At the end of the first act, which comprises seven scenes, the audience views God commanding the void filled with cosmos, beings, life, light, and hierarchy in six days, or six evenings and mornings. This is completed by the seventh scene, which corresponds to the seventh day, at which time God rests. The one-act Creation Play ends. Curtain call.

Creation and Human Origin

In this overall Judaic-biblical religious design, there is no room for science. God issues directives and is happy with the results of his commands, blesses all his creations but gives man the dominant position over all other beings. As it reads, this design makes no room for art and poetics either. The vision of Islamic beginnings is similar in that the universe was created by a supreme being in six "spaces." It differs dramatically, however, in tone and mode of delivery.

One crucial difference is a key premise characterizing the Judaic creation scheme, which concerns the nature of God and man and the relationship between the two. This premise is significant for understanding fundamental and fundamentalist Christian attitudes and particularly regarding responses to the scientific fact of evolution, which are manifested in extremist ways in the United States. It is about the Christian notion that humans were created in God's image, an idea that became the barrier against accepting Darwinian evolutionary thought leading to the strong rejection of the theory of biological evolution by many fundamentalist Christians.[13]

A poll conducted on March 28–29, 2007 by Princeton Survey Research Associates International, reported on the website of the National Center for Science Education, gave results that were broadly consistent with those of previous polls on the issue of creationism/evolution. It used the traditional Gallup question:

> Which one of the following statements come closest to your views about the origin and development of human beings? Humans developed over millions of years from less advanced forms of life, but God guided this process (or) Humans developed over millions of years from less advanced forms of life, but God had no part in this process (or) God created humans pretty much in the present form at one time within the last 10,000 years or so?

Results show that 30% of respondents chose the "God guided process" option, 13% chose the "God had no part" option, 48% chose the "created in present form" option, and 9% offered a different or no opinion. These responses are comparable with previous polls using the question, dating back to 1982. *Newsweek* recorded the results for evangelical Protestants, non-evangelical Protestants, Catholics, and agnostics/atheists. Fully 73% of evangelical Protestants chose the "created in present form" option, while only 39% of non-evangelical Protestants and 41% of Catholics followed suit. Oddly, 13% of the agnostics/atheists who responded chose the "created in present form" option and 27% chose the "God guided process" option (NCSE 2007).

In addition to "man being in the image of God," another barrier in the Judaic-biblical version is the notion of the dominion of man over other beings, as stated in Genesis 1, verses 26 and 28. This proclaimed superiority of man over all beings perhaps stands between biblical belief and the scientific fact of developmental stages generative of forms from earlier forms on the basis of the theories of adaptation and selection.

Once quite comfortable together, science, religion, and temporality were on a collision course. Today we are still experiencing the fallout. "Scientific naturalists who probed the physical processes governing the behavior of the surface of the earth began to realize that the biblical time line, revealed in Genesis to be no more than six thousand years long from creation to the present could not possibly square with the evidence from the geological record" (Aveni 1989: 143). The earth was far older than Judaic writings claim. Not unrelated to the collision course over time, is the collision course over origin of humanity. It is quite remarkable that in this day and age of materialism and secularism, and even by comparison with the rest of the industrial world, polling shows high percentages of Protestant Americans rejecting the notion of evolution as the paradigm that sheds light on the creational scheme universe and humankind.[14]

Islamic Message

Muhammad: Messenger, Mediator, Prophet

> It is God Who has made for you the earth as a resting place, and the sky as a canopy, and has given you form – and made your shapes beautiful, and has provided for you Sustenance, of things pure and good.
>
> Qur'an, Sura 40, Ayah 64

The Christian premise of man shaped in God's image marks a distinctive difference from Islam, not the only one by any means but the most important when it comes to the nature and character of God and the acceptance or rejection of the scientific facts of evolution. According to Islamic principles, the idea of a shared image (that God made man in his own image) would be considered *shirk* (sharing of divinity) or *ishrak billah* (sharing divinity with God). It goes fundamentally counter to the core premise spelled out in the sura called al-Ikhlas (Sura 30) presented below:

> *Qul huwa allahu ahad, allahu samad, lam yalid, wa lam yulad, wa lam yakun lahu kufuwan ahad.* [Say, God is one and only, the eternal and absolute, who does not beget and is not begotten, with no equal or likeness.] (my translation)

This idea is emphatically repeated throughout the Qur'an in different words and contexts. This Islamic principle is unequivocal. It de-anthropomorphizes God and de-divinizes humans. There is no likeness or equal to God. The Qur'an is explicit about God's creation and the notion of likeness. Sura 64 (3), al-Taghayun, states that God has created the heavens and the earth and has given form to humankind, making the image beautiful.

خَلَقَ ٱلسَّمَٰوَٰتِ وَٱلْأَرْضَ بِٱلْحَقِّ وَصَوَّرَكُمْ فَأَحْسَنَ صُوَرَكُمْ ۖ وَإِلَيْهِ
ٱلْمَصِيرُ ﴿٣﴾

Between God and humans in Islam there is a physical, metaphorical, and conceptual separateness, metaphorically expressed in terms of the notion of the *hijab*. In a previous study I analyzed the various usages of the term hijab, which includes its use with reference to separateness between God and human and gender space separateness among other uses, taking the focal concept hijab beyond the narrow reference to women's Islamic clothing (see El Guindi 1999). In the qur'anic text presented below (Sura al-Shura 42:51) is an example of the notion of al-hijab in the sense of separateness:

۞ وَمَا كَانَ لِبَشَرٍ أَن يُكَلِّمَهُ ٱللَّهُ إِلَّا وَحْيًا أَوْ مِن وَرَآيِ حِجَابٍ أَوْ يُرْسِلَ
رَسُولًا فَيُوحِيَ بِإِذْنِهِۦ مَا يَشَآءُ ۚ إِنَّهُۥ عَلِيٌّ حَكِيمٌ ﴿٥١﴾

This ayah from Sura al-Shura translates as follows: "A human can encounter God only through inspiration, from behind a veil, or through a Messenger to whom God willed to reveal a message. He is Most High, Most Wise" (my translation). Islam directs worship by humans only to God. Muslims bow and kneel to God (Allah is Arabic for God).

Muhammad, the Prophet of Islam, is human but has been granted special status as prophet (*nabiyy*) and messenger (*rasul*) whom God chose to communicate the divine word. This message was only revealed to him (the Prophet) orally through the archangel Jibril (*wahy*). The sacred words were later compiled and put in writing to become the Qur'an (the Holy Book of Muslims). The message is sacred, the Qur'an holy, and Muhammad messenger and prophet, who is not himself divine.[15]

Muhammad is very special to Muslims.[16] He is much loved by every believer. That accounts for the passionate reaction of Muslims worldwide, who protested against the Danish cartoons that insulted his memory and distorted his image. Two photos are presented in a collage, Figure 3.2, showing Muslims in public protests affirming their love to their prophet. However, despite such passion for him, in Islam the Prophet Muhammad is not to be worshipped.

As an example of the widespread sentiment after the anti-Prophet Danish cartoons, sticker signs reading "*kulluna fidak ya rasul Allah*" (we sacrifice ourselves for you, messenger of God) could be found everywhere in Doha (Qatar) – on cars, in offices at university, in banks, etc. There is irony and contradiction in arguments made in the name of secularism, which permit secularists to prevent public Islamic

(a)

Figure 3.2 Photographs of Muslim protests expressing love for their prophet. Courtesy of (a) AFP/KHALID DESOUKI/GETTY IMAGES; (b) AFP/TENGKU BAHAR/GETTY IMAGES

(b)

expression yet, at the same time, in the name of liberalism, democracy, and freedom permit expression considered insulting to the Prophet of Islam. Behaviors supported by such arguments are themselves against principles of freedom of expression. The global protests against the Danish cartoons defaming the Prophet

Muhammad and against the ban on the wearing of the hijab in public schools in France and elsewhere in Europe highlight the dilemma posed when public secularism is legally imposed on religious or ethnic groups, thus challenging rights granted by civil freedoms.

While most of Islam is devoid of magical occurrences and miraculous doings, a few are recognized and considered significant. The revelation is one. The other is Muhammad's ascension to heaven in Jerusalem. Both concern the mediatory quality of Muhammad: one as messenger willed by God to bring the revealed word to Muslims and the other in wishing to see God, thus granted ascension, to discover the difference between God and man. Of course Muhammad was the ultimate mediator in his career and community leadership. But he is not mediator between humans and God in matters of worship and communication. Each Muslim is responsible for his conduct.

Humans connect with God, individually or collectively, in a condition deemed appropriate according to the prescription of Islam. Men and women must be in a state of purity, in spaces they fluidly turn from ordinary into sacred, and through the appropriate worship channels. They do so directly, not via prophet or pope. There is no human hierarchy of priests or popes or clergy who have a more direct link to God than humans do. That is what is meant by the phrase "there is no church in Islam." Physically there are houses of worship like most religions have. In Islam they are called mosques (in English, a distortion of the original Arabic word *masjid*). The two terms used to refer to houses of worship for Muslims are *jami'* (*jawami'*, pl., deriving from root *j-m-'*, meaning collective gathering), a usage that becomes relevant as the analysis of Islam progressively unfolds in the final chapters, and *masjid* (*masajid*, pl., deriving from root *s-j-d*, meaning prostrate). One usage stresses the collective nature of the religion and the other the importance of submission to God.

For perspective I mention the usage of the notion of church in Christianity, fully aware that a complex sociohistorical trajectory is being simplified. In Christianity,[17] church has a connotation beyond the physical structure of a house of worship – one that is not applicable in the case of Islam. Church refers to the worldly clerical and governing hierarchy of Christianity. When the phrase "separation of church and state" is used with reference to Christianity, it invokes the factor of authority, that is Christian clerical hierarchy as distinct from from state authority. This makes sense if we look at the history of the development of Christianity in the West and the struggle that ensued between these two authorities. Islam, on the other hand, has no divinely ordained clerical hierarchy or authority empowered to judge believers in religious matters or control them politically. There is a system of justice based on Islamic laws and accepted bodies of interpretation. Scholars of Islam interpret text and jurists codify interpretations in their capacity as human experts into law. They do not form a clerical hierarchy, equivalent to that of priests and popes in Catholic Christianity, or ministers in Protestant

Christianity, who speak in the name of God to the faithful or on behalf of the faithful to God. There are times in Islam's history when religious authorities establish modern political power and adopt national goals, as in the Islamic Revolution in Iran of 1979. This is still worldly rule.

Therefore, the notion of the separation of church and state is based on Christianity's premises that historically allowed their merging. Despite measures to separate them, it is apparent how influential the forces of Zionist and fundamentalist Protestant Christianity can be in the United States. Religion is to be reckoned with in American domestic, moral, educational, and foreign policy issues. The influence and power of Protestant Christianity in the United States is not confined to matters of family and morality, but intervenes in issues of public education, government, international politics, and science.

It is significant that Islam is careful and sensitive to prevent the worship or the appearance of worship of prophets, ancestors, or idols. The Islamic narrative of creation does not have the factor of human likeness to God, as in Christianity, which eliminates a critical barrier against accepting the general scientific fact of the processual development of life. Accordingly, and despite some movements by individuals[18] or groups who are perhaps influenced by Christian fundamentalist thinking on the issue, Islam should be able to accommodate both its vision of creation and the development of science.

Here secularism is revealed as another strong belief system that excludes religion from its space. It is an ideology. From the perspective of freedom and equality, such behaviors are discriminatory expressions against religious beliefs and ethnic behavior and dress. Secularism in this case prevents freedom of choice and ironically stands in contradiction to liberty and democracy. The result is a situation in which dominant groups adopt the vocabulary of democracy but apply it selectively, as we shall see in the next section, on the case of secularism and the French ban of hijab.

Foulard et laïcité In a recent study, Bowen attempts to clarify the issues of the *foulard* (headscarf of Muslim women) in France. In 2003 two commissions were formed to deal with the headscarf issue. One was formed by the parliament and the other (called "the Stasi Commission") was appointed by President Jacques Chirac. These commissions made recommendations that served as the basis upon which a law was passed in early 2004. Bowen describes the situation this way: "In early 2004, the French government passed a law prohibiting from public schools any clothing that clearly indicated a pupil's religious affiliation. *Although worded in a religion-neutral way, everyone understood the law to be aimed at keeping Muslim girls from wearing headscarves in school*" (2007: 1; emphasis added). Bowen goes on to describe the extent of the absurdity: "French public figures seemed to blame the headscarves for a surprising range of France's problems, including anti-Semitism, Islamic fundamentalism, growing ghettoization in the poor suburbs, and the breakdown of order in the classroom" (2007: 1).[19] A vote against headscarves would reinforce the principles of liberty, equality, and fraternity.

Despite all the talk about private religion (discussed in the next section below) and public secularism, it is clear in French daily public life that one cannot claim that religion is entirely private. The extremist and provocative measures against the veil can only be understood as a response to the increased and increasing public presence of Islam in France and the threat perceived therein. In this climate, the lives and feelings of Muslim women who are exercising choice are ignored. These women have to confront stares, harassment, and the implementation of confrontational laws on a daily basis. There is historical context that must be brought to bear for understanding the situation.

Long before the passage of the law in France, known as the law of March 15, 2004, banning headscarves in school, there was a long and brutal colonial occupation of Arab lands by France. The bloody struggles for emancipation left a bitter legacy. France has not really severed domination of its colonies, such as Algeria, Lebanon, etc. The true story, I think, resides in colonial designs and hegemony. Alternatively, we can begin from the first headscarf affair of 1989. Bowen identifies three headscarf crisis points: "At three . . . moments, in 1989, 1993–1994, and 2003–2004, *the headscarf became a convenient, and prominent, symbol of external and internal dangers to France*" (2007: 4, emphasis added). In my book *Veil*, I raised the question about a shift in the primary symbol of Islam from crescent to veil (a concern shared in discussion with colleague Yvonne Haddad). Bowen identifies three concrete fears among the French: "communalism" at the expense of integration, the growing influence of Islam in France and, rather absurdly, "the denigration of women in the poor suburbs" (5).

Fear of the headscarf in France is broadly phrased in terms of *laïcité*. To describe French thinking and politics over headscarf affairs Bowen invokes this key notion of *laïcité*, a relatively recent term in the French language, which, significantly, was not (according to Bowen) employed in the law of 1905 intended to regulate the status of religions in France by not giving any special recognition for one religion over another and controlling funding that subsidizes certain religious activities. The Republican way of thinking in France consists of agreement on basic values. Toward this goal the state sees itself as responsible for integrating citizens (newborns and newcomers) into the Republican mold and does so by deploying public schools to be the socializing agents. "Schoolteachers were the designated agents to make 'peasants into Frenchmen'" writes Bowen (2007: 12). "From the mid-1880s to the mid-1920s, the Third Republic succeeded . . . in removing the Church from the public schools" (12) as it stripped public status from the Church. Much later, this "was to be summed up with the single word *laïcité*" (12). In discussing the headscarf affairs, Bowen (2007) invokes the work of political philosopher Blandine Kriegel. Kriegel states how France is committed to the principle of *laïcité* and that public space transcends individual difference.

This is carried out through public school and public administration. Cultural diversity is accepted and taught and personal rights are respected as universal and human rights, but the French concept of *laïcité* is different from the Anglo-Saxon idea of freedom of religion. The key French idea is *la cité républicaine*, which is rooted in the Greek idea that the citizens were themselves the state. The state sponsors the common good. *Laïcité* is a response to the religion-based conflicts that plagued France historically – Catholics against Protestants and the Catholic Church against secularists. If this is the historical backdrop to the problem, why then is the focus of the recent law on the Muslim hijab?

Culte ou religion? *Cultes* is the term used in France for organized religions. There is a *Bureau Central des Cultes* (Central Office of Organized Religions). Bowen had conversations in 2003 with the Bureau's chief (from 2002 to 2004), Vianney Sevaistre, "to learn about how the French state regulates Islam" (2007: 16). In sum, religion is defined in France as concerning the relationship of the individual to God and thus a sphere that has no place in French law. *Culte*, on the other hand, is used for the set of practices that represent the public expression of that relation between the individual and God, and it consists of three elements: public ritual, its buildings, and the teaching of its principles.[20] Today the term *laïcité* has come to be commonly (somewhat simplistically) translated as secularism. Contradictions in the French system abound. But at issue, from the above discussion and Bowen's remarks, are a number of constructs and concepts such as the primacy of individualism, secularism, and their clash with the nature and character of Islam. These become evident in light of the French definition of *culte* as opposed to religion, the notion of public space and the notion of secularism.

Egyptian Universe

As discussed throughout Parts I and II, notions about space and time and constructions of calendar and cosmology span millennia. We know humans have long gazed at the stars and the cosmos for models for culture, seeking answers to mystery, or in response to processes of thought. It is through the sky, as the Egyptians eloquently told us, that journeys of death are part of the journey of life (not as some scholars claim in order to deny death's finality,[21] but to embrace it in a sacred terrain of spatiality and temporality that gives rich meaning and logical order to everyday experience).

Millennia prior to Judaic formulations, Egyptians envisioned the universe in creative imagery that puts elements of the universe together in a coherent cosmological web of thought as a meaningful whole.[22] Presenting the Egyptian vision for the universe after the biblical narrative of creation puts both in perspective. Prophetically, the second part of Bateson's remark quoted at the beginning of this chapter makes an analogy between earth and egg when he states that the earth is no more tabula rasa than a human zygote, or a fertilized egg – an analogy that was also on the minds of Egyptians of thousands of years ago when they envisioned the beginnings of the universe and wove their own coherent narrative of cosmic order. In contrast to the biblical view of beginnings, the Egyptians looked at their universe as a cosmic egg. This formative and transformative process of building the universe and everything within it is woven in imagery that is reflective of natural, moral, and scientific realities. Metaphors such as eye and egg, discussed below, serve in this process.

Cosmic Egg

The opening scene, as it were, in Egyptian imagery, has its cast of characters: the goddess Nut[23] (female) and god Seb (male) who together produced the Egg.[24] Ra, the sun-god, who is generative of all life, rose from the Egg and journeyed each day from sunrise to sunset. The raising up by Shu, the supreme creative power, of Nut from the embrace of Seb represented the first act of creation (Budge 1969 [1904] II: 105). "The creation of Shu made a space between the heavens and the earth into which the Eye of Nu could rise from out of the waters and shine" (Budge 1969 [1904] I: 299). Nut represents sky and Seb earth. This is the beginning of the creation of the universe and simultaneously with it the beginning of gendering. As element after element unfolds in transformational conceptual embeddings, a rich and complex conceptual order begins to emerge. Analysis of research materials gathered for the visual ethnographic project *El Sebou'* about the contemporary Egyptian birth ceremony led to the insight that a process of gendering accompanies original creation of humans (see El Guindi 1986a: [film]).[25]

From an originary embrace of Nut (sky) by Seb (earth), the Egg (universe) is produced out of which rose Ra, the sun-god of warmth, energy, air, and light. Shu, the supreme creator, separated the two bodies, lifting Nut, the female, from the embrace of Seb, the male – an act resulting in a transformational process by which Nut becomes sky, her limbs (the four pillars) forming the outer boundaries of the cosmos, and Seb, the male, becomes earth. Space, a linking mediatory element, is created in between sky and earth. This space is filled with Ra's rays, hence generating life on earth (Budge 1969 [1904] II: 98); the text of Pepi I, lines 338, 339 is cited on p. 97). For simplicity, this scene of connected happenings can be represented first in an equation of oppositions and correspondence this way:

Seb = male = earth and Nut = female = sky.
Seb's arm : Nut's leg :: Seb's leg : Nut's arm

Their underlying set of isomorphic relations would look like this as equation:

Seb : Nu :: Male: Female:: Earth : Sky.[26]

The process continues. In a heterosexual embrace, Seb and Nut produce the Egg, a symbol in Egyptian imagery that stands for the universe. The supreme creative dual-gendered being called Shu, in creational mode, breaks up the union and breaks down the gendered originary whole into its constituent elements positioned in a duality of complementary relations mediated by the very source of life, the sun.

This imaginative beginning scenario recognizes embodied nature, gender, family, cosmic universe, and the biological process of reproduction in processes characterized by relationality and mediated by the agency of Shu, the dual-gendered creator, with transformational qualities of craftsman and architect, resulting in a mediational space created in between them, a living space that links them in transformational form as a wider union that is generative of universe, life, and other-worldliness.

Simultaneously, a creation and a gendering of the world and the universe were set forth. Two genders in complementary opposition representing, and hence mapped onto, two components of the universe, the earth and the sky, are formed and put in place. That is, so far, relatively easy to represent. Figure 3.3 shows Seb, the earth-god, depicted as lying upon the ground, or earth, with one hand stretched out – the arms of Seb touch the feet of the sky, and the leg of Seb is stretched to touch the hand of the sky. Shu holds Nut up as the sky, with her limbs extending to touch the limbs of the earth. Body is transposed as universe onto space. The sky is depicted in the form of a woman – the goddess Nut – whose body is bespangled with stars. The sky-goddess Nut and the earth-god Seb share many attributes and, together, form a union. Shu lifted Nut from Seb's embrace to form the sky. There are references to them as father and mother (Budge 1969 [1904] II: 95, 99) and elsewhere in papyrus texts the sky-goddess Nut is described as spouse of the earth-god Seb (Budge 1969 [1904] II: 102). It is evident from these references, and others elsewhere, that millennia ago Egyptian imagery of creations recognized a notion of family that is familiar in contemporary conceptual understandings.

A picture emerges of beings personifying nature, and embodiments of a cosmic universe, in which a corporeality of representation includes a genealogy of kinship generation and regeneration and rebirth by passage through a female body, and birth occurring from the bodily substances of tears and blood. An astrological universe is mapped onto the human body: breath, eye, egg, limbs, womb. Of these the Egg and the Eye play a key role. For example, Hathor was born out of the eye of Shu, the sky-bearer, and is also herself the eye of Ra, the sun-god. The sacred world is mapped onto the animal world. Different sacred beings take the attributes of and transform into different animals. Beings of nature and of the animal world are described in the sacred vocabulary of gods and goddesses. We see human institutions, such as primogeniture, heterosexual marriage, and cross-gender sex and

Figure 3.3 Earth-god Seb, sky-goddess Nut, and Shu. © El Nil Research

fertility, moralized by a spiritual world with an afterlife and judgment. An image of the universe that includes a journey to the afterworld, in which Nut, Seb, and Shu are represented, is shown in Figure 3.3.

Nut's arms and legs represent, according to Budge, the four pillars on which the sky was to rest and mark the position of the cardinal points. "The four pillars which held up the sky at the four cardinal points were called the 'pillars of Shu'"(Budge 1969 [1904] II: 92). It is revealing that a female body marks the borders of the universe: Nut's limbs are referred to as the pillars of Shu, who represents the ultimate creative force. Clearly the notion of "mother earth" is not universal, since out of the Egyptian story we have mother heaven or mother sky and father earth. As supreme creative power, Shu separated the earth from the sky (and the waters above) and set forth the process of creation, when the sun filled the space between them. That is, an aspect of the first act of creation and gendering is the emergence of the sun-god Ra.

Several papyri describe creation as having occurred "as soon as the Sun-god . . . appeared in the sky, and sent forth his rays from the heights of heaven[27] upon the earth" (Budge 1969 [1904] II: 97). References in the Book of the Dead (xvii:7–9) confirm that Ra rose for the first time when the heavens and the earth were created. This rising constitutes "the first great act of creation, because as soon as Ra rose he separated the earth from the sky" (Budge 1969 [1904] II: 59).[28]

Mediating, transformative power Shu is the patron of supreme creative power and *the holder of the sky,* who represents *the breath of the sun-god Ra*, whose rays give light and energy. Shu maintains the space between sky and earth, thus linking oppositional spheres, and is the breath of the very life-generative source, Ra. Out of Ra, the sun, other forms came into being: gods, humans, animals, and plants. So Ra stands for life-giving generative power and Shu for a transformative power with overall mediatory functions.

Shu's mediating role extends to death. In death, the souls mount a ladder from the world to heaven. Shu possesses the power to make the deceased stand up by the Ladder and climb to heaven. Instead of direct commands and directives, Shu assists the soul to heaven, thus linking earth to sky, world to heaven, and life in this world to life in the next world (for my discussion of the conceptual significance of mediation and transformationality in understanding cultural systems see my analysis of Zapotec belief and ritual data (El Guindi 1986b).

Shu also fluidly transposes onto and transforms into other manifestations. For example, Shu is described above in some segments as the holder of the sky, whereas we already know it is Nut who holds the sky. Shu is also described as the breath of the sun-god Ra (also emphasized above). We find additional transformational manifestations of Shu as master craftsperson, which is a position represented in the form of two named beings – Ptah and Khnemu (sometimes referred to as Khnum). Figure 3.4 represents the creator Ptah crafting the Egg, or the universe in the form of an egg, using a potter's foot wheel.

Ptah, in turn, appears and reappears, taking on several forms and attributes of other beings. One of these is the all-powerful Ra, the sun-god. Another form of Ptah presents him in partnership with Khnemu as creator, master architect, and

Figure 3.4 Ptah crafting Egg. © El Nil Research

Figure 3.5 Khnemu fashioning human. © El Nil Research

craftsperson of the whole universe – sky, earth, world and heaven, humans and animals and plants. He is described as the father of beginnings, creator of the Egg, of the sun and the moon (for more on this, see Budge (1969 [1904] I: 500–2). Creator Khnemu is described in various ancient texts as the great primeval creative force, the architect of the universe, the builder of humans, the maker of gods, the creator of things, the father of fathers and mother of mothers, the maker of heaven and earth, water and mountains and the raiser of heaven upon its four pillars (Budge 1969 [1904] II: 59). Figure 3.5 shows Khnemu fashioning a human upon a potter's table, with Thoth (the scribe of the gods) standing behind marking the "newborn" life span.

From the universe in the form of an Egg analysis proceeds to another central notion in Egyptian thought: the notion of the Eye discussed next as another key to the overall process of creation and to the generation of life.

Generative Eye

According to the text found in the tomb of Seti I, in the Valley of the Tombs of the Kings at Thebes, in very early times Ra was the ultimate God, who listened to the advice of his first-born god Nu and decided to destroy humankind, who were begotten from his eye, for uttering seditious words against him. After destroying humankind Nu was weary with the earth, mounted upon the back of the goddess Nut (in her form as cow) and stayed there. The cow began to shake and tremble. She complained to Ra, who commanded Shu to support her in the sky. This is, according to Budge, how the heavens above and the earth beneath came into being, and the four legs of the cow became the four pillars of heaven and the four cardinal points (Budge 1969 [1904] II: 93–4).

Within the creation narrative of the Egyptians, the record shows variants representing the cycles of the sun and the moon. Nut, the sky-goddess, first gives birth daily to the sun-god, who then passes over her body until reaching her mouth, into which the sun disappears, then passes through the inside of her body (which is nighttime) until it is reborn the following morning to fill the world with its rays (daytime). This brings up a theme in relation to transitions that recurs cross-culturally, namely the metaphorical cycle from death to rebirth. Ra, the sun, moves across the sky, embodied in Nut's form as a fertile woman, and upon reaching Nut's mouth Ra enters to continue the journey inside her body until rebirth on another journey across the sky. The daily cycle of the sun is marked by the theme of cyclical rebirth from inside the body of the fertile reproductive woman who embodies the sky.

In this rendition, humankind was created out of the eye of Ra prior to the creation of earth and sky. Nu is the first-born son of Ra, and he advised his father to destroy humankind, which he did. Nu is a transformational variant of Seb. In other versions Seb embraced Nut. Nut is a transformational variant of Hathor the cow. So Nu, the son of the Sun (Ra) embraces the cow Hathor (in this version, mounts her). Hathor's transformational variant Nut becomes the sky after Shu in one rendition and Ra in another delinked her from Seb in one rendition and from Nu in another. To clarify, these equivalences are presented in equation form below:

Ra = Shu, Nut = Hathor, Seb = Nu

In one sense, Shu created Ra (the sun) when he created the cross-gendered duality Seb and Nut. The first-born son of Ra asked his father to destroy humankind. A variant on this theme reoccurs with a different cast of characters, much later in time in the Judaic-biblical-Islamic scriptural texts, in the story of Yusuf (Joseph), son of Ya'qub (Jacob), and his siblings.[29] The duality of Seb and Nut not only represents the originary conception, but also together forms the parameters for the universe (earth and sky). Nut's (or Hathor's) limbs form the boundaries of the universe linking sky to earth, and her body is simultaneously the womb which preserves and generates life, when into it the sun sets and out of it the sun rises daily.[30]

The souls of Ra were seven in number and along with their doubles number fourteen. There are deities representing the twelve hours of the night and others representing the twelve hours of the day. Gods represent the different planets. Nut injects power into the deceased who is renewed by journeys with the sun-god from sunrise to sunset (Budge 1969 [1904] II: 107, 110). In the head of Nut, represented as the mother of all mothers, the two eyes take the form of the sun and the moon

(Budge 1969 [1904] II: 111), and Nut through her womb and birth cycle enabled Ra, the sun, to rise in a renewed body for another cyclical journey.

The eye in all these contexts is a source and center of generation. From the eye, humankind is born. And from the eye, life is generated. The Egg is the universe. It was created out of the heterosexual embrace of Nut (or Hathor) and Seb (or Nu) and it is crafted by Khnemu or Ptah, other forms of Shu. In that sense, even as humankind got destroyed once, destruction was not in connection with the eye. Humankind was created out of the eye of the sun. Therefore, the eye is generative of energy, light, and life.[31] We next move on to body in the form of the house that shelters the different parts of the universe.

House

Leroi-Gourhan (1993: 335) reminds us that the form of the shelter should not simply meet the practical requirements of protection and economy but also serve as the hinge between shelter and territory, between humanized space and untamed universe. The "shelter/territory" relationship should be the main term in the formula of spatiotemporal representation. Beyond the physical structure of house, the focus is on the interrelations between physical buildings, people, body, symbols, and ideas. House in Arab culture stands for fundamental aspects of Arab society, family privacy, and group identity. It is common for the term *Bayt* (Arabic for house) to be used as a reference for particular families, lineages, or clans. *Bayt Lehem*, *Bayt Saud*, *Bayt Dawud* would be references to clans of so-and-so. The variants of *Bani* or *Awlad* still refer to the kinship group with the emphasis being on kin affiliation. The physical attributes of the house in Arab societies, including door, are strikingly about identity, family, and privacy. Well studied is the ornamentation of the Nubian house. Louis Werner recently wrote: "the Nubian house, a mud-walled, stand-alone family compound centered on a courtyard and surrounded by an extensive layout of men's and women's quarters. The Sudanese novelist Tayyib Salih has compared such a house . . . to a 'ship that has cast anchor in mid-ocean.'" (2006: 2) Werner goes on to describe the decoration of a Nubian house doorway, or *bawaba*, "which mixes vivid color, adobe brick filigree, figurative and geometric images in mud and white lime-plaster relief, and wall-mounted objects like ceramic plates, automobile headlights, mirrors, cow horns and dried crocodiles" in a strong impulse to "draw attention to one's home, and to its doorway, as a symbol of its family" (2006: 2).

Lévi-Strauss problematized "house," thus introducing a development in kinship and family studies whose time was overdue. Lévi-Strauss (1991) considered "house" in the context of the sphere of kinship and his exploration led him to introduce a new category in his classification of societies, which he called "house societies." Most studies dealing with the phenomenon of "house" prior to Lévi-Strauss were concerned with house as an economic unit of production or consumption, as a source of census of household inhabitants, or a set of political and kinship relationships. The conceptual notion of "house" got relatively little attention. It has not yet become fully centered as a focus of serious discussion. A good critique was published by Carsten and Hugh-Jones in which they included various recent ethnographic-based approaches re-examining Lévi-Strauss's approach (Carsten and Hugh-Jones 1995a, 1995b).

Before Lévi-Strauss, Pierre Bourdieu in 1970 published his seminal and classic analysis of the Kabyle house (1990 [1970]). In his analysis, "house" is an object of thought. It is described as "the principle locus for the objectification of generative schemes" (Bourdieu 1990 [1970]: 89). Bourdieu considered "house" to be significant in that it was an instrument of thought. He wrongly, I contend, made a link between the importance of house in systems of thought and the level of sociocultural organization. He resorted to a sociocultural evolutionary scale when he situated groups who centralize house in their thought in societies which have not developed systems of writing (see also Wilson 1988: 38). In my view any association made between cultures with oral versus literate traditions and centrality of house in thought is erroneous, acknowledging of course that this point was not Bourdieu's central premise.

On the basis of their reading of Bourdieu's analysis of the Kabyle house, Carsten and Hugh-Jones observed in their Introduction (1995b) to a volume they edited on the subject of house (1995a), that the house "gives an appearance of unity to opposing principles made equivalent to each other" (Carsten and Hugh-Jones 1995b: 8). They point out that there is a tendency to focus on ritual aspects of house, whereas it has another side (1995b: 45). To them, the other side is the ordinary group of people concerned with their day-to-day affairs, sharing consumption, and living in the shared space of a domestic dwelling. They go on to say that it is out of these everyday activities, carried on without ritual, reflection, or fuss and, significantly, often by women, that the house is built. This house, all too easily taken for granted, is one that anthropologists have tended to ignore.

Actually, this "kind" of house and orientation in general is replete in anthropology. It is correct in its call for inclusivity of the many aspects of houses, but it shows lack of comprehension and appreciation of the significance of analysis at the conceptual level. This becomes very evident when they invoke Bloch in the statement that "[We] [n]eed . . . an anthropology of everyday life to balance studies of ritual and ideology (see Bloch 1991)" (1995b: 45). Ritual and ideology cannot be grouped together. They are of a very different nature.

The editors rightly challenge Lévi-Strauss's claim that "for peoples without writing, kinship is 'the only language available' (1987: 152)" (Carsten and Hugh-Jones 1995b: 19). They then reiterate that while house is an alternative language, it is not merely about kinship, but also covers economy, subsistence, production, consumption, and property. While true at a certain level, it is possible to engage in analysis of the concept house without reducing it to terms of political economy.

The editors also rightly argue for the value of seeing houses together with the people who inhabit them as mutually implicated in the process of living. But, they state, different aspects of house cannot be understood "*as static pre-given structures,* whether these are *of the material kind or mental projections of a structuralist sort*" (1995b: 45, emphasis added). Here is where they again reveal a confused understanding about the different levels at which analysis can be made. They are right about complexity. They are wrong, however, to think complexity at the concrete level requires complex (complicated) analytic models.

When Carsten and Hugh-Jones stress that houses "are born, live, grow old, die and decay" they are articulating the complexity in nice metaphorical language and simultaneously bringing together house and body. But we need to go beyond metaphoric polemics. They are critical of approaches that give partial rendering of complexity and see that a single theory of the house is fraught with difficulties, just like a single theory of the body. Houses, like bodies, are complex, multifaced entities. In response, I would say that description of complex phenomena can be thick, but theoretical analysis of cultural aspects (as in physics, cognitive sciences, and linguistics) ought to be simple, and its simplicity would reveal the multiple and multilayered aspects and full dynamism of phenomena empirically explored. The analogy between house and body has often been made. But Carsten and Hugh-Jones use the word *houses* rather than "house" and this goes back to the mixing of levels referred to earlier, between concrete material aspects of the house and the more abstract conceptual properties. There is overemphasis on difference, such as when they write that "particular aspects of which are given meaning by different people, in particular cultures, in particular contexts and particular historical conditions. These meanings constantly, shift within cultures, and they have no inherent cross-cultural validity" (1995b: 46). This denies universalities among humans in their unique manifestations of human culture.

They do, however, qualify their stance by recognizing that the processes by which the different meanings are generated are much more general. They also change position somewhat when they state that there should be attempts "to integrate architecture, kinship and cultural categories as they are brought together in the house, exploring the different ways in which houses and people are connected" (1995b: 46).

In support of a conceptual analysis of phenomena through a study of practices but without reducing them to "practice," my own analysis reveals that house would be of key importance in culture, when beginning in 1968 I carried out intensive fieldwork[32] among the Zapotec (El Guindi 1986c). My exploration concerned a major ethnographic study of the system of rituals and of the ritualization of passage into various life-cycle phases and passage into political or religious office (on the latter, see El Guindi 1977b). It was in the course of my exploration of ritual and during fieldwork among the Zapotec of Oaxaca, Mexico[33] that I discovered the focal importance of house in ritual activities, but more importantly its conceptual significance for understanding Zapotec knowledge.

It was found that in Zapotec socio-moral space (El Guindi 1973, 1977a, 1977b, El Guindi and Read 1979a, El Guindi 1981, 1982, 1983, 2006b; see also El Guindi and Read 1979b, 1980) "house," which was culturally conceptualized as closed, moral, and bounded, is culturally defined, not simply in its physical, social, or material manifestations but as a concept that stands in opposition to the concept of "field," conceptualized as open, amoral, and unbounded (on this particular subject, see El Guindi and Selby 1976).

To the Valley Zapotec the notion of house represents qualities of sacredness, safety, morality, authority, and family, all embodied in their social-kinship behavior and in the centrality of a sacred household shrine – the altar. The altar is ritually sanctified – it would contain candles and an image of a saint, and becomes the official-ritual entry into, and exit out of. This is explicitly manifested on ritual occasions (on this, read the ethnographic detail of ritual activities collaboratively authored with the late Abel Hernández Jimènez in El Guindi 1986c). The house altar plays a focal role in all rituals but particularly in the rituals of the Day of the Dead (El Guindi 1977a).

In El Guindi (1982: 178–9) I make the simple observation that rituals are bounded by space. They take place somewhere, in some location, such as in a house, church, village plaza, or the like. Among the Zapotec, when the spatial locus of a ritual is a house, the people of that house become categorized as *caseros* (literally, people of the house) and are called and referred to as caseros. They are the hosts for the duration of the ritual. They are distinguished from other people attending or participating in the ritual by the fact that they are "los que mandan" (in charge). The people in charge in the house (caseros) are in a position of certain authority. Caseros see to it that jobs and errands are done, obligations are met, and conflict is avoided or resolved.

The content of the category caseros, however, is not fixed. That is to say, the individuals categorized during the particular ritual as caseros vary from ritual to ritual and sometimes from rite to rite within one ritual. This variation depends on the point of the domestic cycle at which the ritual occurs and on the residence rule. For example, in the Angelito ritual associated with the death of unmarried individuals (who are mostly children) those who become caseros during the ritual would typically be the parents of the deceased, since they are usually the adult persons of the house when an unmarried child dies. Similarly, in Difuntos (funerals for adults) the caseros would typically be the surviving spouse and/or adult children living in the same house.

Likewise in weddings, the people of the house become caseros. But whereas in a death "the house" is that of the deceased, in a wedding it is less obvious since two persons are equally getting married: the groom and the bride. Hence the house of the bride's parents seems equally important, and either house might "qualify" as the wedding house. The Zapotec "choose" the house of the groom's parents to be "casa del fandango" (wedding house) in consistence with the prevalent virilocal residence rule. Thus in weddings the groom's parents become the caseros and their house serves as the physical base for the wedding activities.

This dynamic transformational quality of ritual suggests that looking at "house" simply as a physical structure or at the level of physical boundary can obscure the enormously significant dimension that unfolds in ritual; a dimension that leads us to a conceptual level of local knowledge and the way the people's spatial domain is mapped onto their kinship, social, and moral domains (El Guindi 2006b). Various significations of "house" reveal themselves. At a concrete level, there is the label casa (house) which is used to refer to: first a room, built with concrete material, as opposed to a hut; or, second, the whole house, including the solar (courtyard) and physically bounded by a fence, wall, bush, or the like.

At an abstract level, the Zapotec conceive of casa as a conceptual category "House," in opposition to "Field." The importance of House and Field as a contrasting pair of categories in their conceptual system is made evident through analysis of their myths, rituals, daily activities, and statements. House has boundary, is central to most rituals and accompanies life-cycle passage from one phase to another and political passage from one office to another. But for the Zapotec there is more. House has a sacred dimension in local knowledge. In rituals and ceremonies of a religious nature, related to the birth of Jesus Christ, the village community participates in collective events of making and unmaking the house and the raising and lowering of the house. Clearly there is more to house than being a dwelling to sleep and eat in. Approaching house conceptually reveals interesting dynamics to spatiality and temporality.

In the ancient Egyptian narrative, it is insightful to look at the connection that Bourdieu made between house and body. He observed that when Berbers cross the threshold and move from the outside to the inside of the house, their whole world is reversed (1990 [1970]: 40). Others object to notions of opposition and homology and see the relation between interior and exterior to be one of movement, a continuous movement of goods and people between the inside and the outside, a movement sometimes represented as one through the orifices of the body, attesting to the processual and animate qualities of the house (Carsten and Hugh-Jones 1995b).

Both ideas – that of the metaphoric expression of a conceptual link between house and body and the more concrete idea of movement expressed processually in expressions of journeys into and out of orifices of the body – very aptly describe the Egyptian narrative of creation. In my description earlier I followed Ra, the sun, as it moved across the sky which is embodied in a woman's form as goddess Nut, a fertile woman, and upon reaching Nut's mouth Ra enters to continue the journey inside her body until rebirth out of her vagina on another journey, another day, across the sky. In other words, the daily cycle of the sun is at once an astronomical event and a human birth event. It invokes the theme of cyclical birth and rebirth, into and out of the body of the fertile reproductive woman who embodies the sky. Seb was the god of the earth, and the earth is his house and was called the "house of Seb," just as the air was called the "house of Shu" and the heaven the "house of Ra," and the Underworld the "house of Osiris."[34]

House and body are in dialectical relations, at once sacred sanctuary and created space. In my exploration I find no mention of house in connection with Nut (representing sky).[35] However, my analysis shows that house is used in four contexts: Seb or earth (one of a pair: Seb–Nut), Shu or air (dual gendered), Ra or sun (heaven), and Osiris or afterworld. The four houses are the earth (Seb), the air (Shu), the heaven (Ra), and the Underworld (Osiris), the core spaces of the universe. Nut who embodies sky, herself houses heaven by giving birth to Ra.[36]

House therefore stands with egg and eye to complete the complex universe of the Egyptians. In order to clarify the whole Egyptian creation narrative I analyzed[37] the several variants and different elements. A relational structure emerges which integrates form with function, structure with process and meaning, thus looking at these expressions in terms of a process of creation, of gendering and of regeneration. This is presented in graphic form in Figure 3.6.

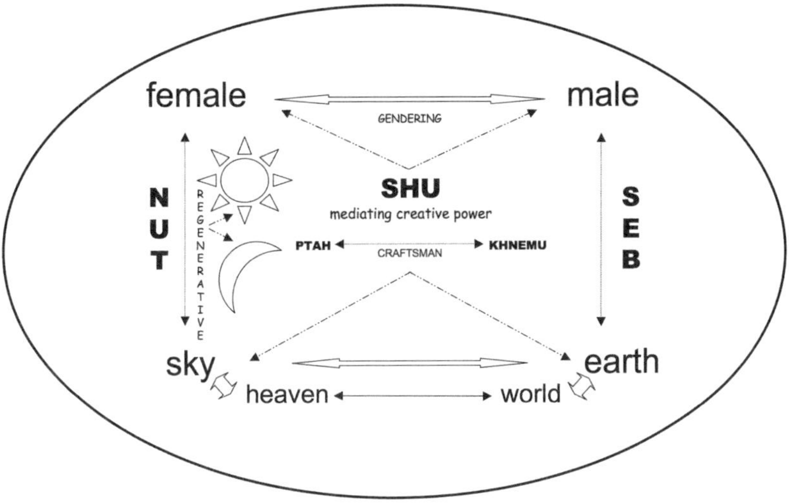

Figure 3.6 Universe as egg. © El Nil Research

Power of the Sacred

For Augustine in the fifth century AD, time comes out of mind, not out of space. Bateson would agree. Space, however, also comes out of mind. Clearly as evident in the ancient texts, imagery of sexuality and fertility is linked to birth, creation, and corporeal manifestations. It embodies ideas about nature, life, universe, and the sacred. Woven masterfully together in a coherent imagery are the human body, the daily passage into rebirth, sexuality in a gendered universe anthropomorphized in the form of Nut and Seb, an animal world (bull and cow), a natural world, cycles of the moon and the sun, the cardinal points, immortality through the soul's journey into afterlife, from a life nourished by sky-goddess – all folding onto notions of time that connects with space through creative and transformative powers. Gods are correlates to humans. Both possess similar component parts and qualities: a physical body, a double, a heart, intelligence, power, a shadow, a spiritual body, a name (Budge 1969 [1904] I: 299–300). It is the sacred linked with the ordinary. Animals are endowed with sacred powers and become incorporated into the world of gods and humans.

Behind all this there seems to be a philosophy containing the idea of a "wisely conceived humanism" suggested by Lévi-Strauss when he writes "that human beings, animals, and plants share a common stock of life" and that beliefs and rituals that respect that serve to "keep a human group in harmony with the natural environment" (1985: 14).[38] What is, for instance, the plethora of gods, goddesses and creators among Egyptians of the ancient world really about? All these gods and goddesses in ancient Egyptian cosmology are not merely about religion or political authority, but rather reflect an orientation that, instead of establishing the supremacy of man over nature or other beings, brings all aspects of life together in one whole.

Are these god and goddesses symbolic manifestations of power or representations of a religious system of polytheism? Do the terms "gods" and "goddesses" commonly used by Egyptologists as translations of hieroglyphic terminology best represent the Egyptian conceptualization of their cosmic universe? I would argue that the elaborate construction of a universe filled with beings, as the one spun by ancient Egyptians, suggests something deeper, more comprehensive, and more complex than the terms "gods" and "goddesses" invoke.

As André Leroi-Gourhan put it:

> Technical rhythm has no imagination; it does not humanize behavior but only raw matter. Thousands of years ago figurative rhythms brought the Moon and Venus within the confines of a human-controlled world and turned them into reassuring actors upon a vast stage where humans made and unmade their gods; but technical rhythms are only just beginning laboriously to penetrate sidereal space. Yet the slow invasion of technology has little by little placed the imagination in a new situation. The gradual erosion of mythological thought has set societies upon a course which disguised the crisis in figurative representation. Individuals today are imbued with and conditioned by a rhythmicity that has become a total mechanicity (as opposed to humanization). The crisis of figuralism is the corollary of the dominance of machinism. (Leroi-Gourhan 1993: 310)

The Egyptian notion of deities goes beyond expression of power manipulated by the elite or of absolute authority over humans, and it goes beneath a literal understanding of the polytheistic worship of multiple gods. Rather than manifestations of power or literal polytheistic worship, I contend that the many "gods" and "goddesses" of Egypt in ancient times are woven as a symbolic system that imposes order upon their universe by mapping multiple spaces, forms of time, and conceptual worlds. It is a system of mappings or relations among the material cosmos, the animal world, and the human universe. It connects time and space. It creates space, opens space, and closes space. It also creates life, genders it, and regenerates it in cyclicity with death.

As evident in the discussion of Egyptian cosmology, elements of calendar have already been emerging. The calendar, as we read in the next chapter, is not merely about keeping time and marking space but becomes a terrain in which politics of time and space are played out, leading to global politics of economy, religion, and empire.

–4–

Science, Religion, and Business of Temporality

Time for All Seasons

It is interesting how the whole world was led to observe televised celebrations of the new millennium, but not everyone considers the Gregorian calendar the dominant marker of time. There is hegemony behind the pressure for a globalized Christian calendar. Attempts by the United States to pressure the United Nations to officially impose a World calendar on the world looked promising during the late 1950s or early 1960s, with prospects for adoption by the United Nations. Aveni writes: "In 1954, the Vatican endorsed [the plan] provided it could be demonstrated that 'there were a general desire for reform, motivated by serious requirements of the economic and social life of the peoples of the world'" (1989: 163). One asks whether behind such attempts is a desire for real reform to improve the conditions of the people. If there is, it is not obvious. We know that the Roman Catholic Church had adopted the Roman system of timekeeping and, "like the Romans, used it to perpetuate and maintain the church's increasing power" (138). And as Aveni further points out, regarding the proposed World calendar of contemporary times, "even the headquarters of the Catholic Church regards time management as primarily a civic rather than a religious concern" (163).

Clearly there is more to calendars than time, or even religion as the case of the Vatican support of a world calendar shows. There are the factors of politics, economics, and hegemony. By the fifteenth century, Western Christianity had pervaded Europe and "had a tenacious grip on the European way of thinking about time, creation, and history" (Aveni 1989: 138). Proponents of the World calendar predicted that it would be instituted in 1961, *because in that year January 1 fell on a Sunday*. In other words, it would have been a Western Christian calendar imposed on the world. There were strong objections from many cultural/religious groups against such an imperial time system based strictly on Western Christian values. It is no surprise that Muslims opposed it. The significance of Muslim opposition will become clear when Muslim temporality is discussed in Chapters 5 and 6.

It is not the only failure. Instituting calendars has a long history. The French Revolution attempted to institute a calendar reform by which the Republican era was to replace the Christian era. "In a single stroke," writes Aveni, "all connections to the past were erased, and all unites of time abolished and replaced with new, more uniform ones" (1989: 144). The count of the years would begin with 1792, and the New Year's Day would be 22 September – the equinox. But French Revolutionary time ended as abruptly as it began. In 1806, after only fourteen years, Napoleon brought the French Revolutionary era to an end and restored the Gregorian calendar.

Formal Calendars

Formal systems of keeping time developed gradually in the form of official calendars and from the start their function and meaning went beyond organizing activities and regulating public time. Calendars were intertwined with authority, economics, politics, and religion. The practice of keeping and marking time precedes both developments by millennia. Enough evidence shows that keeping time is a practice that may go back more than 20,000 years, when hunters of the ice age notched holes in sticks or bones, possibly to track the days between phases of the moon (Stix 2006:4). Fraser observes that the unceasing rotating of the heavens, the regular changing of the seasons and other cyclicities are why humans measure all activities in terms of suns, moons, and climatic seasons (Fraser 1975). "The famous Paleolithic paintings found in caves . . . [suggest] . . . people were operating 20,000 or more years ago with teleological intent in terms of past, present, and future" (Whitrow 1989: 21). Human pictorializing can be traced back 30,000 years to the cave and rock art referred to earlier, in which humans used rudimentary tools to produce a vast pictorial record of life and ideas, assuming that human pictorializing never ceased paralleling the beginning of culture itself (El Guindi 2004). "As humankind pictorialized its universe," El Guindi writes, "it memorialized itself and made its ideas part of the visible material world to be learned, decoded, and studied" (2004: x).

Archbishop James Ussher pegged the origin of the world at 4004 BC by tabulating Old Testament genealogy – a period of a few thousands, as opposed to hundreds or millions, of years that may be more representative of the perceived dividing line between human and divine history than of reality. A hundred generations amounts to only 2,500 years, an interval not beyond imagination in contrast to the millions and billions of years offered by paleontology and astrophysics. Is time beyond history and religion? (Aveni 1989: 134–5) Maybe this is the wrong question. Perhaps framing origins as Archbishop Ussher did was the wrong framing to begin with.

Whitrow writes of evidence of ritual burial going back at least to the Neanderthal period, possibly earlier. The Neanderthal burial 60,000 years ago in a cave in northern Iraq appears to have included flowers. In terms of the present human species, evidence going back to 35,000 BC shows the presence in burials of tools, weapons, ornaments, food, and deliberate body preparations, a practice revealing deeply held convictions about the transitionality of death (Whitrow 1989: 23). And it has been suggested that markings found on upper Paleolithic artifacts and in caves are probably calendrical or astronomical in nature. Research on upper Paleolithic bone and stone artifacts has revealed tool marks showing patterns that correspond with the cycle of lunations. If this is true, we are then looking at human ancestors who about 35,000 years ago were turning regular processes in time into a set of static symbols representing patterns in nature (Fraser 1975: 48). It has also been proposed that Stonehenge, a place of Druid worship, represented a sophisticated lunisolar calendar.

While archaeological evidence from prehistory awaits more evidence, we are on more solid ground with the civilizations of Egypt and Babylonia and their written records.[1] About 5,000 years ago the Babylonians and Egyptians devised calendars for organizing central activities, particularly those that are time-based, such as agricultural. "Early chrono-technologists traced natural cycles: the solar day, the lunar month and the solar year" (Stix 2006: 4). The earliest known device employing the diurnal rotation of the sun for the measurement of time is the Egyptian shadow clock dating from the tenth to the eighth century BC. A sun-stick placed parallel with the axis of the earth comprises a sundial. Placed this way, its shadow indicates the time of the day not by changing length but by changing direction. The earliest known version of a sundial (borrowed by the Romans) was used to tell time when the shadow of its pointer moved against its inner surface. This invention is attributed to the Babylonian astronomer Berossus about 300 BC (Fraser 1975: 48–9).

The Sumerians of about 3500 BC divided their days into twelve hours, starting at sunset; the Babylonians into twenty-four hours starting at midnight. The Egyptians found correlations between social and natural events. "In Egypt, where everything depended on the Nile, the coronation of a new pharaoh, was often postponed until a new beginning in the cycle of nature provided a propitious starting-point for his reign" observes Whitrow (1972: 24). Besides marking time by official calendars, the Osiris narrative embodied a cycle of birth, death, and rebirth and "gave the promise of immortality", which, to Whitrow meant that the Egyptians had a definite concept of time; "since [they] believed that Osiris had actually lived in their land long ago . . . a particular historical event, in this case the death and resurrection of Osiris" this would serve as archetype for perpetual repetition of the past. Time was regarded as a succession of recurring phases. The Egyptian view of time is connected to their conceptualization of chronology. "The years were not numbered in linear succession but according to a particular pharaoh's reign, each mounting the throne in the year 1, and also according to the levy of taxes. The treasury officials numbered the royal possessions every two years, so that the years of a given reign were designated as the Year of, say, the Third Numbering, or the Year after the Third Numbering, and so on (Whitrow 1972: 25).

Calendar: Origin and Beginnings

The early calendar of the Roman Empire was lunisolar, containing 355 days divided into 12 months beginning on January 1. To keep it more or less in accord with the actual solar year, a month was added every two years. The system for doing so was complex, and cumulative errors gradually misaligned it with the seasons. By 46 BC, it was some three months out of alignment, and Julius Caesar oversaw its reform. Consulting Greek astronomers in Alexandria, he created a solar calendar in which one day was added to February every fourth year, effectively compensating for the solar year's length of 365.2422 days. This Julian calendar was used throughout Europe until AD 1582.

In the Middle Ages, the Christian liturgical calendar was grafted onto the Julian one, and the computation of lunar festivals like Easter, which falls on the first Sunday after the first full moon after the spring equinox, exercised some of the best minds in Christendom. The use of the epoch AD 1 dates from the sixth century, but did not become common until the tenth. Because the zero had not yet reached the West from Islamic lands, a year was lost between 1 BC and AD 1.

The Julian year was, nonetheless, 11 minutes and 14 seconds too long. By the early sixteenth century, due to the accumulated error, the spring equinox was falling on March 11 rather than where it should, on March 21. Copernicus, Christophorus Clavius, and the physician Aloysius Lilius provided the calculations, and in 1582 Pope Gregory XIII ordered that Thursday, October 4, 1582 would be followed by Friday, October 15, 1582. Most Catholic countries accepted the new "Gregorian" calendar, but it was not adopted in England and the Americas until the eighteenth century. Its use is now almost universal worldwide. The Gregorian year is nonetheless 25.96 seconds ahead of the solar year, which by the year 4909 will add up to an extra day. Though they share twelve lunar cycles – months – per solar year, the *hijri* calendar uses actual moon phases to mark them, whereas the Gregorian calendar adjusts its nearly lunar months to synchronize with the sun.[2]. Let us first begin from the beginning: with the Egyptian calendar.

The Egyptian Calendar[3] Scholars agree that the Egyptians made an outstanding contribution to the science of time. They devised "the only intelligent calendar which ever existed in human history" (Otto Neugebauer, quoted in Whitrow 1972: 26). The Egyptian civil year consisted of twelve months, each of thirty days, with five additional days at the end of each year, making 365 in all. It originated on practical grounds based on the rising of the Nile. They continually observed and averaged time intervals between successive arrivals of the Nile flood at Heliopolis. At first, the Egyptians assumed the astronomical year consisted of 365 days. When they realized that there is an extra fraction (about a quarter) of a day, they introduced another calendar, which corresponded better with the astronomical cycle. It was noted that the rising of the Nile occurred when the last star to appear on the horizon before dawn obscuring all stars was the dog star Sothis, or Sirius. This rising came to be regarded as the natural fixed point of the Sothic calendar. Astronomical computations show that the first day of the two calendars agreed in the year 2773 BC, the year claimed to be the time the Sothic calendar was formulated. This, according to Whitrow, is associated with the Minister of King Zoser of the Third Dynasty, Imhotep, later deified as the Father of Egyptian science.

The Sothic calendar kept pace with the seasons, but the civil calendar did not. The two coincided at intervals of 1460 years. The civil year was divided into three conventional "seasons" – called time of inundation, sowing time, and harvest time each divided into four months. These are not connected to the moon. Despite the linguistic anomaly that the season called "the time of inundation" would in due course fall in one of the other seasons, the Egyptians retained the 365-day calendar right down to the Roman period. This was the most suitable calendar for astronomical calculations. The Egyptian calendar was later adopted by Hellenistic astronomers and was even used by Copernicus in his lunar and planetary tables. Salzman, who specializes in Roman calendars, has a different interpretation of the Egyptian calendrical achievement (1990: 126–7). He considers the Egyptian calendar to be based on geophysical considerations rather than simply on astronomical patterns. By this, he means that Egypt's dependence on the regular rising and flooding of the Nile, which brings down soil from the mountains to the Egyptian plain, enabled the people to establish an agricultural system, which supported the civilization. So, he stressed, it was around the flood, as well as around solar and lunar motion that the early Egyptian calendar and its attendant religious observances was built, rather than the astronomical observations and calculations farther to the east across the Red Sea and the Persian Gulf.

In Egypt, observation of the sun was a useful way of telling time. Therefore, it was in Egypt that the earliest known solar clock was invented. A fragment of an Egyptian sun-clock dating from about 1500 BC has been found.[4] Shaped like a T-square, it was placed horizontally with the crosshead laid towards the east in the forenoon, thereby casting a shadow along the stem, which was graduated with marks for six hours. As the sun rose higher in the sky the shadow shortened until noon, when it disappeared at the sixth hour mark. Then the instrument was replaced with the crosshead towards the west so that the lengthening shadow gradually moved back along the hour marks to the twelfth.

The earliest clocks of this type were correct only at the equinoxes, and not until much later was it possible to take due account of the seasonal changes in the position of the sun. Eventually a series of hour scales, seven in number, was devised to accommodate these changes, but even then this timepiece was seldom accurate. The warrior pharaoh Tuhutmus III referred to the hour indicated by the sun's shadow at a critical juncture of one of his campaigns in Asia, and it would therefore seem that he carried with him a portable sun-clock. Another form of sun-clock employing the direction rather than the length of the sun's shadow was the sundial, but the Egyptians who invented it were not ready for the precisions involved in perfecting this instrument, which needed to be calibrated for the latitudes of different locations.

To measure time at night, the Egyptians invented the water-clock. Two main kinds were developed, depending on whether water flowed out of or into a graduated vessel. Inflow clocks were usually cylindrical; outflow clocks were in the form of inverted cones with a small hole at or near the bottom the time being indicated by the level of water. This invention was also borrowed by the Greeks and the Romans. For time at night, the *merkhet* was also used to determine the time. They observed the transits of selected stars across the meridian as they came into line with two merkhets. A merkhet on permanent display in the Science Museum in London[5] is thought to date from about 600 BC. According to the inscriptions on it, it belonged to the son of a priest of the Temple of Horus at Edfu, in Upper (southern) Egypt.

Because, as the Egyptians discovered, the sun not only participates in the daily rotation of the heavens from east to west but also has its own slow annual motion relative to the stars in the opposite direction, different heliacal risings occur throughout the year. The Egyptian priests were primarily concerned with the timing of the nightly service in their temples. Instead of choosing a different star daily they made a fresh choice every ten days, a period of time and a stellar constellation known as a "decan."

Whitrow observes that the oldest astronomical texts now known are found on the lids of wooden coffins dating from the Ninth Dynasty (*c.*2150 BC). They are called "diagonal star-clocks" or "diagonal calendars," and they give the names of the stars associated with the respective decans. These star charts were provided to enable the deceased to tell the time of night or the date in the calendar. It is recognized in scholarly and scientific circles that the present way of dividing up the day into hours, minutes, and seconds owes its existence to Egyptian scientific exploration and inventions in matters of time, calendars, and clocks, combined with Babylonian numerical procedures. This system went through some Hellenistic modification. The Egyptians also had a lunar calendar to regulate festivals by phases of the moon. They found that 309 lunar months (or lunations) were almost equal to twenty-five civil years.

The Roman Calendar According to Parise (2002), the earliest Roman calendar, traditionally ascribed to the legendary founder of Rome, Romulus, consisted of ten months – extra days or months were added to fill out the remaining 365 days of the solar year. When Numa Pompilius became king of Rome around 715 BC he reformed the calendar, added 50 days to the 304-day calendar of Romulus, and adopted a lunar calendar of 354 days but for superstitious reasons, having to do with even numbers and bad luck, added an extra day to make the year 355 days. This improvement was not sufficient, however, since every four years there were four days too many. "The Roman year had thus grown from a humble agrarian time count" (Aveni 1989: 112). But the number of days in the year could not accommodate all the traditional market weeks. Extra days were inserted into the calendar, a process known as intercalation. "It had taken nearly six hundred years from the time of the inception of the calendar before Roman chronologists took on a challenge that was to occupy them, if not with equal intensity at all times, through the zenith of their empire" (Aveni 1989: 112–13). The challenge, which was also to haunt Arabs in Arabia long before Islam, was how to devise a manageable, lasting method for inserting days into the calendar in such a way that it would keep in step precisely with the both the moon's and the sun's cycles. Why? For market purposes. But more importantly in the case of Rome, the Pontifex Maximus, who had charge of the calendar, began using intercalations for political purposes – for extending the terms of prominent politicians or giving extra holidays. The "politics of intercalation became an issue in the development of the calendar, for the pontiffs, those Romans responsible for the administration of the cults of the state, ordered the calendric observances. Periodically they allowed the full years to be those during which their friends were in office" (Aveni 1989: 114). These corrupt Roman practices rendered the calendar almost meaningless, and when Julius Cesar undertook reform, developments led to the Julian calendar (Parise 2002: 62). The Julian reform would suffice for 1,600 years.

Salzman (1990) explored the topic of Roman time to find out the functions a Roman calendar served in society. He observes that by modern standards "Roman methods of counting time were extremely imprecise" (1990: xxi) and yet they retained their awkward system of calculating time, suggesting its purpose was not merely to increase efficiency. Salzman relates events that shed light. "A wealthy Christian aristocrat by the name of Valentinus received an illustrated codex containing a calendar for the year AD 354 . . . The calligraphy was of exceptional quality . . . [but] aside from its handsome physical appearance, the codex was of great utility for an aristocrat living in Rome" (3). It marked that year's important events and celebrations, including "pagan holidays, imperial anniversaries, historical commemorations, and astrological phenomena" (3).

Salzman notes that the Romans recognized early in their history the need to regulate their activities, a function that would be the first step in establishing a calendar. Attribution of the origins of the first calendar to honored founders, hence giving it an ancient pedigree, reflects the importance given to the calendar as a Roman institution. Its content and organization "remained generally the same for the six centuries of the Roman calendar's usage" (11). The influence of astrology was reflected in the inclusion of lunar and solar week cycles. Christian holidays were omitted from the calendar as they were not yet of civic importance in Rome. The seven-day weekly cycles were not a result of Christian influences. They "came to Rome via an interest in astrology as early as the first century B.C." (13). Various sources contend that the seven-day week came to Rome from Babylonia.

An official Roman calendar in the fourth century (AD 354) recorded public holidays, which were state-recognized and state-supported. Salzman notes that the Latin terms for holidays (*feriae*, *dies festi*, or *dies feriati*) include the notion of honoring the gods and abstaining from work. It was the priests, however, who were charged with carrying out prescribed rites, not the public at large. The public had no obligation to perform acts of worship. Despite continuity with earlier calendars in Rome, the calendar of 354 does show certain developments. The most striking is the significant increase in the number of days devoted to holidays and festivals. Other than sheer increase in number, more and more festivals were combined with games. So there was change in quality as well. The situation had become so excessive that a commission eventually formed to remove from the calendar some festivals (Salzman 1990: 118, 178).

In a later publication Salzman concludes that both pagans and Christians in the fourth century were familiar with and used a seven-day cycle and were also aware of astrological associations in the naming of days. They were much more alike than Christian preachers, who justified use of planetary names for the days of the week perhaps to maintain continuity, were willing to admit. However, evidence shows that pagans and Christians had different notions of Sunday. For Christians it was a weekly day of worship. Pagans continued to celebrate a traditional Roman holiday in honor of Sol, begun by Constantine, with circus games and market days. Sunday to them was the day of the Sun (*dies Solis*) not the day of the Lord (*dies Dominica*), that is a day of religious observance, through the end of the fourth century (Salzman 2004: 207).

It is important to note that adopting Sunday as a day of celebration was neither swift nor sudden. It came about as a gradual process. Seven- and eight-day market cycles have a long history in the Roman Empire. In fact, market cycles varied by region. There was also the ten-day lunar cycle. Evidence suggests that these systems overlapped into the fourth century. "The *Codex Calendar of 354* had three weekly cycles of seven, eight and ten days each" (Salzman 2004: 205). Some Christian writers noted that, while both pagans and Christians used lunar days, the Christian time-reckoning was superior. The reason given for this superiority was that Christians use lunar days because they were given by God not because they determined the nature of the day (2004: 193). So the seven-day week had not become at that time the only way people organized their time and activities. It would be safe to say that it was in the fifth century that there was in the West "uniformity in using the seven-day week in regulating people's activities" (2004: 207)

Origin of the Seven-Day Week

It is quite common around the world today to live according to a seven-day week cycle. We take it for granted. But it has not always been this way. Salzman follows the historical development of the seven-day week cycle: "In the only extant 4th century Roman calendar to survive, the Codex Calendary of 354, there were not fewer than three 'weekly cycles,' one of eight-days, to record the traditional Roman market week, one of seven-days to record the planetary week, and one of 10 days to record the lunar cycle" (Salzman 2004: 185). It is a calendar filled with pagan holidays intended for use by Christians in Rome. It was Constantine who established the day of the Sun (*dies Solis*) or Sunday as a holiday. The law of 321 said "the day of the sun deserves veneration." The clergy in Rome and Italy were eager to make Sunday the Christian day of worship. But "[i]t was not until 65 years later that we hear in law an emperor specifying that Sunday is intended as a holiday for Christians" (Salzman 2004: 201). The law was dated between 368 and 373.

However, as historians pointed out, the seven-day week itself is not a natural cycle, and the question becomes where has that idea originated? From the viewpoint of Judaic and Christian belief, the idea of the seven-day week is anchored in divine commandments, that is, the notion of creation as imagined in Judaic cosmology. The biblical account of creation relates God's commandment to work for six days and rest (not worship) on the seventh: the Aramaic term Sabbath, equivalent in Arabic to *Sabi',* was adopted by Jews and made into a day of worship.

Conceptually and historically, however, the idea and convention of the seven-day week can be traced back to much earlier than biblical accounts, to the Egyptians, Sumerians, and Babylonians. The notion of seven for temporal spatiality for creative beginnings is integral to Egyptian cosmology and thought. Further, the seven-day cycle relates to the seven planets of ancient astrology. Evidence from Babylonian/Chaldean records point to a development around 500 BC that links the planets to the seven gods of each day. It may be rooted in earlier Babylonian beliefs in a universe that was a "sevenfold entity governed by a fusion of seven deities" (Zerubavel 1985: 7).

But direct evidence of a seven-day astrological week comes from Egypt. Salzman, citing Roman writers, observes that "[t]he custom of referring the days to the seven stars called planets was instituted by the Egyptians" (2004: 189). In the first century BC the idea spread in the Roman Empire. Once Imperial Rome adopted it, this convention was instituted in European time-reckoning. Whitrow observes that "[i]n Imperial times . . . the custom became popular, under astrological influence, to use the seven-day week with the different days named after the respective 'planets.'" (1989: 68) These were Saturn, the Sun, the Moon, Mars, Mercury, Jupiter, and Venus. It is from these that the modern European days of the week derive. *Dies Solis* (the day of the Sun) was the name of today's Sunday. The Christians at first adhered to the seven-day week in which the days were numbered not named. Table 4.1, adapted by El Guindi from Aveni (1989: 102) shows the English language names of the week and corresponding Latin and Anglo-Saxon names.

Table 4.1 Seven weekdays named in Latin, Anglo-Saxon, and English

Latin	*Anglo-Saxon*	*English*
Dies Solis	Sun's Day	Sunday
Dies Lunae	Moon's Day	Monday
Dies Martis	Tiw's Day	Tuesday
Dies Mercurii	Woden's Day	Wednesday
Dies Jovis	Thor's Day	Thursday
Dies Veneris	Frigg's Day	Friday
Dies Saturni	Seterne's Day	Saturday

Modified from Aveni 1989: 102

The basis of numbered weekdays is rooted in pre-Islamic Arab calculation and it might be the source for the Christian week. Eventually, astrological influences from pagan converts to Christianity led a shift in which a planetary week was adopted. The planetary week was officially adopted in AD 321 by the Emperor Constantine, who adhered to the Christian practice regarding Sunday as the first day of the week. "He formally decreed that magistrates, citizens, and artisans were to rest from their labours 'on the venerable day of the sun'" (Whitrow 1989: 69). January 6 was considered the major Christian celebration, Epiphany, or anniversary of Christ's baptism believed to have occurred in the river Jordan (the Dead Sea area in what is now Jordan) on his thirtieth birthday.[6] The origin of January 6 is traced to the early Christians of Egypt, and is purported to correspond to the blessing of the Nile.

The first mention of Christmas Day was in the Roman calendar in the year 354 (Whitrow 1989: 69). In the latter part of the fourth century, the Emperor Theodosius, abolished the pagan Roman calendar, and in 386 he reaffirmed his decree, and invoked sanctions against those who desecrate the Lord's Day. This marks the beginning of a uniform calendar that corresponds to the needs of what was then a universal society, one based on the Christian year.

Julian and Gregorian Calendars In 46 BC Julius Caesar reformed the Roman calendar on the advice of astronomers. He discarded the concept of a lunar calendar with its intercalated months and established a completely solar calendar of 365¼ days with the extra day added every four years. Caesar added 90 days to the year 46 BC (between November and February). Spring therefore began in March in 45 BC. In order to maintain this seasonal position, he rearranged the number of days in each month. January, March, May, July, September, and November were all to have 31 days. All other months except February would contain 30 days. February was to have 29 days in common years and 30 days in leap years. The year began on January 1.

After Caesar's death, the number of days in each month was rearranged. February was reduced to 28 days in common years and August was given an extra day. In order to avoid three successive months of 31 days, September and November were reduced to 30 days, and October and December were given 31 days. The calendar was again changed during the reign of Augustus. The priests in charge of the calendar around 10 BC had added the leap day every third year rather than every fourth. To correct this no further leap years were added until AD 4.

In AD 325 the Council of Nicaea adopted the Julian calendar as the official calendar of the Church. The Council changed the era to the birth of Christ, AD 1. It was adopted as part of a project to fix a common date for Easter. Prior to that, local calendars had been used in Christian areas not under Roman control. Parise (2002) notes that during the seventh and eighth centuries, England and other areas conquered by the Scandinavians and other "barbarian" tribes employed a unique calendar – one with a peculiar construction known as a "week-year," consisting of fifty-two weeks of seven days. The major festivals, most celebrated for a week, occurred at the beginning of the winter season, the Winter Solstice, and at the beginning of the summer season at the Summer Solstice. The year began with the start of summer.

The Celts developed another form of this calendar, dividing their year into quarters of thirteen weeks each, with approximately seven weeks before each of the solstices and equinoxes, and approximately six weeks after August 1. Interestingly, although the moon does not figure prominently in most versions of this calendar, the Celts apparently ran another time count simultaneously with the solar one. Evidence shows a reckoning of a 62-month period with two intercalations to adjust it to the solar year, dividing each lunation, or month, into the waxing (light half) and the waning (dark half) of the moon (Parise 2002: 293).

Gradually earlier calendars were replaced by the Julian calendar. There was pressure to unify the Roman Empire, both Eastern and Western, consolidating the date for celebrating Easter by Christians. In addition to Coptic (Egyptian) agrarian-based months, the months mostly used in the East by Semitic-speaking peoples (today the Arabs) were Aramaic months, used by Christian Arabs and other Orthodox Christians, which was based on lunar cycles. The date had been fixed as the fourteenth of the Arabic month of Nisan,[7] which began with the appearance of the crescent of the spring moon, the one nearest the spring equinox. Empire was instituting an alternative to Eastern Christianity. "The *computists*, specialists in charge of Christian calendric computations" were in charge of fixing the problem. But the religious issue of standardizing Easter Sunday was also "an astronomical problem of fixing the place of the vernal equinox in the zodiac" (Aveni 1989: 115). More importantly it was an issue of empire.

But intercalation was not sufficiently rigorous. Aveni mentions debates after the Middle Ages centering on the extent to which religious festivals really needed to be calculated with astronomical accuracy. The German astronomer Johannes

Kepler is reputed to have said, "Easter is a feast, not a planet." "The Julian calendar . . . was eleven minutes a year too long, and by the sixteenth century the error had accumulated to ten days . . . compounded by lunar discrepancies [which] meant that the Easter of the church often failed to correspond with that indicated by the heavens" (Poole 1995: 106). The surplus time of six hours over the 365 days gradually moved the vernal equinox from March 21 to March 11 by 1582. Easter Sunday began to fall later and later in the season. The equinox needed to be restored to its proper place in the year cycle and a mechanism to be devised to hold it fixed.

The Coptic Calendar The Coptic calendar, which is sometimes called the Alexandrian calendar, is based on the ancient Egyptian calendar. It is used by the Coptic Orthodox Church. To avoid discrepancy between calendars, a reform of the ancient Egyptian calendar was introduced at the time of Ptolemy III (Decree of Canopus, in 238 BC) which consisted of the intercalation of a sixth epagomenal day every fourth year. However, this reform was opposed by the Egyptian priests, and the idea was not adopted until 25 BC, when the Roman Emperor Augustus formally reformed the calendar of Egypt, keeping it forever synchronized with the newly introduced Julian calendar. The Egyptian calendar, however, remained in use by some astronomers until medieval times. To distinguish the reformed calendar from the Ancient Egyptian calendar, it is referred to as the Coptic calendar. Its years and months coincide with those of the Ethiopian calendar but have different numbers and names.

The Coptic year is the extension of the ancient Egyptian civil year, retaining its subdivision into three seasons, of four months each. The three seasons are commemorated by special prayers in the Coptic Liturgy. This calendar is still in use all over Egypt by farmers to keep track of the various agricultural seasons. The Coptic calendar has thirteen months, 12 of 30 days each and an intercalary month at the end of the year of 5 or 6 days, depending whether the year is a leap year or not. The year starts on August 29 according to the Julian calendar or on August 30 in the year before (Julian) leap years. The Coptic leap year follows the same rules as the Julian calendar so that the extra month always has six days in the year before a Julian leap year. To obtain the Coptic year number, one needs to subtract from the Julian year number either 283 before the Julian New Year or 284 after it.

From Julian to Gregorian In the year 1582 Pope Gregory XIII reformed the calendar. He suppressed ten days in 1582 (October 5 became October 15). The Gregorian calendar was accepted quickly by Roman Catholic countries – Spain, Portugal, parts of Italy with Rome. France adopted it in December 1582 and the Catholic states in Germany began using it a year later. The Protestant countries were slower to accept it. Protestant areas in Germany instituted it in 1700, as did most sections of Scandinavia. Sweden took a cautious path, making gradual changes. It was not until 1844 that the Gregorian calendar was adopted, which meant that Sweden celebrated Easter on a different date than other Christian countries (Parise 2002: 294–5).

As Christianity expanded throughout Europe so did the calendar. However, the Julian calendar remained in use among remote groups in Lapland and Iceland – despite conversions to Christianity – until the twentieth century. Iceland officially adopted the Gregorian calendar in 1700 but the earlier forms of reckoning remained in use until the nineteenth century. These died out after World War II.

England, Work, and Puritanism Prior to 1752, England began the new year on March 25 (Lady Day). It is one of the Quarter Days still used in legal circles, which divide the year in quarters (the others being Midsummer Day (June 24), Michaelmas Day (September 29), and Christmas Day (December 25)). So in England the day after March 24, 1642 was March 25, 1643. Britain waited until 1750 to adopt the Gregorian calendar and actually put it into effect in 1752, changing the legal year from March 25 to January 1, whereas Scotland had done this in 1600, so year dates between Britain and Scotland varied for the period 1600 to 1752. Russia continued to use the Julian calendar until the Revolution.

According to Poole, calendar reform in England resulted in skipping eleven days. In 1752 the British government decided to alter the calendar so as to bring it into line with that adopted by most other countries. It was decreed that the day following September 2 would be September 14. Whitrow describes how people thought their lives were being shortened. Workers actually believed they were going to lose eleven days' pay. The people rioted. It was worst in Bristol, in those days the second largest city in England, where some were killed. Workers demanded "give us back our eleven days," which became a famous slogan. This was so despite, as Whitrow notes, the fact that the Act of Parliament was carefully worded so as to prevent any injustice in the payment of rents, interest, etc. (1989: 1). Although the incident and how it was reported and interpreted became the subject of reconsideration,[8] I would like to stress the implications of internalized time. Constructed calendars organize time in a way that eventually becomes real to people. Any change in that constructed time is considered a change of real time, which impacts real lives.

There is a sense of order, writes Aveni, in reckoning history by the years. Maya kings numerically linked their ancestral origins to the birth of the gods thousands of years in the past. By giving numbers to their years they were able by mathematical calculation to predict eclipses and other natural events. In the West the numerically based liturgical calendar permitted the setting of the celebration of Christian holidays. Formally, the serial numbering of the years did not actually begin until the sixth century. The sequence of the years before Christ was not initiated until more than a thousand year later, in AD 1627. This abstract, rational, arithmetical scheme serves as the framework within which most of the world orders events.

The next section presents an ethnographic account of the struggle that contemporary traditional methods face against the encroaching Gregorian calendar.

Moon, Sea Worms, and Kodi Priests

Emile Durkheim (1961 [1912]) tells us that the notion or category of time is an abstract and impersonal frame, which surrounds humanity. He states that all things are temporally located (23). We have shown different manifestations of this idea. Using detailed ethnography, Janet Hoskins recounts the situation in which the modern calendar is overtaking traditional modes of temporality mastered by the Kodinese who are simultaneously being Christianized (Hoskins 1993). Hoskins summarizes the battleground: "a calendar is not a piece of paper to be hung on the wall but a highly charged arena . . . the politics of time . . . with conversion came the new Christian time unit of the week (the naming and defining attribute of the church)" (1993: 333). The Kodinese, according to Hoskins (1993: 335–6), speak of these changes as a "shift in the temporality of the heavenly bodies themselves or *the sun now sets differently, the moon now rises strangely*."

There is a disjunction between traditional and recently introduced modes of reckoning time. This is seen in events surrounding the timing of festivities. It is the priest of the calendar who is the symbolic anchor of the whole polity. It is within the authority of the guardian of time to measure months and count out the year. But pressures were brought to bear to "rationalize" the timing of Kodi calendrical rites to correspond to the Roman calendar, hence meddling in the traditional system, ignoring the flexibility and negotiability of Kodi time-reckoning. It is an example of a failure to appreciate the importance of the Kodi calendar in a regional system. This intrusion has caused festivities to become out of synch with the ecological rhythms[9] they were supposed to mirror. The sea worms are supposed to swarm during the ritual performances, but they often do not swarm because the days of the ceremonies are imposed, so frequently they take place without the presence of the worms that are the reason for the performances.

Janet Hoskins describes the politics of sea worm festivities; how the highest-ranking ritual specialist in all of Kodi, the holder of the new year, the guardian of a sacred tradition as designated by divination by the great priestess, a person who knew the secrets of the months and the years, the carrier of important knowledge and mythological narratives, and their shaper, is no longer in control of the events. The traditional leaders were visited by officials from the governor's office regarding a new policy to "improve and upgrade" the quality of traditional ceremonies. The local population would need to report to the governor the dates of the ceremonies ahead of time so that distinguished outsiders could be brought to witness the spectacle.

Traditionally, the date of the swarming was not announced until seven days before the event, at which point the people could begin preparing their foods to take to the coast for the festivities, beginning with the first day of the seven-day countdown after the full moon. But the district administrator was impatient with delays and uncertainties. Hoskins quotes him: "I can count the days and nights as well as anyone." He needed a calendar telling him when the new moon would appear in February.

The Kodi people protested his claim. The district administrator is not the priest who holds on to the year. Kodi months are not the same as the foreign months. The administrator cannot have this knowledge because he has not been watching the stars and the seasons as the priests have (Hoskins 1993: 337). February was usually the month when the performance was held, but by imposing the Western calendrical system on the traditional ceremonial season, the district administrator was trying to establish an exact correspondence that was not, in fact, possible. He knew that the Roman months did not begin with a new moon. But he countered: "we know the worms come in the second month of the year, so why should we wait for the priests to count it out?" (338).

The priest could not fight this kind of external power. He felt that it was not his "business to tell the government when they should invite their guests . . . *but neither should they tell us how to count the moons*" (359; emphasis added). He summed up the hegemonic situation overtaking the traditional system this way: "The *pasolo* of our ancestors was staged to greet the sea worms as they swarmed on our shores from across the sea. If we do it without their presence, we are not keeping our promise to the ancestors. *Now that so many people are Christian, however, they may not care*" (359; emphasis added). Ceremonies begin and close by "government" order.

The priest would not stop government intervention but at least he tried to make it understand. He asked the anthropologist to make a chart for him of the Kodi months to show to government officials, so when they set the dates they could do so more accurately. He wanted to explain to officials how the system worked (339). Hoskins sees that the purpose of any calendar, lunar or otherwise, is to measure the progress of the seasons and predict them (340). But the concept of the year as a fixed number of days (365.24 for the solar year) is an artificial temporal development and that it is the periodicity of the seasonal cycle that is appreciated first, by all early chronologists, and not the duration between successive periods.

This, as Hoskins points out, relates to the situation of the Trobriands. Leo Austen, the resident magistrate whose description of Trobriand calendars formed the basis of Leach's discussion, systematized the Trobriand garden times in terms of European months and dates. By doing so, Austen effectively destroyed the functions of the traditional astronomer and garden magicians – rationalizing the calendar in the name of progress and increased productivity. Whether the Kodi priest was subordinating to hegemonic pressure or saving dignity, when he decided to ask the anthropologist to provide him with a chart to give the government officials using the Western calendar, he wanted to familiarize them with local lunar temporality. But, as Hoskins rightly sees it, he was in reality engaged in a process of intercalating the lunar calendar and the solar year.

Currently the Gregorian calendar is used in most of the world either as the primary calendar or in conjunction with other calendars and different temporalities. It is the primary calendar for international business and diplomacy. Yet, we will see in Part III that in the Arab and Islamic World another temporality dominates life, thought, and business. It is a temporality that has been heard regularly, five times a day, for fifteen centuries, throughout most of the world, from a human voice from the top of minarets. To Muslims this is more powerful than mechanical and digital clocks and more meaningful than other calendars. An Arab recently told an American during the contemporary Anglo-Israeli-US wars on Muslim countries (1990–present): "Yes, you have clocks, but we have time." The time that this anonymous Arab meant is not the "time for money" that developed in the West and which is discussed next.

Time for Money

Today Americans feel good "gaining an hour" when the clocks "Fall back" and cheated of an hour when clocks "Spring forward" every year. With daylight saving time, "we simply make an instantaneous leap to the time zone directly east of us. Then, everything, including the setting of the sun, happens an hour later by clock time, giving us the illusion of having more daylight" (Aveni 1989: 97). Humans today in urban industrialized communities are dominated by time. "During our daily routine we are continually concerned about time and are forever consulting our clocks and watches. . . . [w]e even tend to eat not when we feel hungry but when the clock indicates that is meal-time" (Whitrow 1989: 17, 18). We live in the West "by legalized time," to use Aveni's phrase. How did this attitude, which Tom Blakely called draconian time, come about? For convenience, uniformity, and money, we move away from nature. Using a fictive sun in machines gives us equal hours and days. Evans-Pritchard (1940) remarked how the Nuer have no linguistic expression equivalent to "time" and so would not, as people do in the West, speak of time as it is being wasted, saved, spent, etc. Aveni says: "There is no choice: if you want uniform hours in the day, then you must cast your eyes away from the sun in the sky, and so in the eighteenth century, astronomers banished the *apparent sun* and put in its place *the mean sun*" (Aveni 1989: 97).

The link between industrialization, standardization of calendar, and changed notions of time is clear. But the general climate that allowed for the familiar Western notion of "time" to develop had been forming over an extended period of time and was influenced by many factors. As steam power became the driving force of industrialization, the character of work changed. Factory workers had to be punctual, becoming "the slaves of the clock" (Whitrow 1989: 160). Whitrow stresses the "puritanist" factor, meaning the role Puritans of England played in turning happy time into "draconian time." Puritan writers castigated the "vice of 'wasting time.'" The idea was that time is unrecoverable – when it passes it is gone forever. By the nineteenth century this idea had become more widespread. In England there was the Victorian work ethic, a premise that led to the notion of "spare time" – earning it after hard work. When they were in power for over a decade in the middle of the seventeenth century, the Puritans, who regarded the traditional Christmas festivities a pagan relic, removed the many intermittent holidays in England. In Scotland, the Puritan influence persisted and, adding sentiments against Roman Catholic leanings, Christmas became less and less important. This led to the abolition of holidays based on religious festivals. In place of the holy days, four compulsory "bank holidays" were eventually instituted by law. Physical recreation, such as competitive football, was organized on a weekly basis.

In an ethnographic study on the relation between time and work values in Bucharest, Romania, Heintz (2005: 172), in a section called "Time Discipline," evokes E. P. Thompson's study on work-discipline and industrial capitalism (Thompson 1967) for the analysis of the link between the organization of work and the perception of time. The study shows how the demands of the capitalist organization of work gradually imposed a new understanding of time during the process of industrialization in England and how impressively individuals resisted the change in their perception of time – the complete "conversion" to the new notion of time taking some centuries. The introduction of clocks and timepieces in factories became an early tool for imposing the new work discipline. On that note, interesting clock images displayed in a museum on clocks in Germany I visited recently are combined in a collage in Figure 4.1.

This imposition was reinforced by a moral endorsement from the Protestant ethic, while other notions of time were condemned. "Waste of time is thus the first and in principle the deadliest of sins," declared Richard Baxter's Christian Dictionary (Weber 1984 [1904]: 157). In the nineteenth century there was a proliferation of pocket watches. Putting it all together money making was "the new religion" that determined work and play. Distraction was provided by organized sport, which was not separate from profit making. Not only did workers clock in and clock out, but timekeeping permeated organized sports as well. Clocks were everywhere and determined everything. Anxiety about time led to worrying that a delay of a few moments might destroy lifetime plans. A process of dependence on time developed. This kind of time was fostered by the mercantile class and the rise of a money economy.

Time was becoming money. Benjamin Franklin is quoted from his published letters as having said: "Remember that *time* is money. He that can earn ten shillings a day by his labour, and goes abroad, or sits idle, one half of that day,

Figure 4.1 Clocks. © El Nil Research

though he spends but sixpence during his diversion or idleness, ought not to reckon *that* the only expense; he has really spent, or rather thrown away, five shillings besides" (Franklin 1748). The economic-utilitarian philosophy of time presupposes a quantitative perspective. Whorf points out that Western time-units are objectified as counted quantities (Whorf 1956). Scheduling is possible because of the notion of "time slots," which are quantities of duration into which we "fit" activities and events (Zerubavel 1981: 60). Time-keeping became time-saving and time-accounting became time-rationing. It is interesting in this regard to evoke observations by Martin Mills (2005: 349–66) in which he mentions the British tradition of stopping or covering up clocks upon a death in the family (Cohen 1985: 315). He sees that as perhaps one of the most obvious symbolizations of a "fracturing" of time and "ordinary self . . . and of the social (and temporal) disempowerment that attends upon the mourning of families." The lyrics of the song "Grandfather's Clock" come to mind:

> My grandfather's clock . . .
> It was bought on the morn of the day that he was born,
> And was always his treasure and pride
> But it stopp'd short, Never to go again,
> When the old man died.
>
> ("Grandfather's Clock," Henry C. Work, 1876)

Experiences resulting from altering time conventions or familiar calendars are disruptive and feel intrusive or strange because they challenge familiarity and comfort zones. These zones allow people to experience time as if it is absolute, real, permanent, and universal. However, this is not a culturalist attempt at white-washing the forces behind reform. There are important political and economic motives, often hegemonic, behind official reform of time and calendars by manipulation of clocks and calendars. Recently, there has been a development to manipulate how people use their time. Reform is contemplated in Spain today to end the "siesta" custom. A *Washington Post* story in April 2006 stated that the national government of Spain "has launched a campaign to break Spaniards of their traditional midday meal and nap, arguing that the old-fashioned custom is bad for business, bad for families and out of step with Spain's image as an emerging European dynamo" (Anderson and Green 2006: A12).[10]

The "bad for business" trope is already familiar and reveals itself in different places and at different times. We have seen examples of time at the beginning of the industrialization process in Europe. It is still debatable since we can argue about different ways of doing business. The paradigm of business is the one that found support by the Puritans. As to the second aspect of the rationalization for reform of time in Spain, that the custom of "siesta" is bad for families, it finds resonance in the manipulative language of "family values" used by US politicians during election time while in reality meaning opposition to abortion and gay marriage rather than support the tradition of family. US values give priority to individualism over groups. Individualism is good for consumerism in a corporate consumerist economy. It is good for business. The third phrase is also of interest. The notion of an "emerging European dynamo" should remind us of the glorious promise of the emerging industrialized states of centuries past.

Travel across time zones presents a most dramatic challenge to the notion of time absoluteness. Nothing is more challenging for Muslims than praying and fasting across time zones and while crossing time zones. Time within a day is measured by the sun cycle, and the month within a yearly cycle is measured by lunar movement. Yet, modern clocks got tamed into accommodating Islamic time just as compasses were directed toward Makka for prayer direction.

What does Yamamoto (1975: 235) mean by "clock"? To him "clock" does not literally mean the mechanical clock or wristwatch, but rather he uses it in a much broader sense, meaning "the alternation of day and night, the change of shape of the moon, the rotation of the four season, the birth and death of men, and the rise and fall of dynasties," phenomena that were occurring long before even the water clock or the sundial were invented. Yamamoto challenges the reification of time; in the process he sees a connection between time and clocks, "not that a clock is made because time exists, but that time appears because we use a clock" (235). Toda urges us not to mix "timers" with "clocks." He spells out the difference. Timers "set off predetermined activity patterns at the prescribed moments in the recurring cycles of time" (Toda 1975: 319). He observes that animals possess fairly precise timers, which are often adjustable to external cycles of events. They are context-bound, fixed interval signaling systems. "A clock," Toda writes, "is something that allows a context-free evaluation of the passage of time of virtually any length within a limit" (319). We know that time is not absolute, or real, and definitely not universal. Linearity of time is not universal; noon is different in different cultures and so are meal-times.[11]

Non-anthropological works on time cite anthropology often as the source for the hierarchical view of difference – observations that small-scale social groups have no abstract sense of time. They cite Evans-Pritchard and Clifford Geertz among many others who have been studying time-reckoning in non-Western cultures. What do we make of Clifford Geertz's observation that in Bali they "don't tell you what time it is, they tell you what kind of time it is" (1973 [1966]: 33, n. 55)? Non-materiality and nonlinearity of time is not confined to the Balinese or the Chinese or the Indian or the Egyptian. Lee (1973) invokes the Trobriands studied by Malinowski (1927, 1935). Instead of using the past tense, they use non-temporal verbs, and place events situationally.

The nonlinear pattern of temporality is part of the coherence of experienced Trobriand reality in which activity is relational to other aspects in a patterned way. When the Zapotec community in Oaxaca admonished the newly evangelized Zapotec man for his materialization of temporality and when Egyptians construct coherence in their universe in accordance with cognitive processing we find notions of linear and material time devalued and alien. Johannes Fabian sees such dichotomies as a way of distancing the unfamiliar. We magnify the differences between us and them and append human values to each side (Fabian 1983; Aveni 1989).

The character of sacredness as it interweaves with the ordinary to weave an Islamic rhythm is developed next in Part III, "The Ecology of Arabo-Islamic Rhythm," in which the notion of rhythm is conceptualized in a discussion of Islamic temporality and spatiality to bring together, in Chapters 5 and 6, the concepts of *khususiyya* (privacy), *qudsiyya* (sacred), and *jama'iyya* (collectivity) in a unified theory of rhythm that allows the unique character of Islamic life and the living pulse at the core of its culture to unfold in analysis.

Part III
The Arabo-Islamic Ecology of Rhythm

–5–

Marking Time, Carving Space

> In the twenty-odd years I lived in England, I never found out how the English mourn. There seems to be a funeral and then – nothing. Just emptiness. No friends and relatives filling the house. No Thursday nights. No Fortieth Day. Nothing.
>
> Ahdaf Soueif, *The Map of Love*, p. 38[1]

Egyptian novelist Ahdaf Soueif grew up in a culture (Egypt) that humanizes time and collectivizes space. Even after several decades living in England, she could not locate the familiar markers of comfort in this different environment – one that mechanizes time and individuates space. As we have seen in Parts I (Cosmos and Temporality) and II (The Anthropology of Time and Space), humans have been imposing spatial-temporal order on the universe and on themselves for thousands of years. The order of the cosmos is conceptual. Human culture, writes Aveni, emerges as the great processor of time, as people sensed the orderly biorhythms of natural time – the beat of the tides, the coming of the rains, the swarming of worms, the movements of the moon. Paradoxically, Aveni writes, "our mechanical way of repatterning time has led to a way of knowing it that is totally divorced from the real world" (Aveni 1989: 338–9).

Expressing an ordered nature was done in oral and written tradition, through poetry and song, through astrology and science, and as Aveni puts it with "hammer and chisel." Aveni continues: "*We* have framed it [time] in tiny blocs and hung it on a wall. *We* have linearized and circularized it, endowed it with a quality of irreversibility, even artificialized it by wrapping it around *our* wrists, and exalted it in the turrets of *our* religious buildings" (Aveni 1989: 135; emphasis added).

Expanding on this materialist thread, Whitrow writes:

> All the elaborate mathematization of time comes down to the desire to put time to work. Once a new technology has been invented, it tends to proceed with its own relentless logic and thus may have a lasting effect on a whole civilization. We have seen that this is what happened after the invention of the mechanical clock and this is what is now happening since the deep mathematical insight of Alan Turing (1912–1954) and of J. von Neumann (1903–1957) has led to the invention of the modern digital computer, perhaps the greatest achievement of twentieth-century technology. (1972: 181)

Perhaps not all societies put time to work or even put work to time. Some regulate time to balance their integrated spheres of life.

In the above statements, both Aveni and Whitrow seem to speak from ethnocentric/Eurocentric postures when they use the word *we*. "Putting Time To Work" is not a universal priority, nor is time's materialization. Small-scale local groups like the Kodi people, described in Chapter 4, struggle against hegemonic time impositions to maintain their own balanced system, which harmoniously links ecology, ritual, politics, and society. Nor do certain civilizational people, like the Arabs, necessarily accept interventions of methods or calendars that destabilize the harmonious balance between the sacred and the ordinary, values and trade, life and market. Twice in their long history as Semitic-speaking peoples "Arabs" had visionaries: Jesus in Palestine threw the money-changers out of the temple, and Muhammad in Arabia threw the intercalators out of business. What is the story behind such moral outrages? What is the impact of such interventions? The discussion in this chapter should shed some light on these questions.

In other words, some groups stress the ideational over the corporeal, the conceptual over the material. Bateson is clear on what comes first. He writes that the corporeal universe is a spin-off from the forms and ideas, but "*in the beginning was the idea*" (Bateson 1979: 4, emphasis added). The validity of this view can be seen in Part I, "Cosmos and Temporality," where ancient texts were explored to reveal ideas about nature, life, universe, and the sacred, all woven coherently, folding culture onto nature, in lunar and solar cycles, and journeys from life to afterlife. Notions of time connect with space through creative and transformative powers. Cosmic order is time and space. From cosmic temporalities in Chapter 3 we went to formal calendars in Chapter 4. There we discovered "Arab" (region) roots to time – conceptualizing it and measuring it. We end in Part III with the ecology of Islamic time and space. Ecology refers to a comprehensive conceptual framework for a comprehensive understanding of Islam – an understanding that transcends great and little traditions and goes beyond the "Five Pillars of Islam." Basic principles of ecology use the language of nature and its relation to culture within a new framework. Toward this framework, new ways are explored by which Arabs and Muslims have been marking time and carving space in order to creatively build a coherent system, we begin by tracing the roots of Arab time.

Roots of Arab Time

By way of putting Arab calendars and the Islamic notion of time in historical space and cross-cultural perspective, this section begins with a skeletal overview of the development of the Western calendars, specifically the Julian calendar followed by the switch to the Gregorian calendar, discussed in detail in Chapter 4. The Julian calendar, as discussed earlier, was based on the calculation of the time the Earth takes to be under exactly the same constellations, which is 365.256 days. In AD 1582 it was ten days short. Pope Gregory XIII issued an edict which replaced the Julian calendar by the Gregorian calendar. Conversion to the Gregorian calendar began from AD 1582, but it was slow and gradual. England accepted it two centuries later.

Today, the Gregorian calendar is widely used for global communication of temporality, but often alongside other more culturally meaningful calendars. It measures the time it takes for the Earth to rotate completely around the Sun, 365.2422 days. It is referred to in Arabic as *sana miladiyya* which is abbreviated after the year by the Arabic letter (م). The lunar cycle is considered central in organizing ordinary and sacred life for the Arabs. However, the Arabs have always used and continue to use both the lunar cycle and solar calculations. Together, the two make up their calendrical system, which has always been and continues to be lunisolar, rather than purely lunar or purely solar.

A lunar calendar measures the time it takes for the moon to orbit the earth twelve times, 354.3667 days. The lunar year is eleven days shorter than the solar year. Because of this discrepancy and to make adjustment between the two cycles a technique was devised called "intercalation." The Islamic calendar is called *sana hijriyya* in Arabic. It is known as the Hijra calendar and is abbreviated as AH in Western languages, deriving from the Latinized *Anno Hejirae*, which means "in the year of the Hijra." The Hijra is an Arabic word, derived from the root *h-j-r*, and refers to the time and act of the emigration of Prophet Muhammad and his companions, the *muhajirun* (emigrants) from Makka, his home of birth, to Madina where he built the beginnings of an Islamic community, the *Umma*, and the development of a state in Arabia (for different perspectives on this, see al-Biruni 1879, 1998; Wolf 1951: 86; Aswad 1963, 1970). Two trajectories characterize the process of organizing time in Arabia. There is the Arab trajectory which folds into the Islamic one, yet remaining two distinct parallel calendars. Both continuity and discontinuity mark the path of Arab time-reckoning.

It must be noted that for primary data I draw heavily on the work, *Al-Athar Al-Baqiya,* by the eleventh-century Muslim scholar Abul-Rayhan al-Biruni, particularly for information on Arab pre-Islamic and Islamic time and calendar. I would have preferred to use al-Biruni's original Arabic text but due to its inaccessibility at this time the source used for data here is the English version translated/edited by philologist and Orientalist C. Edward Sachau (al-Biruni 1998 [1879]). Sachau states at the outset in the Preface that his role merged translator and editor (1998 [1879]: vi).[2] It is worth noting that al-Biruni derived his data from his own observations and calculations, from Arabic poetry,[3] and from written and oral sources.

Arab Time and Real Events

Before Islam, Arabian Arabs marked time and space by the happenings of specific events. This, of course, is quite common at all times, but would be one of the primary ways in which groups marked time and space before the advent of clocks. Aveni remarks that "[b]efore the advent of clock time, people thought of time as distance traveled" or as has been happening around the world "we can think of time having been created out of the journey of the sun and moon among the stars" (1989: 136). It is informative to note at this point that "the first watch was made by Qutby, a renowned watch-maker of his time." During the Abbasid reign, the use of watches became quite common and the famous Harun ar-Rashid, it is reported, once dispatched a watch as a gift to his celebrated contemporary, the French Emperor Charlemagne. At that time a watch was considered a novel object in Europe and was regarded with wonder (see mutmainaa/history/muslim_inventors.html).

Al-Biruni recounts the instances in which Arabian Arabs would have said "From the time x till the time y the years have turned round one cycle" (1998 [1879]: 73). In a section labeled "Epochs of the Ancient Arabs," al-Biruni notes that

> The Ishmaelite[4] Arabs used to reckon time and date from the construction of the Ka'ba by Abraham and Ishmael till the time when they were dispersed and left Tihama. Those who went away dated from the time of their exodus, whilst those who remained . . . dated from the time when the last party of emigrants had left. But afterwards, after a long course of time, they dated from the year when the chieftainship devolved from 'Amr ben Rabi'a, known by the name of 'Amr ben Yahya, who is said to have changed the religion of Abraham, to have brought from the city of Balka the idol Hubal, and to have himself made the idols of 'Isif and Na'ila. (1998 [1879]: 39)

Al-Biruni goes on to write:

> Afterwards Arabs dated from the death of Ka'b ben Lu'ayy – till the *Year of Treason*, in which the Banu-Yarbu' stole certain garments which some of the kings of Himyar sent to the Ka'ba, and when a general fighting among the people occurred at the time of the holy pilgrimage. Thereupon they dated from the *Year of Treason* till the *Year of the Elephants*, in which the Lord, when the Ethiopians were coming on with the intention of destroying the Ka'ba, brought down the consequences of their cunning enterprise upon their own necks, and annihilated them. Thereupon they dated from the era of the Hijra. (1998 [1879]: 39)

Some Arabs used to date from famous accidents, and from celebrated days of battles. As such epochs the Banu-Kuraish, for example, had the following:

- The day of alfijar in the sacred month

- The day of the Confederacy of Alfudul, in which the contracting parties bound themselves to assist all those to whom wrong was done. Because the Banu-Kuraish committed wrong and violence against each other within the holy precinct of Makka.
- The year of the death of Hisham ben Almughira Almaqzumi for the celebration of his memory
- The year of the reconstruction of the Ka'ba, by order of the Prophet Muhammad.

Al-Biruni (1998 [1879]: 70) mentions an earlier set of Arabic names used by Arabs for their months, which according to his record, passed on to them by their ancestors. They seem to have been gathered from different sources (and thus he encountered differences in the ordering of the months), one source being poets who mentioned the names in their poems. The meanings of the names are given on pages 71–2, with a reference that dictionaries were used as the source of translation. The phrase is: "according to the statements of the dictionaries" (71), so it is not clear which dictionaries and whether this was the translator/editor Sachau demonstrating his own attempt at giving Arabic meaning to Arabic words. What is interesting is that in none of these sets of names are heavenly bodies, celestial symbols, or astrological references used. They used mostly situational terms from relevant events, climate conditions, geography, and ecology.

A particular group of people in the same region known as the Thamud is mentioned by al-Biruni as having assigned distinct names to twelve months. The Thamud are also mentioned by Bamyeh to make a completely different point – as an example of a group that is divided by *fitnah*, to illustrate Islam's disapproval of discord and factionalism which, to him, is a sign of an emergent reaction during the period of Madinian community formation to what he considers to be an "emerging inegalitarian disharmony of sedentary life" (1999: 204).[5]

In general, Al-Biruni (1998 [1879]: 74) relies on a number of contemporary sources for gathering his data. Regarding names of weeks and months, he mentions how he found the names of the Thamud months in "Kitab al-Wishah and in through Abu-Bakr Muhammad ben Duraid Al'azd," which were in turn verified by Abu-Sahl Isa ben Yahya Almasihi. Al-Biruni found the names presented in different orders. They are organized here in table form in Table 5.1. The year began with the month Daimur, which, according to al-Biruni, is equivalent to the Arabic month of Ramadan. If so, then al-Biruni did not present the names in their chronological order. Daimur, in the order he gave, would be the ninth month, which makes it equivalent to the Arabo-Islamic month Ramadan. He claims, however, that Daimur is in fact the first month of the year.

Table 5.1 shows the month names used by the Thamud in pre-Islamic Arabia, based on al-Biruni's calculation, changing the sequence of months in order for them to correspond to Islamic months. Placing the month of Daimur, which is the

Table 5.1 Thamud months corresponding to Islamic months

1	Mujib	7	Haubal
2	Mujir	8	Mauha
3	Murid	9	Daimur
4	Mulzim	10	Dabir
5	Musdir	11	Haifal
6	Haubar	12	Musbil

ninth month in the changed sequence, as the first month of the year, as al-Biruni states it ought to be, Table 5.2 shows the "original" sequence.

Arabic Months

In pre-Islamic Arabia, various official systems of measuring time were used. In South Arabia, some calendars apparently were lunar, while others were lunisolar,[6] using months based on the phases of the moon but intercalating days outside the lunar cycle to synchronize the calendar with the seasons. At the time of the birth of Islam in the seventh century, the Himyarites of southern Arabia appear to have used a calendar based on the Julian form, but with an epoch of 110 BC.

In central Arabia, the course of the year was charted by the position of the stars relative to the horizon at sunset or sunrise, dividing the ecliptic into twenty-eight equal parts corresponding to the location of the moon on each successive night of the month. The names of the months in that calendar have continued in the Islamic calendar to this day and would seem to indicate that, before Islam, some sort of lunisolar calendar was in use, though it is not known to have had an epoch other than memorable local events.

It must be noted that there is strong resemblance in the names of months among living Semitic languages contemporary at the "time of Jesus in Palestine," which is no surprise since these are related Semitic languages (which some linguists might even consider dialects) belonging to the same family of languages and sharing ancestral roots. They share common linguistic origins. At the historical time of "Jesus" in Palestine, Aramaic was the mother tongue of the entire Semitic-

Table 5.2 Thamud months in original sequence

1	Daimur	7	Murid
2	Dabir	8	Mulzim
3	Haifal	9	Musdir
4	Musbil	10	Haubar
5	Mujib	11	Haubal
6	Mujir	12	Mauha

speaking region. As mentioned earlier, scholars propose that Aramaic has evolved into the Arabic of the Arab/Islamic region today. Evidence suggests that the present form began to develop around the fourth century in Arabia and elsewhere. The names of the months in the Arabic calendar today do not differ much from their Aramaic origins.[7]

In the contemporary Arab world several month systems overlap formally and informally. In all Arab countries the Islamic months are used for religious and often for general purposes as the dominant calendar. Egypt uses the Islamic months, Arabized Gregorian months (for example, *Aghostos* for August), the Arabic months derived from Aramaic roots, and Coptic months, derived from Egyptian roots, for agricultural and climatic references and Coptic religious purposes. This is discussed in more detail in Chapter 3. It is worth noting that Coptic month names are used by ordinary Egyptian folk, Muslim and Christian, talking about the weather or climatic conditions. The names[8] of the Coptic months are: Thout,[9] Paopi,[10] Hathor,[11] Koiak,[12] Tobi, Meshir, Paremhat, Paremoude, Pashons, Paoni, Epip, Mesor, Pi Kogi Enavot.

Regarding Arabic names for months, Arabians used the names in use by Aramaic-speaking groups in the region, such as the Nabateans and others. The same names are used today by Arabic-speakers throughout the Arab world, for example, Syria, Lebanon, Palestine, Egypt, Iraq. The names of the Islamic months are also used by these populations. Among many of these, all three calendars are used: the Gregorian (in Arabized form), the Arabic, and the Islamic. It is revealing, I think, that Al-Biruni (1998 [1879]: 70) refers to the twelve Islamic months as "The Months of the Arabs." It seems that the names used for Islamic months were the same names already in use by Arabs prior to Islam for lunar months.

The names of Arabic months, derived from ancestral Aramaic, are organized into a table of twelve months, one column for Arabic months and one column for equivalent Gregorian months, shown in Table 5.3.

Month Day Names It is interesting that in the West only months and weekdays are named. Month days are not named, as in the case of Persia according to al-Biruni (1998 [1879]: 74). Interestingly, ancient Egyptians assigned names for all the days of the month, thirty in all (see Budge 1969 [1904] II: 320 (XIX)). But, al-Biruni tells us, Arabian Arabs had "special names for each three nights of every month, which were derived from the state of the moon and her light during them." The engagement with the moon, its movements, cycle, properties, and pattern was so intimate that Arabians had an additional system of names, which are associated with the properties of the lunar phases during the month. They gave a name to every three nights in each month. Al-Biruni gives us the names but due to space limitations their etymological interpretations are not included here. The names for each set of three days are given here in Table 5.4; ten Arabic names, one for every three days of a month, describing the lunar phases.

Table 5.3 Arabic months (ancestral Aramaic) and corresponding Gregorian months

	Arabic months	*Gregorian*		*Arabic months*	*Gregorian*
1	Kanun Awwal	December	7	Hozayran	June
2	Kanun Thani	January	8	Tammuz	July
3	Shbat	February	9	Ab	August
4	Athar	March	10	Aylul	September
5	Nisan	April	11	Tishrin Awwal	October
6	Ayar	May	12	Tishrin Thani	November

Overall, there are ten names, each describing the characteristics of the moon in that phase of those three days and thus covering thirty days. Further, certain nights of the month were identified by special names, as for example the last night of the month which was called *sirar* (because, according to Sachau's translation of al-Biruni, "the moon hides"); it was also called *fahama*, (which would derive from *f-h-m*, with reference to black tar in modern significations, and which al-Biruni interprets as a name meaning "being no light in it"). There is also *bara'* (from innocence), because, according to al-Biruni, the sun has nothing to do with it.[13] The last day of the month was called *nahir*, because it is in the *nahr* (throat) of the month. The thirteenth night is called *sawa*; the fourteenth, the night of *badr*, because it would be the full moon and her light would be complete. *Badr* in Arabic refers to full moon, and in some metaphoric expressions would describe a human face as healthy, glowing, and beautiful. Interestingly, *badr* shares the same root (*b-d-r*[14]) with *badra*, a sprinkling of grains or money. The ultimate compliment to a woman in modern Arabic is to describe her as "'*amar arba'tashar*" (which, in Egyptian colloquial Arabic, means the moon on the fourteenth day, the full moon).

Arabic Week

The Arabic week is a seven-day week. We have earlier discussed, particularly in Chapters 1 and 3, the conceptual origins and organizational roots of the seven-day week. The number seven and related conceptualizations pre-date Judaic and

Table 5.4 Arabian month day names

Days	*Names*	*Days*	*Names*
1–3	Ghurar	16–18	Dura'
4–6	Nufal	18–21	Zalam
7–9	Tusa'	22–24	Hanadis
10–12	'ushar	24–27	Da'adi
13–15	Bid	28–30	Mihak

Christian influences, and the seven-day week was not invented by the Romans. Rather, the records point to Rome having adopted the construct through astrological influences coming from Egypt and Mesopotamia, probably early in the first century BC. Various sources contend that the seven-day week came to Rome through Babylonia.

Conceptually, "seven" as a symbol can be found in many cultures around the world, but it is clearly present in the region of the Arab East, marking creative time and space for the formation of the universe and the creation of life in it. From the viewpoint of Christian belief, the idea of the seven-day week is anchored in divine commandments, i.e. the notion of creation as formulated in the biblical account (see Chapter 3). The biblical account of creation relates God's commandment to work for six days and rest (not worship) on the seventh, the term in Aramaic and Arabic being *Sabi'*, the basis for the popular usage *Sabbath*. Jews turned the day of rest on the seventh day of the week into a day of worship.

Conceptually and historically, however, the idea and convention of the seven-day week can be traced back to much earlier than biblical accounts – to the Egyptians, Sumerians, and Babylonians. The notion of seven for temporal spatiality for creative beginnings is integral to Egyptian cosmology and thought. Further, the seven-day cycle relates to the seven planets of ancient astrology. Evidence from Mesopotamian records points to a development around 500 BC that links the planets to the seven gods of each day. It may be rooted in earlier Babylonian beliefs in a universe that was a "sevenfold entity governed by a fusion of seven deities" (Zerubavel 1985: 7; also see 1981, 2003).

This can be traced to very old roots in the cultural region and particularly to Egyptian cosmology. Historical continuity in conceptualization of a worldview symbolized in cosmological ideas is not unique to Egyptians, Arabs, or any other group of people throughout history. But in the Egyptian case one can discern continuity through some practices that can be best analyzed in terms of past ideas.

According to al-Biruni (1998 [1879]: 75), Arabs identified seven days of the week and assigned Arabic names to them early on. It is not clear when or how long before the seventh century (the advent of Islam) these names were used. The names given to early Arab days of the week were descriptive, although the exact etymology and meaning will have to await further exploration. At a later date, the Arabs changed the names of the week to the names that are still in use today. The days are numbered, as it were, except that in the Islamic week one day of the week, the one equivalent to Friday in English, does not use a number as a name.

The sixth weekday in the Islamic week (equivalent to Friday in the English week) is called *al-Jum'a*, and is derived from the root *j-m-'*, referring to the notion of collectivity or gathering rather than number six. The name *Jum'a* for Friday is used generally by all Arabic speakers. The implications of adopting this name, as opposed to continuing with numbers, are discussed and analyzed in Chapter 6.

Table 5.5 lists weekday names in early and later Arabic with an additional column giving present-day English weekday names for comparison and perspective.

Months, Seasons, and Market

In agricultural communities the calendar tends to be based on seasonality. We have seen this reflected in the seasonal calendar of Egypt (and the Coptic calendar based on it). But in desert or border desert communities this becomes less meaningful. Aveni links man-made year cycles to agrarian economies in which "festivals for invoking or paying debt to the gods are positioned strategically in relation to periods of work" (1989: 334). In his discussion of early Arab trade and sedentarization, Bamyeh (1999) uses the classic Ibn Khaldun terminology of *badawah* and *hadarah* to refer to nomadic versus sedentary, but in a much more simplified sense than the full dynamic sense intended by Ibn Khaldun integrating the duality within a paradigm of cyclicity and processual change. Bedouin life is rich and nuanced. It is unfortunate that Bamyeh seems to have adopted an ethnocentric posture toward badawah, from the perspective of hadarah, which biases his account of them.[15] He has not consulted the rich ethnography on Bedouins, such as Lancaster 1981 [1997] or Young (1996), or on the dynamics of family among Arab sedentary groups (Antoun 1972, among others).

Describing Bedouin life as if static, timeless, routine, monotonous, one of "eternal subsistence" and "similitude of past and present", their economic activities as structurally disjointed (53), idealization of past and negation of present (59–60) suggests that the perspective taken by Bamyeh (1999) regarding Bedouins ethnocentrically carries with it the biases of the sedentary lifestyle and urban folk. This bias is seen in comments such as: "One of the major features of nomadic ideology, therefore, entailed denigrating an unattainable hadarah (sedentary) lifestyle while at the same time morally exalting the timeless ethics of the badawah (nomadic) lifestyle" (Bamyeh 1999: 53). This follows a familiar pattern known in anthropology which conditions us to look down on difference using the label "traditional," or as in this case badawah, to imply sameness in a static, unformed,

Table 5.5 Weekdays in early Arabic, later Arabic, and English

	Early Arabic names	*Later Arabic names*[†]	*English names*
1	Awwal	al-Ahad (one)	Sunday
2	Ahwan	al-Ithnayn (two)	Monday
3	Jubar	al-Thalatha' (three)	Tuesday
4	Dubar	al-Arba'a (four)	Wednesday
5	Mu'nis	al-Khamis (five)	Thursday

[†]These are the names used to this day by Arabic-speakers.

undeveloped, lifestyle. Badawah is a fully formed social organizational system that is integrally linked in the process of development of civilization in the Arab region to sedentary lifestyles. Biases by hadarah against badawah or badawah against hadarah should be recognized by, but not carried into, scholarship.

The strength of the study by Bamyeh (1999: 29) lies in his exploration of commercialism in Arabia. He describes the centrality of Makka in the trade activity in Arabia and particularly in connection with the emergence of long-distance trade side by side with intertribal trade within Arabia. This intertribal system of trade developed around the seasonal *suqs* (marketplaces) in and around Makka. Bamyeh makes the point (1999: 274, n.22, citing Rostovtzeff 1966: 95) that the opening of a direct maritime route between Egypt and India during the first century AD led to the flourishing of a hadarah lifestyle, which could have negatively affected the economic position of Makka.

But, he suggests, it could be that the development of this intertribal trade within Arabia may have cushioned this lifestyle from the side effects of the new trade route (Bamyeh 1999: 30). Intermediary trade became the most important capital-accumulating occupation in the otherwise largely barren land of western Arabia. The trade driven capital accumulation led to social transformation. Long-distance trade gradually transformed social and political life. It involved India, East Africa, Egypt, Persia, and Byzantium. For at least two centuries preceding Islam, Arabia witnessed an increase in sedentarization and complexity of social organization. Stability was necessary for sedentary marketplaces.

This complex of processes was very evident in Makka, which relied exclusively on trade. It wanted to maintain absolute neutrality and to preserve peace in the town at all cost (31). The strength of the populous tribe of Quraysh was sufficient to guarantee peace within the boundaries of Makka and its *haram* (Bamyeh 1999: 275, n.29). Bamyeh cites al-Alusi (1964 I: 227) in suggesting early roots to the commitment to the preservation of order in tracing the name Makka to the ancient word *bekka,* which connoted a certain and swift punishment for anyone who violated its peace (31).

Quraysh was the tribe most interested in preserving peace in general and during the sacred months in particular, the period when the most important commercial activities in the peninsula took place. Through a process of successive elimination of the city's potential and actual competitors, Makka emerged as the supreme trade center. Makka did not herself participate in or initiate such elimination, but ended up being the beneficiary of surrounding developments: disuse of the trade routes in Asia, problems with the maritime route in the Red Sea, the decline of Yemen, struggles in the northern frontier cities, etc.

*Sacred Months (*Ashhur Haram*)* Significantly, according to Bamyeh (1999: 29), the *suqs* forged regular, organized links between the sedentary societies of the peninsula, furnishing the material backbone for the emergence of a set of semi-legal, semireligious rules that prefigured the later formation of the Islamic central state and its apparatus. Most importantly, such rules included the "prohibition of fighting and raiding for four months of the year (Ashhur haram, 'the forbidden months') which *happened* [emphasis added] to be the months during which all of the *suqs* of Hijaz and more than half of the *suqs* in the peninsula were held." Bamyeh further adds that

> [s]ome religious concepts entailing a regularity of path or time, such as pilgrimage, developed parallel to the trade cycle and in a way that acknowledged the central role of Mecca in both regards. The commercial activity increased rapidly around Mecca as the pre-Islamic pilgrimage season neared, culminating in the great suq of 'Ukaz, whereafter the pilgrimage to the nearby haram (sanctuary) in Mecca took place. (1999: 29)

The concept was that peace should be observed during "forbidden"[16] months as a pseudospiritual accompaniment to trade.

But it was often difficult to enforce. For many nomads, the concept meant little, especially if the specified months coincided with periods during which they needed to resort to raiding as a means of survival, or if they were excluded from the trade involved (Bamyeh 1999: 275, n.31). Bamyeh (275, n.32) draws on both Ibn Khaldun (1961: 405) and al-Mas'udi (1965 II: 197) as sources indicating that the sacred months failed to garner much reverence among many Arabs prior to Islam. There is also some evidence to suggest that some Arabian groups, even while accepting the principle of having months as sacred, contested the arbitrary designation of specific months as being forbidden (275, n.33).

Prior to the instituting of an Islamic pilgrimage to Makka, there was Arab pilgrimage to Makka related to trade cycles. Al-Biruni describes the calendar of this earlier Arab pilgrimage as having gone "wandering around through the four seasons of the year" (1998 [1879]: 73). That is, pilgrimage occurred at different times of the year each year, shifting around the seasons. It was in the interest, it seems, of the economy and those Arabians in power at the time, prior to Islam, to find a way to coordinate pilgrimage and market – that is, to hold pilgrimage when "their merchandise (hides, skins, fruit, etc.) was ready for the market" (73). They wanted to fix pilgrimage times to coordinate with "the most agreeable and abundant season of the year" (73). The purpose was to have the most beneficial conditions to maximize benefits from trade and commerce. The solution was to be found in the procedures of intercalation, by which the discrepancy between the sacred months of pilgrimage and the calendar of seasons is removed.

An-Nasi' *(Intercalation)* Mathematics, the gift of the Egyptians, Babylonians, Greeks, and Arabs, seemed to assist elegantly as a way of expressing the motion of the moon. In a section called "On The Nature of Months and Years," al-Biruni mentions how the Semitic-speaking peoples of the region used a lunisolar year. He states that they "derived their year from the revolution of the sun, and its months from the revolution of the moon." This way, he writes, "their feast and fast days might be regulated by lunar computation, and at the same time keep their places within the year" (al-Biruni 1998 [1879]: 13). They were keeping both calendars and sought correspondence between them.

Accordingly, pre-Islamic Arabs "intercalated 7 in 19 lunar years . . . in the derivation of their cycles and the different kinds of their years" (13). They observed "the difference between their year and the solar year, which is [roughly] 10 days and 21 1/5 hours . . . adding it to the year as one month as soon as it completed the number of days of a month." This was rounded to be 10 days and 20 hours (13).

This business of calculating differences between the two cycles, the lunar and the solar, was administered, according to al-Biruni, "by specialized Arab people known as the *an-Nasa'a*[17] (the intercalators) who tended to come from the tribe of *Kinana*, known as the *Kalamis*, a plural form of *Kalammas*[18]" (14). He specifically mentions Abu Thumama and his ancestors, all of whom were intercalators. Interestingly, intercalators were recognized and highly valued, as contemporary poetry shows.

Poetry in Arab culture and long before Islam was not simply an exercise in aesthetics, but was and continues to be a highly valued mode of expression that valorizes oral tradition and serves as a depository of form, values, memorable sayings, and genealogical information. In poetic expressions one locates historical events and heroic deeds. Poetry among Arabs developed in their early history into central tribal institutions and continues until today to serve as a vital mode of expression. Al-Biruni refers to Abu Thumama as "the last of them" and cites an anonymous poet of that era as follows:

> The difference between the revolution of the sun and new-moon
> He adds together and sums it up
> Till it makes out a complete month

Another anonymous poet cited by al-Biruni (73) demonstrates the centrality of intercalators in pre-Islamic Arabia:

> We have an intercalator, under whose banner we march;
> He declares the months "ordinary"[19] or sacred, as he likes"

Ibn al-Athir (1965; cited by Bamyeh 1999: 275, n.33) reports that the Arab *an-Nasa'ah* (intercalators) using their calendar as the standard, "exchanged one of the forbidden months for the following one because they needed to raid during the month designated sacred by the Quraysh." Al-Mas'udi (1965 II: 30–31, 188) reports about a month, *an-Nasi,'* that *an-Nasa'ah* added to the lunar calendar once every three years in order to make up the discrepancy between the lunar and the solar calendars. In terms of the sacred months, this would result in an increase once in three years of a month in which fighting was permitted.

It appears that Arabian Arabs adopted a system of intercalation for at least two centuries before the Hijra. It involved "adding the difference between their [referring to lunar] year and the solar year, when it had summed up to one complete month, to the months of their year" (al-Biruni 1998 [1879]: 73). That is to say, lunar months and solar months are never in synch. Their "intercalators . . . the *Kalamis* of the tribe Kinana, rose, after pilgrimage had been finished, delivered a speech to the people at the fair, and intercalated the month, calling the next following month by the name of that month in which they were. The Arabs consented to this arrangement and adopted the decision of the *Kalammas*, This proceeding they called 'Nasi,'" i.e. *postponement*, because "in every second or third year they postponed the beginning of the year for a month, as it was required by the progression of the year" (73).

Al-Biruni elaborates: "a month progressed beyond its proper place in the four seasons of the year, in consequence of the accumulation of the fractions of the solar year, and of the remainder of the *plus-difference* between the solar year and the lunar year" (73–74). They add the "plus-difference," thus making a second intercalation. The Arabian Arabs were able to follow such progression by recognizing "the rising and setting of the Lunar Mansions," when the turn of intercalation had come to Sha'ban. Now Sha'ban was called Muharram, and Ramadan was called Safar.

To illustrate this technique a list of the names of twelve months reported to have been employed centuries before and into the seventh century (i.e. prior to and into the birth of Islam) is provided here in table form to simplify al-Biruni's explanation of how intercalation works. Note that in Table 5.6 the twelve Arabic month names are the same names used today as Islamic months.

Lunde (2005: 3) observes that because the Islamic lunar calendar is eleven days shorter than the solar, it is therefore not synchronized to the seasons. Its festivals, which fall on the same days of the same lunar months each year, make the round of the seasons every thirty-three solar years. This eleven-day difference between the lunar and the solar year accounts for the need to convert dates from one system to the other.

Al-Biruni (1998 [1879]: 73) describes how the system of month changing worked: "The first intercalation applied to Muharram; in consequence Safar was called Muharram, Rabi' I was called Safar, and so on; and in this way all the names of all the months were changed." He goes on: "The second intercalation applied to Safar; in consequence the next following month (Rabi I) was called Safar. . . . this went on till intercalation had passed through all twelve months of the year and returned to Muharram. Then they commenced anew what they had done the first time." This domino style name changing is how Arabian Arabs are reported by al-Biruni to have "fixed their dates," "counting the cycles of intercalation" (73).

Table 5.6 Arabic month names (adopted as Islamic)

1	Muharram	7	Rajab
2	Safar	8	Sha'ban
3	Rabi' Awwal	9	Ramadan
4	Rabi' Thani	10	Shawwal
5	Jamad Awwal	11	Thu l-Qa'da
6	Jamad Thani	12	Thu l-Hijja

Islam Rejects Intercalation The Arabs, following the leaders who were controlling both market and sacred activities, continued to "fix their sacred months" using methods of intercalation until Prophet Muhammad made his "Farewell pilgrimage" (al-Biruni 1998 [1879]: 14) during which he delivered his well-known speech, addressing the people: "Time has come round as it was on the day of God's creating the heavens and the earth," and continuing, he recited to them the verse above on the prohibition of the Nasi' (i.e. intercalation). He recited a revealed qur'anic passage. In al-Biruni's translated work the ayah identified as recited by the Prophet to support his position was Ayah 38 of Sura 9. But Ayah 38 would not make sense in this context. In al-Biruni, Sachau translated Sura 9, what seems to be Ayah 37 (rather than 38 as he claims), in this awkward phrase: "Intercalations only an increase of infidelity, by which the infidels lead astray (people), admitting it one year and prohibiting it in another." Let us review Sura 9: 37 (At-Tauba [The Repentance]), retranslated:

> Verily the transposing (of a prohibited month) is an addition to Unbelief: the Unbelievers are led to wrong thereby: for they make it lawful one year, and forbidden another year, in order to adjust the number of months forbidden by Allah and make such forbidden ones lawful. The evil of their course seems pleasing to them. But Allah guideth not those who reject Faith. (9:37)

Note that the term used is *kufr*, which translates more accurately as unbelief, and not as infidels, as Sachau claims. *Infidels* is a term usually used against the Arabs and was originally used in the context of the Catholic Crusades against them, and continues to be propagated by misguided Orientalists. It sees *an-Nasi'* (Arabic for intercalation, Aramaic for both intercalation and usury) as an expression of unbelief and an act against faith. The violation is in declaring a month sacred at one time and ordinary at another and also in the very declaring by humans of what is sacred and what is not. Identifying a dual meaning, intercalation and usury,[20] in the word's original usage in dialects of Aramaic makes the announced displeasure even more pertinent. The lunar cycle is determined by nature (which, in Islam, is of God's making) and is hence divine.

Pilgrimage created a pattern of regularity in the path of time. The four sacred months during which pilgrimage took place were regulated by a prohibition against fighting and raiding. However, clearly from the sources cited so far, the sacred months did not, as Bamyeh states, "happen" to be the months during which all of the *suqs* of Hijaz and more than half of the *suqs* in the peninsula were held. Nor, as he assumes, has the pilgrimage and other forms of religious worship develop in parallel to trade cycles. He is right, however, in his observation that the central role of Makka was validated by it. This parallelism was constructed. The change of the lunar months was by manipulation of the sacred months exactly for the purpose of bringing them to correspond to seasonal markets. And that is what Islam objected to.

As Muslim leader, prophet, and messenger of Islam, Muhammad clearly was not happy with intercalation. He made his displeasure known. Bamyeh interprets the disapproval of intercalation by using his paradigm of a tension between badawah (nomadism) and hadarah (sedentarism). He claims that the Islamic verdict against intercalation is, in fact, against factors that would disrupt the hadarah style from facilitating trade and commerce. The extent to which Arabs prior to Islam disapproved of the arbitrariness of the system was evident in a number of sources. They, however, were following the lead that privileged trade over sacredness of time, or at least subordinated sacred months to make pilgrimage correspond with trade.

But it was Islam, through Muhammad, that took a firm stand against the intercalation technique, seeing in it sacrilegious implications. There are other qur'anic passages that support Islam's critical position on this. Relevant would be Sura 9: 36 (At-Tauba [The Repentance]), which says:

> The number of months in the sight of Allah is twelve (in a year) – so ordained by Him the day He created the heavens and the earth; of them four are sacred: that is the straight usage. So wrong not yourselves therein, and fight the Pagans all together as they fight you all together. But know that Allah is with those who restrain themselves.

Its original Arabic is below:

إِنَّ عِدَّةَ الشُّهُورِ عِندَ اللهِ اثنَا عَشَرَ شَهْرًا فِي كِتَابِ اللهِ يَوْمَ خَلَقَ السَّمَاوَاتِ
وَالأَرْضَ مِنْهَا أَرْبَعَةٌ حُرُمٌ ذَلِكَ الدِّينُ القَيِّمُ فَلا تَظْلِمُوا فِيهِنَّ أَنفُسَكُمْ وَقَاتِلُوا
المُشْرِكِينَ كَآفَّةً كَمَا يُقَاتِلُونَكُمْ كَآفَّةً وَاعْلَمُوا أَنَّ اللهَ مَعَ المُتَّقِينَ (٩:٣٦)

(9:36)

Here it is confirmed that there are twelve months in a (lunar) year, and the sacredness of four of these months is reaffirmed. However, it also states that when attacked by the polytheists or pagans Muslims need to defend themselves, although God is with those who exercise restraint. Then there is the passage that is directly about the cycles of the moon and the sun in Sura 23: 40, which states: "It is not permitted to the Sun to catch up the Moon, nor can the Night outstrip the Day: each (just) swims along in (its own) orbit (according to law)."

لَا ٱلشَّمْسُ يَنۢبَغِى لَهَآ أَن تُدْرِكَ ٱلْقَمَرَ وَلَا ٱلَّيْلُ سَابِقُ ٱلنَّهَارِ ۚ وَكُلٌّ فِى فَلَكٍ
يَسْبَحُونَ ﴿٤٠﴾

This describes the natural (divine) order, recognizing both moon and sun each in its orbit, which Islam reaffirms as the guide to time and space. Prophet Muhammad's concern was about restoring the stability of nature, the divinity of sacredness, and the morality of values. In other words, he was "throwing the money changers out of the temple," again.

From the time when the Prophet of Islam announced the end of calendar manipulation, Muslims stopped using intercalation, which had led to "months . . . [receding] . . . from their original place, and the names of the months . . . no longer in conformity with their original meanings" (al-Biruni 1998 [1879]: 14). Intercalation was abolished and forbidden. Sacredness of religious activity was restored and, if we look at historical developments since the seventh century until today in the Islamic region, this sacredness had not compromised the symbiotic coexistence between religion and market that does not subordinate one to the other, nor feel the need to do so.

The Moon

> It is he who made the sun to be a shining glory, and the moon to be a light (of beauty) and measured out stages for her, that ye might know the number of years and the county (of time)
>
> The Qur'an, Sura 10: 5 (Yunus)

> Joseph said to his father: "O my father! I did see eleven stars and the sun and the moon: I saw them prostrate themselves to me!"
>
> The Qur'an, Sura 12: 4 (Yusuf)[21]

The Arabic original is as follows:

إِذْ قَالَ يُوسُفُ لِأَبِيهِ يَٰٓأَبَتِ إِنِّى رَأَيْتُ أَحَدَ عَشَرَ كَوْكَبًا
وَٱلشَّمْسَ وَٱلْقَمَرَ رَأَيْتُهُمْ لِى سَٰجِدِينَ ﴿٤﴾

Sura 10: 5 above, which is usually taken to stress the lunar cycle, is in fact about both sun and moon. The sura below it, 12: 4, is about Joseph's dream recounted to his father, also mentioning both sun and moon. Evidence recurs demonstrating how both moon and sun guide the Islamic cycle of life; for example, the following

Sura 71: 16, Sura Nuh:

> And made the moon a light in their midst, and made the sun as a (Glorious) Lamp
>
> وَجَعَلَ ٱلْقَمَرَ فِيهِنَّ نُورًا وَجَعَلَ ٱلشَّمْسَ سِرَاجًا ﴿١٦﴾

This does not lessen the centrality of the moon in Arabo-Islamic life and thought. In Sura 54: 1, Sura-t al-Qamar, the passage says:

> The Last Hour draws near, and the moon is split asunder!
>
> ٱقْتَرَبَتِ ٱلسَّاعَةُ وَٱنشَقَّ ٱلْقَمَرُ ﴿١﴾

Here it is reaffirmed that the position of the moon is central to the conceptualization of time. The appearance of the moon to Muslims marks the beginning of time and, as represented in Sura 4: 1, the end of time.

Scientists estimate the age of the moon to be 4.5 billion years (with a margin of error of 10 million years) and it is not showing signs of aging yet. This lunar "permanence" and eternal existence with humanity is evident in cosmology, belief, science, and popular expression. *Qamar*, *Badr*, *Hilal* are among a diverse and rich Arabic vocabulary denoting moon. There is a saying used in the context of describing a beautiful person: *wa hal yakhfa al-Qamar*? Can the moon be hidden? As described in Chapter 3, the ancient Egyptians considered the moon to be central in the workings of the universe. It is interesting in this regard to look at ancient Egypt's representation of the cycle of the moon, its waxing and its waning as presented in Figure 5.1.

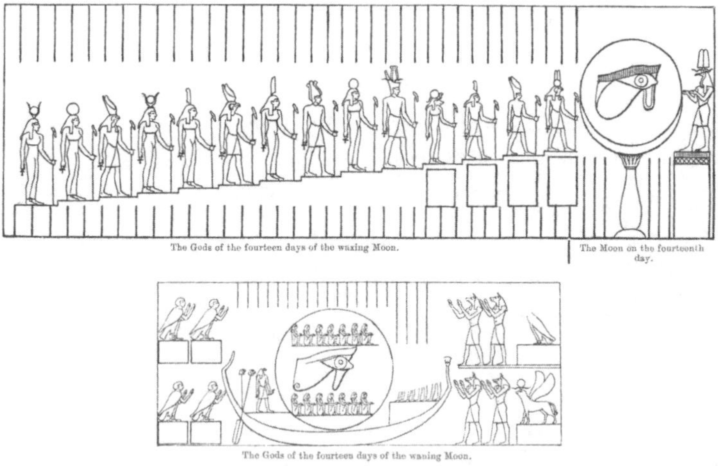

Figure 5.1 Waxing and waning of moon in ancient Egypt. © El Nil Research

The peoples of what is now the Arab world are tuned to the moon, whether peasants in rural fields, Bedouins in tents in the desert or semi-settled in border desert towns, or urbanites in cities, from badawah to hadarah, to use Ibn Khaldun's sophisticated terminology for a continuum of development and change. They feel it, live it, and as an Iraqi archaeologist recently poetically phrased it at a dinner, "we used to sit in Iraq and look at the big beautiful moon, which was so close, we stretched our hands to touch it." Arabs touch, are in touch, and are touched by the moon in intimate ways. To them, the moon does not phase out.

Aveni describes its cycle thus: At the beginning of its cycle, the moon is a thin, sharp-horned crescent suspended above the western horizon, its cusps always pointing away from the sun, which has already set. On succeeding twilights, it waxes, or grows, appearing at sunset farther away toward the east from where it was at the beginning of the month. It passes its quarter phase and takes on that familiar "D shape" it always exhibits when it rides high on the meridian (the imaginary north–south line that passes overhead) in the south at sunset. Still later in the month, it enters the gibbous phase, when more than half its visible disk is lighted, and can be seen high in the east late in the afternoon. After half a cycle, when it reaches the full phase, the moon is most prominent of all, rising opposite the setting sun, illuminating the sky with a flood of pale yellow light all night long" (Aveni 1989: 86).

After two weeks, the moon backtracks in its cycle, slowly eroding away in reverse, passing through gibbous phase, and then back toward quarter as it wanes. At month's end, the disk is reduced once again to a thin crescent, the vanishing sliver of which can be glimpsed low in the east before sunrise. Then it vanishes altogether for a couple of days as it becomes lost in the low of the sun's light.

The whole cyclical lunar process takes 29½ days – a synodic month. If we look at the wall calendar hanging on the wall of any Western home we will see vertical divisions and named columns. Is that a Western invention? Looking back at the various chapters in this book we know that these divisions are founded on early discoveries from the east about nature and agriculture and creative constructions about concepts of time and space that began thousands of years ago, and especially in an organized "scientific" sense in Egypt and Babylonia (Iraq), to be borrowed by Greece and Rome culminating with Western imperial designs to organize time to control capital. In the process, the people in the West lost touch with nature's rhythms in the struggle to wade through the maze of religion, politics, and economic intrigue and control. Aveni puts it this way: "With the development of technology – from sun watching at the horizon to weight-driven clocks to atomic timekeeping devices – we have removed our marking of time from nature's realm and in the process, become ever less in touch with the events that occur there" (1989: 118). Time has become money. The moon has receded behind the clouds of market and technology.

Perhaps, as Aveni invokes, there is in all humans some recognition of the parallels between natural and sacral periodicity. As we have seen in Chapter 3, cosmogonic myth was molded to re-create the creation, to bring time-past into time-present, to regenerate the world. Do we need to raise the issue of whether sacred time preceded utilitarian time or whether the two are the same or different? He observes that the constant in the study of calendars and time is that "time captivates not as a pure fact of nature but instead as a dimension of life that ultimately can be submitted to cultural control" (Aveni 1989: 336). Submitting nature to culture control, however, is not what Arabs and Muslims wish to do.

In the Arab-Islamic East the story is different. The moon remains as bright and shining as it has for millennia, guiding people's lives and inspiring their creative imagination. How? This is so today because of the firm stance by the leader of Islam who stood in public, facing a congregational gathering of pilgrims in Makka, in the seventh century, and recited divinely revealed passages to validate his mission, gave an extended khutba in which he laid out the fundamental principles of Islam, then announced the end of "playing" with time, the end of subordinating the sacred to market trade. He asked believers to leave nature's rhythms alone and to re-embrace the moon to shine on their path, in sacred glory and in its natural synergy with the sun, in and out of the rhythm of Islam. The moon was back in center stage in Arabia then, and around the world of Muslims today.

Al Hilal (The Crescent) It is said in the Qur'an that when asked about the crescents, we should say they are times for people and pilgrimage. Aveni writes that "When we see no moon, we speak of the 'new' moon, but the moon is not visibly renewed until we see its crescent again in the evening twilight" (87). As al-Biruni writes: "They fixed the beginning of the new month by the appearance of new moon" (1998 [1879]: 75). Seeing the "new" moon, or sighting, is pivotal in the Islamic cycle of sacred rhythms. Other than sighting, however, most Arabs and Muslims (as I am sure other groups around the world) are very connected to the moon at most times. My reaction to Aveni's phrase "we speak of the new moon" is that he must mean it metaphorically, as I never heard any American of any age, ethnic tradition, lifestyle, or career (even farmers today whose agriculture has become mechanized and their time mechanicalized) during my forty years plus in the United States notice or speak about the moon. No one, especially in urban or metropolitan environments, follows its phases or uses the word in ordinary speech or conversation. It is not much of a subject of poetry or prose, song or humor. It is not integral to popular culture[22] or the public psyche. The moon is simply not there.

Aveni himself puts it this way: "There is nothing in the universe quite like the moon. If we were freed from the fetters of indoor lighting, telescopes, and abstract scientific explanations, we all might be a little more familiar with its apparent behavior" (Aveni 1989: 86). In contrast, to an Arab or a Muslim the moon is there, forever and everywhere in absence of presence of artificial lighting and urban distractions. It is in poetry, in popular expressions, in ordinary conversation, in metaphor, in folk and sacred life. The crescent is the symbol *par excellence* of Islam.

Mushahra I relate the following ethnographic content to demonstrate how people are connected to the moon in such a way that much of their life and ritual activities become constructed according to its cycles and phases. Although such beliefs may not be approved by scriptural Islam, it nevertheless represented a reality on the ground for many folk who find comfort in having such beliefs. And, while I am using an example from field research that I carried out among the Nubians, many Egyptians of non-Nubian origin also believe in the complex. *Mushahra* is a word that stands for a complex of beliefs and associated practices that surround the idea that there are moments in a month when individuals are vulnerable and need protective measures. Some of these moments are related to the phases of the moon. It derives from the same root *sh-h-r* that yields *shahr*, meaning month.

During my fieldwork in Nubia and among Nubians (1962–4), I was invited to attend the circumcision event[23] including the excision procedure and ritual celebrations for an eight-year-old girl who was the daughter of a migrant woman who had returned to visit her relatives in Dahmit (Nubia in Egypt south of Aswan prior to relocation). The procedure and ceremony took place in the mid afternoon in the courtyard of the house in which the family was staying during their visit to the home village. It was held on the twenty-eighth day of *Shawwal*, the tenth month in the Islamic calendar.

This was considered a propitious time in the lunar cycle. The belief is that phases of the moon mark many sacred beginnings as well as thresholds of endangerment. This day was chosen to reduce the risk of harm during the period of mushahra, a liminal state that lasts from the waning of the old moon until the appearance of the new moon. Celebrating a ritual on the twenty-eighth of the month reduces the mushahra period to two days before the beginning of the next month (El Guindi 2006a).

The Islamic Calendar

There was no official Islamic calendar during the lifetime of the Prophet Muhammad. But after his death, in AD 638, the second caliph (successor), 'Umar Ibn al-Khattab,[24] recognized the necessity of introducing a calendar in order to govern the affairs of Muslims efficiently. One reason was purely practical: running affairs and conducting correspondence with military and civilian officials in the then expanding lands of Islam necessitated official dating. The issue was complicated by the fact that different regions within the Islamic world had their own established calendars.

Persia, for example, used its own calendar, which was different from that of Syria, where the caliphate was based; Egypt used yet another. Each of these calendars had a different starting point, or epoch. The ruling dynasty of Persia, the Sassanids, used as starting point the date of June 16, AD 632, which coincides with the date of the accession of the last Sassanid monarch, Yazdagird III. Syria, which was part of the Byzantine Empire until Muslim conquest, used a form of the Roman "Julian" calendar, beginning with an epoch of October 1, 312 BC.

Egypt used the Coptic calendar, which marked its beginning as August 29, AD 284. All these calendars were solar and contained 365 days. They were based on the agricultural seasons. Each also had a different system for periodically adding days to compensate for the fact that the true length of the solar year is not 365 but 365.2422 days. This was one factor in the decision to devise an Islamic calendar. But, according to Lunde (2001), there were two other reasons given for why 'Umar rejected the existing solar calendars.

The Qur'an, Sura 10 (Yunus), Ayah 5, which was fully presented earlier, is claimed to state that time should be reckoned by the moon. In fact, upon careful reading of the original in Arabic and its Arabic *tafsir* (official interpretation) this interpretation is not that apparent. I examined the tafsir given for this ayah and explored all the qur'anic ayahs in which the moon is invoked. Considering one ayah outside the context of other ayahs can distort intended meaning. Based on this examination, I disagree with Lunde's interpretation as to why Caliph 'Umar opted for a lunar calendar. Looking at moon in the context of all the surahs mentioning it and their tafsir I can make the following observations: (1) moon is almost always mentioned along with sun (Sura al-Qiyama 75: 9, al-Rahman 55: 5, Nuh 71: 16, Yasin 26: 40); (2) when sun is mentioned alone it is in terms of its rising and setting (Sura Qaf 50: 39); (3) both moon and sun are described in terms of systematicity of movement, measurement, and precision, the moon described in terms suggesting marking and measuring (Sura al-Rahman 55: 5); (4) moon and sun are described in antonymic language that describes sunlight using the word *siraj* and *diya'* and moonlight using *nur* (Sura Nuh 71: 16); (5) each moving in own orbit following its course, paths not overlapping (Sura Yasin 26: 40), which is further explicated in tafsir in terms of sun and moon each in its *sultan*, the sun reigns in the morning and the moon reigns at night. Taking all this together it becomes evident that Islam embraces a relationality between moon and sun in such a way that binds the polarity in patterned movements used to mark time for Muslims.

Another factor given by Lunde as to why Caliph 'Umar wanted to institute an Islamic calendar was the fact that the calendars used at that time by the Persians, Syrians, and Egyptians, the populations who are now within the Islamic fold, were identified with other religions and cultures. An alternative calendar was created specifically to serve the Muslim community. It would be in part lunar, and it would have twelve months, each with twenty-nine or thirty days. This gives the lunar year 354 days, 11 days fewer than the solar year. It was named the Hijra calendar.

The Hijrah

According to Lunde (2005: 3) it was Khalifa (Caliph) 'Umar who chose as the epoch for the new Muslim calendar the *Hijrah*, which became the name of the calendar, but also refers to the emigration of the Prophet Muhammad and seventy early converts to Islam from Makka to Madina, where Muslims first attained religious and political autonomy. The event of the Hijrah (migration) from Makka to Madina (or at that time Yathrib) by Prophet Muhammad and the early followers marked the creation of a new kind of community the likes of which the region had not seen and also allowed them to escape persecution by the people of Makka (primarily the dominant and powerful clan of al-Quraysh, which was the clan that the Prophet Muhammad was born into) who rejected and doubted the message of Islam. Hence the Hijrah calendar.

The Hijrah thus occurred on Muharram 1 according to the Islamic calendar, which was named "*hijri*" after its epoch. (This date corresponds to July 16, AD 622 on the Gregorian calendar.) Today in the West, it is customary, when writing hijri dates, to use the abbreviation AH, which stands for the Latin *anno hegirae*, "year of the *hejirah.*" Parise (2002: 71–72) concurs that the Islamic calendar is computed from the Hijrah, the emigration of the Prophet Muhammad and *al-muhajirun* (Muslims emigrating with him) from Makka to Madina. The epoch is their arrival in Madina, considered to be sunset July 16, AD 622 by the majority of Muslims (a minority of Muslims reckons the day from midnight to midnight using July 15 as the epoch). While computed from the events of the Hijrah, it started to be actually used from the seventeenth year of Hijrah. Many consider the Hijrah calendar to be purely lunar, that is, the year contains 354 days, which does not take into consideration the solar revolution, thus it is consistently 11 days behind each solar year. Its months contain alternately, twenty-nine or thirty days. The last month may have either number of days. Periodically one day is added for a leap year, because the moon's orbit is just over 29½ days long. Otherwise the intercalations are the same.

Some disagree with the way the notion of hijrah is defined. Rather, it is considered to mean neither flight nor fleeing. It shares the root *h-j-r*, which yields the verb *hajara*, meaning break off or abandon. Using this rendering, the suggestion of using discontinuity – a distinctive characteristic of Christianity (Robbins 2007: 3–38) – would not be valid in the case of Islam. Both factors, continuity and discontinuity, mark the processual phases of Islam and Islamic movements.

Islamic Months

It is worth noting that the advent of the Islamic calendar in the seventh century of the Christian era, was not marked by battles or war victories, nor with the birth or death of the Prophet of Islam. Nor does it start at a time that commemorates the revelation itself. It starts with Hijra. Some consider Hijra to represent the sacrifice for the cause of Truth and for the preservation of the Revelation.[25]

The Islamic calendar contains one major fast period, for the duration of the month of Ramadan, and two major feasts. During the month of Ramadan no food or drink may be taken from sunrise until sunset. Muslims during the fast also refrain from sex. Ramadan is marked by good deeds and spiritual thought and action. A sense of community is re-affirmed. Ramadan ends as it starts, with the *ru'ya* (crescent sighting) (see pp. 112–13). A feast period follows known as Eid al-Fitr. It lasts for three days, or from the first through the third of Shawwal. The other major feast, called 'Eid al-Adha (the feast of Sacrifice or al-'Eid El Kabir), is celebrated from the tenth through the thirteenth or fourteenth of the last month of the Islamic year, Dhu-l Hijjah. Perhaps Parise's report that "it continues for three or four days is determined by whether or not there is an intercalary day added to that year" (72) may have been true in the past but it certainly is not the case today. It lasts for five days. This feast celebrates Prophet Ibrahim's attempt to sacrifice his son, Ismail.

Al-Biruni discusses a possible etymology for the names of the Islamic months (70–1). Muslims use the names presented below, in Table 5.7, for the Islamic months.

The Islamic month begins when two responsible witnesses claim they can see the first crescent of the new moon. They then go before the qadi (judge), who, if he decides they are correct, informs a mufti (interpreter of the law). He, in turn, announces that the new month has begun. Prior to the coming of the telephone and telegraph, complications could arise if the weather was cloudy. Each local group decided independently just when the month actually started, and the day could, on occasion, be later than the calendar indication. This issue continues to be debated in the Arab world in seminars, conferences, on Islamic talk shows on television, in the press, and so on. While, in the past, it had become customary among Muslims

Table 5.7 Names of Islamic months

1	Muharram	7	Rajab
2	Safar	8	Sha'ban
3	Rabi' Awwal	9	Ramadan
4	Rabi' Thani	10	Shawwal
5	Jamad Awwal	11	Thu l-Qa'da
6	Jamad Thani	12	Thu l-Hijja

to accept the verdict of Cairo on when the month begins, today some follow Saudi Arabia and some follow Cairo.

This ambiguity regarding the source to follow on sighting, *al-ru'ya*, is commented on by Dr. Shaykh Yusuf al-Qaradawy. In a televised interview that took place on October 6, 2005, he stated that Ramadan is confirmed by the appearance of the *hilal* (the crescent). This is a sign accessible to all Muslims. It is incumbent upon able Muslims to fast, as the Hadith says the Prophet said "fast to its sighting and break fast to its sighting" and in another "do not fast until the crescent is sighted and do not break fast until it is sighted." Asked whether the difference in sighting by different Arab countries and groups will ever be resolved, he said:

> Note that al-ru'ya is a means not an end. The *ummah* is large and widespread and now there are those who begin their fast according to Egypt-Tunis-Algeria, others according to Morocco, There are Muslims in the United States, others in Europe, in Pakistan etc. If we cannot reach a unity in this area at least maintain unity with your own people in your own country. Become an *ummah* in your own country. I say, fast to your own sightings. I tell Muslims if Muslims worldwide cannot be united in this act it should not be reason to divide Muslims who are ahl (kin) in one country.

Islamic Week

Zerubavel reminds us that "whereas the day and the year are essentially based on natural cycles, the week is most clearly a purely artificial cycle" (1981: 27). Nothing in the natural world can provide a clue to people as to whether this or that day is Monday or Tuesday. But for Muslims, the cultural clue for one particular day in the week is very obvious and is prepared for and lived in differently from the rest of the days. That day is the one called Friday in English.

The Islamic calendar uses a week of seven days, the names of which are now standard among Arabic-speaking people. Even when variations in names of week-days exist among certain groups there is one day that remains unchanged. That name is *al-Jum'a*, or the "day of collective gathering"[26] – equivalent to Friday. Parise (2002: 72) states that Friday "is considered the first of the week" giving as reason the incident that Prophet Muhammad entered Yathrib (now Madina) at sunset. I could not verify this story. Nor is it true today that the week begins on Friday. Friday is the day of collective worship. The *jum'a* prayer in the mosque marks a sacred interval of the day. While it has become a holiday in most Islamic countries, it is the collective jum'a prayer that is the sacred moment of the day.

The week in the Islamic world today is a work week. It begins after the weekend holiday ends. Since liberation from nineteenth-century European colonial occupation[27] of Muslim lands (between the 1950s and the 1970s) when Friday was not even acknowledged as the day of worship to be given off from work, many Muslim countries instituted Friday as the official weekend holiday and added either Thursday or Saturday[28] to grant a two-day weekend.

Parise mentions that the Muslim day runs from sundown to sundown. Therefore the week begins at sundown on Friday and runs through to the sundown of the following Friday (2002: 72). It is interesting that this very point provokes heated debate among Muslims today. Contemporary Algerian astronomer Dr. Loth Bounatiro, chief research scientist at the astronomy laboratory and astrophysics department at Algeria's Centre for Research in Astronomy, Astrophysics, and Geophysics, won a medal for design and another for respect of environmental standards for his project on anti-seismic buildings at the British Invention Show on October 21, 2006. He also won an award at last year's show for inventing the *universe clock*, a timepiece that can be used universally, but more importantly it follows nature. In an interview in Arabic on al-Jazeera Satellite TV channel aired on February 27, 2007, he related the following: "Time (*zāman*) has its high value in the Arabo-Islamic civilization and Muslim scientists considered time as an aspect of a science of time-reckoning. Western culture has a variable and changing time like all things that change" Bounatiro invented what he calls a "universe time clock," which follows a 24-hour cycle instead of a 12-hour one according to the exact solar pattern, mathematically showing the duration of the *ash-shafaq al-ahmar* (twilight or sundown). The most significant feature of the universe clock is that the day is from sundown to sundown, instead of the Western system used today from midnight to midnight. He goes on to say that the West follows solar considerations but not mathematically, inventing instead the fictive Greenwich time line, which is mathematically inaccurate. In the past all peoples followed the lunar cycle, then they adopted a lunisolar cycle for agricultural purposes to match the climatic seasons and herein lies the error, dealt with by patching up. It is patching up because it is mathematically incorrect and does not follow scientific standards. The lunar calendar that follows the Makka–Madina line (as opposed to the mythical Greenwich line) is regular and eternal without needing reform. "That alone is a scientific accomplishment," Bounatiro said. However, some Muslims consider establishing the day from sundown to sundown as contradicting the sacred cycle of sunrise to sunset. Since fasting during Ramadan starts with sunrise and ends at sunset, this is considered by Muslim adherents to be the Muslim daily cycle.

"Five Pillars of Islam" Reconsidered The most common response to the question "What does Islam constitute?" is a rapid recitation of the *Five Pillars of Islam* (*Arkan al-Islam*). They are: *shahada* (declaration of faith), *salat* (prayer), *sawm* (fasting), *hajj* (pilgrimage), and *zakat* (charity). This approach to Islam is accessible, simple, and effortless. There are five pillars that every Muslim must adhere to, which constitute a list of five obligations known as *fard* or *farida* in Arabic. Fard (also farida: obligation, duty) is an Arabic term that denotes an

Islamic religious duty. It is synonymous with *wajib*, which is one of the five qualifications (*al-ahkam al-khamsa*) into which *Fiqh*, the Islamic religious law, categorizes all human acts. The law distinguishes two sorts of duties: individual (*fard ayn*) and collective (*fard kifaya*). The first relates to tasks every Muslim as an individual is required to perform, like the daily prayer (salat) or the pilgrimage to Makka at least once in a lifetime (hajj). The second is a duty that is imposed on the whole community of believers (*ummah*). *Jihad* (which means struggle in general, extending to struggle in defense of the community) is a fard kifaya. This means that not each individual is required to do it. It is not required as long as a sufficient number of community members fulfill it.

Ahkam (from the root *h-k-m,* meaning to judge or evaluate) in Islam refers to judgment or evaluation of individual Muslim acts. Propriety of acts and behaviors of Muslims is determined in accordance with Islamic law by being identified along a gradation ranging from obligatory to forbidden. They are five as follows: *wajib* (obligatory), *mustahabb* (recommended), *mubah* (permissible), *makruh* (undesirable), and *haram* or *muharram* (prohibited).

What is interesting is that even in this range of five characterizations of judgment there is flexibility and leniency. Any resulting hardship would be taken into consideration. The same act can be identified as one of the five in one situation and as another under other circumstances or in specific situations. For example, fasting which is obligatory for all adults during the month of Ramadan can be declared prohibited to a sick individual whose condition can worsen from fasting. Consideration is also given to social and public effects of a certain action. A general Islamic requirement for the community as a whole might differ for individual persons under different conditions.[29]

Wonder Woman or Prayer?

A rerun episode of *Wonder Woman* was playing on Egyptian television during the early afternoon hours. It was in the 1980s during my fieldwork project among college students about the Islamic movement. A college woman majoring in veterinary medicine in Cairo University, who had become "religious" and adopted the "Islamic dress" had just returned home as her semi-retired father was sitting in the sitting room engrossed in watching *Wonder Woman*. Within minutes after her arrival and after a brief exchange of greetings, the *athan* from the nearby mosque was heard. She said that she was going to cleanse and pray. There was no response from the father. He did not seem to have any intention of leaving *Wonder Woman* in order to pray. The daughter reminded her father that prayer was called. Traditionally, the father would have been the one to do this. He would have been letting his daughter know that it was prayer time. He would be the authority figure in the family and an exemplar in Islamic matters. Instead, without looking away from *Wonder Woman* he casually remarked that there was still time in the prayer interval and that he would be praying later after the program was over. Prayer interval is the period within which a particular prayer is performed. The daughter persistently kept the pressure and made references to Islamic sayings stating priorities, in this case between watching *Wonder Woman* and praying. The father lost that battle, turned off *Wonder Woman*, and got up to pray.

This incident of *Wonder Woman* is not about a purist or fundamentalist morality against watching *Wonder Woman*. Rather it concerns priorities in the face of the rhythm of Islam. What is new for Arab society in this example is not only that there is a new Islamic consciousness among urban youth, but that it enabled a shifting in the direction of authority and pattern from the previous top down to the emergent bottom up. In the recent past (in Egypt up to the 1970s) youth and women looked up to adult men in the family for guidance in Islamic behavior, and everyone looked up to Azhari scholars for judicious and sagacious decisions on Islamic matters.

The movement of the 1970s shook many out of apathy and into a renewed vigor about Islamic obligations and public appearance and morality. The direction from which this vigor came shook Egyptian society to the core. The fact that the shake up came from "below," from ordinary Muslim believing folk and not from al-Azhar, from young Muslim men and women and not from their adult parents, from college youth and not from their professors and teachers, sent tremors across Egyptian society, which was unprepared for such a challenge to its authority structure. It is a movement that took root and kept growing, shaking society to the core. It is now routinized, as it enters its fourth decade. Predictions that it was a passing trend or fad proved wrong. It is not that this Islamic awakening introduced a new rhythmic pattern for Muslims. The pattern is fundamental to the ordinary daily and annual cycle of life for Muslims. But there is a difference. The new awakening has brought about wider participation by women and men in public Muslim life, a change in public appearance and behavior, increased mosque activity by women, and renewed assertiveness about adherence to Islamic obligations.[30]

Extensive participation of women in public Islamic activity began in Egypt in the mid 1970s as part of the new Islamic awakening. More ordinary people, and more women of all status groups, having acquired formal education and original Islamic knowledge directly, began this movement and innovated forms of participation and "appropriate" dress. Many factors underlying this general phenomenon are discussed in my earlier works on the topic. But the phenomenal increase in, and equal access to, free formal education by all strata since the 1952 Egyptian Revolution of Gamal Abdul Nasser may have worked as a major catalyst for such a change. Islam is a religion in which general participation by ordinary folk becomes enhanced by increased literacy and access to formal education.

Another story in the *Los Angeles Times* in February 2007 described how Asia is experiencing a new austere Islam as a result of migrant labor to the Gulf. According to the *Los Angeles Times* story (Daragahi 2007: A1, A12), trade winds across the Arabian sea have carried merchants between the Arab-Persian Gulf and southern India since antiquity. "The migration to oil-rich Persian Gulf monarchies of as many as one in five men from India's Kerala province has brought an influx of money that pays for food, shelter and education. It also funds dowries for their daughters and gifts for their wives. But like many of the world's millions of economic migrants, the men bring back more than money." They bring back from the original home of Islam Islamic ideas about the proper way to worship, simple green mosques with minarets to replace the ornate and bulbous temples of India, which Muslims have long used for worship, and Arabic writing. In other words, Arabic Islam, in purer form, as well aspects of Arab culture travel back with the returning migrants. A globalized transnational labor force is carrying Islam and Arab culture around as it spreads wealth from rich to poorer nations.

In Chapter 6, Islam's specific and distinctive rhythm will be examined in the context of the notion of rhythm in general and Arabo-Islamic cultural conceptualizations in particular. An empirically based theory of Islamic rhythm is proposed.

–6–

Khususiyya, Qudsiyya, Jama'iyya: A Theory of Arabo-Islamic Rhythm

> Rhythms are the creators of space and time . . . Space and time do not enter lived experience until they are materialised within a rhythmic frame. Rhythms are also the creators of forms.
>
> André Leroi-Gourhan (1911–86), *Gesture and Speech*, 1993: 309 [trans. from original French *Le Geste et La Parole: Memoire et les Rhythmes*]

The Notion of Rhythm

Edmund Leach was criticized in his analysis of time for bringing up the question of "sensing" time. But analysis of Muslim life cannot leave out this factor. There is no doubt that a Muslim feels and lives Islam and experiences time and space in interweaving rhythm. This is what immigrants in an adopted homeland must miss – Islam's rhythm. They might be missing it despite regular praying at home and in mosque, fasting, participating in Islamic community life. One could empathize with the comment made by novelist Ahdaf Soueif (quoted at the beginning of Chapter 5) regarding the vacuum and silence following a death in England. Whitrow brings up what might seem obvious to some – that although "time does not constitute one of the human senses like smell, taste, etc. it certainly is seriously experienced" (1972: 109). Muslims experience time intimately and move comfortably in and out of Muslim space.

I was recounting to an American woman how in the States, when I gave students a break during class they would go to vending machines and bring back with them sodas and fast food. When I gave students at Qatar University a break they all went to pray, that is, perform the prayer of that time of day. The woman's response was: "Pray? Pray for what?" She was sincerely curious. Unprepared, I said "just pray, pray to God." "Yes," she persisted, "but pray for what?" Need prayer be for a specific request from God? Mauss, in his original French work of 1909, is cited by Morphy as having stated that prayer "has taken the most varied forms, but turns adoring and coercive, humble and threatening, dry and full of imagery, immutable and variable, mechanical and mental. It has filled the most varied role: here it is a brusque demand, there an order, elsewhere a contract, an act of faith, a confession, a supplication, an act of praise" (Morphy 2003: 141).

Morphy goes on to contextualize Mauss's view of prayer in anthropological knowledge: "The most elementary forms of prayer are ones in which the performers demand action . . . [T]he higher forms of prayer are more supplicatory" (2003: 146). This division, "praying for" versus "praying to" remained with anthropology up to the 1970s and was taught in classes of comparative religion. The "praying for" was often classified as magic. Due to the evolutionary paradigm that influenced early anthropology, "praying to" became associated with Protestant individualist Christianity. This classification proved unsustainable and anthropologists ultimately dropped it.

It is noteworthy to stress, however, that Muslim prayer challenges the classification in another way. It is "praying to" but it is not individualistic. It is not about specific requests from God. It is about obedience to God, following "the right path" carved by God, belonging to the community of believers and about Islam's rhythm. Once in a cleansed state, facing the appropriate direction, and in proper dress code a Muslim person can pray anywhere according to Islam's time pattern. Rhythm is a focal notion for understanding Islam and is centered in the new paradigm presented here. It is conceptual, yet lived and felt. Communities of immigrant Muslims try hard to, but cannot, reproduce the rhythm which exists "naturally" in the homeland. They create community, social and legal services, mainstreaming campaigns, place for worship, religious forums, but cannot reproduce the "rhythm." André Leroi-Gourhan, in the above quote, states that "rhythm" is itself the creator of space, time, and form. I would add that in the case of Islam, it is the creator of Muslim life. Without rhythm, Muslim life becomes clinical, routine, prescriptive, and dry.

Rhythms of Nature, Rhythms of Culture

Rhythm of Nature

In the year AH 10 there was the Farewell Pilgrimage (*Hajjat al-Wada'*) during which Prophet Muhammad gave the Last Sermon, known as *Khutbatul Wada'*.[1] This sermon is considered significant not only for its historical moment, being the last one before his death, but also for its rich content. The Prophet is reported to have summarized the Islamic message and asked the congregants to pass his words to those unable to attend. In this *khutba* Prophet Muhammad defined what is sacred, namely "this month, this day, this city, life, and property." He forbade usury and interest on loans and declared any outstanding interest on loans waived. He warned Muslims to protect the safety of their religion. He stressed the rights of women and their status as partners in marriage. He reminded Muslims of their obligation to worship: five daily prayers, fasting Ramadan, giving wealth in zakat, and, if possible, performing hajj. He situated Muslim believers, who constitute a brotherhood, in the context of wider humanity: all humankind comes from Adam and Hawa, the Arab is not superior to a non-Arab nor is a non-Arab superior to the Arab, a white is not superior to a black nor a black superior to a white – the difference lies in piety and good deeds. Finally, he advised Muslims not to stray from the right path, and to follow the Qur'an and the Sunnah. In sum, he summarized Islam's innovation: its community, morality, and rhythm.

One important element in this khutba, however, concerned morality and rhythm directly. This has to do with the Islamic calendar. Chapter 5 presented the details of how Arabian Arabs introduced intercalation to make sacred months correspond to market season. In his qur'anic commentary, Yusuf Ali comments in footnote 1295 on Sura 9: 36 regarding the pre-Islamic Arab calendar and intercalation to match seasons: it may be noted that the Arab year was roughly lunisolar like the Hindu year, the months being lunar and the intercalation of a month every three years brought the year nearly but not accurately up to the solar reckoning. However, from the year of the Farewell Pilgrimage and specifically in the Last Sermon, the Islamic year was definitely fixed as a purely lunar year of roughly 354 days, the months to be calculated by the actual appearance of the moon. Islam went back to nature.

Islam's recounting of the ending of intercalation is dramatic. It is a story about continuity, discontinuity, the sacred and the economic, nature and culture. Much scholarly debate surrounds Sura 9 and this particular event. Arabian and surrounding Aramaic-speaking people (Jewish "Arabs," Christian "Arabs," or polytheist "Arabs") shared many customs and practices. The historical record seems to suggest that since at least since AD 412, about 200 years before Islam, and also during Muhammad's life at the beginning of Islam, sacred rites were celebrated around the *Ka'ba* or *Maqam Ibrahim* (the monument of Ibrahim) in Makka, which had shifted from a lunar-based cycle that fixed sacred months to an intercalated cycle that subordinated the sacred to the seasonality of trade. Instead of performing the rites of hajj during sacred months as they shifted across the seasons, sacredness was fixed to the seasons, and rites were performed annually in the spring. Sacredness stipulated that during those times there would be no wars, battles, or any bloodshed. It was a time for pilgrimage rites and equally the season for active trade.

The dramatic moment came when Prophet Muhammad made a proclamation that the shifting of lunar months to coincide with the spring season would cease. He declared a return to the lunar cycle. Some scholars (see Rubin 1982) suggest as reason for this change the severing of worship from other groups. The real concern for Prophet Muhammad, according to the evidence, was not to follow the moralities of the *mushrikun* (the polytheist Arabs of the region). It was the "mushrikun" who concerned him, not "the people of the book." The pre-Islamic hajj was also the time of hajj for the Bedouins (Rubin 1982: 243).

Inasmuch as Jewish, Christian, or Muslim Arabs may have followed traditions propagated by mushrikun then they would be included in the chastising. The focus of reform was those who shared the patterns established by polytheists or supported ones that violated the sacred. The Prophet of Islam disapproved of the subordination of the sacred to market demands.

The pre-Islamic groups of the region introduced the institution of *Nasi'* (intercalation) in order to regulate the operation of pilgrimage, such that it would become parallel with the main markets in the vicinity of Makka. It is precisely this "priority" of market over the sacred that Prophet Muhammad was taking action against. As I put it earlier in this book, Muhammad was throwing the money-changers out of the Temple again. It is at that moment that an Islamic rhythm began to take hold and take root for all Muslims.

Moon When religion married economy, with its secular dictates of commercial production and trade in a world market economy, the Christians of the West invented the notion that "Time is money." With that "the money-changers had re-entered the Temple." This is what Muhammad stopped fifteen centuries ago. He put an end to intercalation, which was unleashed on the people to change the ashhur haram (sacred months) to correspond with seasonal markets. Since its abolition, Muslims have maintained the separation and the sacredness of lunar months to this day. The goal was not so much to oppose market or capital as to preserve the sacrality of sacred months and by doing so life itself, not just market, is subordinated to Islam's rhythm.

The Islamic calendar is commonly perceived as one of the few remaining purely lunar calendars, the year being just over ten days shorter than the tropical year, or year of the season. The Islamic era began on July 16, AD 622, the first day of Muhammad's flight to Madina. The circumstances in which this was adopted as an epoch, instead of the time when the Prophet was either born or entrusted with his divine mission or died, are explained by al-Biruni (AD 973–*c*.1050) (1998 [1879]: 34–6) in his work *The Chronology*. The fundamental instant in Islamic life occurs with the new moon, which must be watched for and established by two "witnesses of the instant." The "perfect instant," however, is the Hour of the Last Judgment, for the "witness" of this instant is the divine Judge himself.

Whitrow describes this as the eschatological view of Islam (1989: 80), and goes on to contrast it with the Christian case. The eschatological basis in conceptualizing time led to the periodization of history, a chronological method that we still use, although nowadays we approach history from a purely secular point of view. Medieval historians followed the scheme devised by St. Augustine for dividing world history into six ages corresponding to the six days of creation described at the beginning of Genesis. Prophecy had it in the tenth century that the world would come to an end in the year 1000. Such millenarian belief arose from combining the idea expressed in Psalm 89:4 that "A day with the Lord is as a thousand years" with the interpretation of the Sabbath, or seventh day in Aramaic and Arabic, as a symbol of heavenly rest.

The most influential exponent of millenarian beliefs in the Middle Ages was Joachim of Fiore (1145–1202). He was a monk and abbot in southern Italy where cultural influences fused Greek culture, Arab culture, and the Roman church with cross currents of thought and belief. In this environment, Joachim of Fiore "had moments of intense spiritual illumination that led him to formulate a new millenarian philosophy of history, which combined prophecy, history and the end of the world, an idea which influenced prophecies down to the end of the seventeenth century" (Whitrow 1989: 82; on millenarian connections, see Stowasser 2000). Whitrow notes that in the Middle Ages, European people did not give much significance to time mostly because they were ill-equipped to measure it. The practice of the liturgy and the regular tolling of church bells had accustomed them to a more precise knowledge of the rhythm of the hours than judges or ordinary folk. There was lack of precision. Aveni uses biologists' terms when he writes how circadian cycles are the principal cycles that make up human time. "We in the West," he goes on to say, " have re-envisioned them as intervals of calendar and clocks" (1989: 88).

> By the late Middle Ages, a new kind of public time system had been, created. Born out of religion, commerce, the rise of towns, and the bureaucracy that accompanied them, the "work clock" slowly began to dominate life. Bells of different pitch and duration pealed from the turret that marked the center of town. They tolled when to begin and end work, when to open and close the market, when to call the people to assembly or to begin the curfew. Only in remote rural areas did folks still keep time by the natural course of the heavens, which served well enough to organize a set of daily farm activities such as milking time, meal time, market time. (Aveni 1989: 93)

In his Wiles Lectures of 1956 John Nef concluded that if we seek the origins of our modern quantitative-mindedness, we must concentrate on the last decades of the sixteenth century. Earlier we find little trace of it generally – it was missing in the ordinary person's consciousness. Until the fourteenth century, only the Church was interested in temporal measurement and division. Even the concept of the hour was not used as a unit of duration before the time of Middle French. In the popular tongue it was used only to indicate a point in time.

Change in this mental outlook was slow – even after the introduction of the mechanical clock in the fourteenth century most people were unconcerned in their daily life with the passage of time. In England, parish registers providing dates of birth were instituted by law in 1538. Pressures on recording time were largely economic (Whitrow 1989: 83–4). It is interesting that in the process of "economizing" thought and practice about time, Europe also injected a gendered notion of domesticity of time. This is clearly embodied[2] in the old Anglo-Saxon nursery rhyme:

This is the way we wash our clothes,
Wash our clothes, wash our clothes,
This is the way we wash our clothes,
So early Monday morning.
This is the way we iron our clothes, etc.
So early Tuesday morning

And so on through Wednesday (mending), Thursday (scrubbing the floor), Friday (sweeping the house), Saturday (baking bread), and Sunday (going to church).

This is an altogether different pattern from that of Islam, which neither domesticates nor genders its rhythm. Instead it integrates time and space to interweave for both sexes between sacred and ordinary throughout the day, the week and the year, the moon and the sun. Parise (2002) describes the cyclic regularity of the moon and how this played an immense part in the elaboration of cyclical concepts in many cultures. The moon represents more obviously than other heavenly bodies the changing and permanent aspects of time. It is dark, then increases, it is full, then decreases, then vanishes and reappears, yet it remains identical with itself. One may guess why lunar periods must have been regarded as very important by early humans. All sea creatures have periods that coincide with the tides which, in their turn, contain a fundamental cycle of a period that corresponds to one half that of the moon's apparent revolution around the earth, as well as many other astronomical cycles, such as those corresponding to the conjunction and opposition of the moon with the sun. Menstrual periods of women average twenty-nine days thus, even in our epoch, they coincide, on the average, with some phases of the moon. Pregnant women of the Tiv in Nigeria count lunations to determine the status of their pregnancies (Bohannon 1967: 318). Land animals also display many lunar periodicities. Perhaps the moon was the most obvious and reliable natural clock, with a period appropriate for man's memory. Many calendars are lunar, or lunisolar.

The Islamic calendar is based on twenty-eight lunar mansions, which make up a solar year of 354 days. The lunar months retrogress with respect to the seasons making one complete cycle every 32½ years (Parise 2002: 51). While some scholars claim that the day for Muslims begins at nightfall, Muslims consider the beginning of the day to be sunrise. They pray and fast at sunrise.

In fact, however, when we take a closer look at the lived rhythm of Muslims we find that its "calendar" not only integrates temporality and spatiality in interweaving patterns of sacrality, it integrates the two natural phenomena that have captured the imagination since ancient times: the moon and the sun, such that the Islamic cycle follows the moon in its monthly pattern and the sun in its daily pattern.[3]

Sun According to Fraser (1975: 2) the sun is not the only astronomical body whose motion has been judged sufficiently regular to be used as a basis of timekeeping. The Egyptian *merkhet* was a device for telling the hour of the night by the culmination of stars, attesting to Egyptian familiarity with the elements of astronomy in remote prehistory. Nocturnal dials which told hours by means of the fixed stars were first made in Europe in about 1520 and were commonly used during the seventeenth and eighteenth centuries. Such night dials are simplified embodiments of the oldest scientific instrument, the astrolabe, which was the chief astronomical instrument of both Arab and Latin astronomers of the Middle Ages and was known as "the mathematical jewel."

In its simplest form, that of the panispheric astrolabe, it may be described as a flat model of the heavens. It may be put to one of three uses: (1) to compute the position of heavenly bodies at any given time; (2) to determine the time of the day from the altitudes of the stars or the sun, provided the position of the observer is known; and the stars or the sun, provided the position of the observer is known; and (3) if the position of sun or stars as well as a reference time are known, to determine the position of the user. Thus, an astrolabe may be described as a memory device upon which the laws of planetary motion and the motion of the earth are engraved as functions of the observer's position. In simplified ways, the same holds for a nocturnal dial – or for a sundial.

Rhythm of Culture

Daily prayer Shaped by solar temporality, the five prayers are: dawn (morning), noon, afternoon, sunset, and evening. At specific times the call for prayer is publicly chanted. It marks the beginning of an interval, a period, within which performing the particular prayer is valid and preferred. When unable to, one can perform prayers at the end of the day. The preference in Islam is not to miss prayer during its active interval. Muslim life maintains the rhythms of nature and the rhythms of culture in a seamless whole that characterizes the community. The daily prayer interweaves intervals of sacred and ordinary. Figure 6.1 demonstrates graphically the daily prayer pattern.

The *fajr* prayer begins the daily rhythm. Its *athan* (from *a-th-n*, which denotes both announce and permit) is unique. It is the only one that includes the phrase "*as-Salatu khayrun mina al-nawm*" (prayer does more good than sleep). A Muslim accumulates more good if, in addition to the fajr, he/she prays the *shuruq* (when the sun appears on the horizon) and the *duha* (later morning) pre-noon morning prayers. Noon prayer falls during work hours in urban centers. It is also in some Muslim countries the prayer to bid the dead farewell. It is when the prayer of the dead is performed in the mosque prior to burial. This is followed by the afternoon prayer, sunset prayer, and evening prayer. The whole week keeps that pattern. The days of the week are numbered, that is they follow numbers from one to seven (skipping six): *al-Ahad* (one, equivalent to Sunday), *al-Ethnayn* (two, equivalent

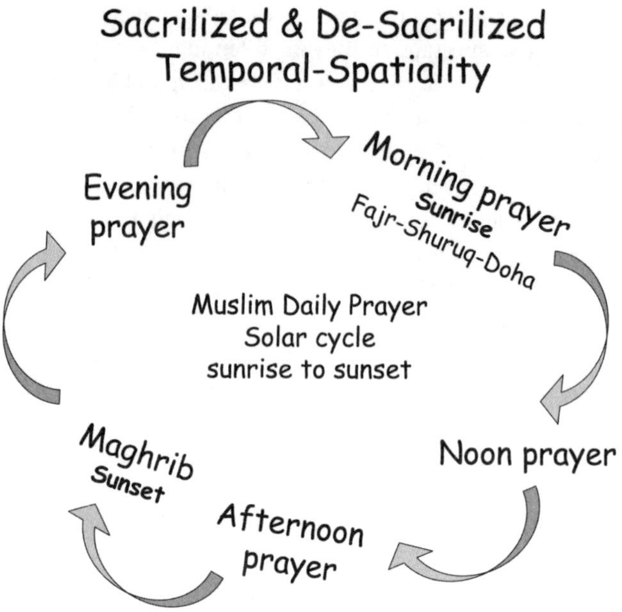

Figure 6.1 Daily prayer – solar cycle. © El Nil Research

to Monday), *al-Thalatha* (three, equivalent to Tuesday), *al-Arba'a* (four, equivalent to Wednesday), *al-Khamis* (five, equivalent to Thursday), and *al-Sabt* (a variant of Sabi' or seventh, equivalent to Saturday), except the day of worship, *yawm al-jum'a* (the day of collectivity, equivalent to Friday), which is the one day of the week that is not named as a number and is for collective worship. There is a qur'anic reference to *salat al-jum'a* (Friday prayer) in two ayahs of Sura al-Munafiqun (62: 9, 10). It tells believers that once the call is made for prayer on Friday they should leave business and proceed to prayer (ayah 9), and that on completion of prayer they may return to pursue their livelihood (10).

This was ethnographically demonstrated recently on the Alexandria–Cairo highway on a Friday. The ethnographic photo collage, Figure 6.2, captures the sense of rushing at Friday prayer time to find room to park by the side of the road and hurrying to the roadside mosque, where at the door they removed their shoes and entered the mosque to perform salat al-jum'a. The scene prior to that was of trucks carrying produce crowding both sides of the highway, taxis carrying passengers, people driving cars. It was time for salat al-jum'a. I parked nearby to observe. After prayer and sermon, *al-musallun* (people who have been praying) were slowly heading out the mosque door, putting on their shoes, and going back to their vehicles. Trucking of produce and certain business is not interrupted on Fridays.

The special place of salat al-jum'a to Muslims was seen on a colleague's face when I asked him hypothetically at Qatar University about missing Friday prayer

Figure 6.2 Friday prayer. © El Nil Research

and whether it would be a substitute to perform noon prayer at home instead. His face expressed anguish at the thought of missing Friday prayer at the mosque. When I persisted in asking why not pray it as a noon prayer, he oversimplified it in his answer, "then there will be no *khutba* (sermon)" (on the importance of sermons in collective prayer, see Antoun 1989). He seemed afterwards to be reflecting on the matter, which he could not articulate to me at the time I asked.

Daily Ramadan Fasting

رجب لله، شعبان للرسول، رمضان للأمة

I once asked a Muslim who was fasting in the Islamic month of *Rajab* why he was fasting. His answer was that fasting *Rajab* is for God, fasting *Sha'ban* is for the Prophet, and fasting *Ramadan* is for the Ummah (the Muslim community). The link between Ramadan and the Ummah is a powerful one. An individual fasting Ramadan, breaks fast every day alone or with family and friends, but at some level would be joining a seemingly tangible community of folk across global time and space who would be fasting and breaking fast following the same pattern at equivalent time. This becomes the open and unbounded Islamic community in its contemporary transformation of the form already conceived fourteen centuries ago in Yathrib.

Today this is a community of over a billion Muslims in different parts of the world in Africa, Asia, Europe, and the Americas, most of whom are adhering to patterns of fasting. It becomes a powerful bond underlying an intangible worldwide community, undivided by clerical authorities or church organizations. There is genius behind the seventh-century construction of a community of monotheists in Arabia, which turned into a worldwide community of Muslims. It was to be a community built on faith instead of kinship. That was the radical contribution. It is a strong common belief that in fact it was built in the seventh century entirely on the basis of faith. However, it managed also to accommodate kinship loyalties. It has never completely dropped the kinship bond. Instead of denying it, it transcended it, perhaps due to countering the big threat it posed to the established structure of Makka and its political and economic base. Most of the first Muslims were relatives of Muhammad one way or another. But so were those who rejected Islam and persecuted the first Muslims. Kin bonding was and continues to be very strong in Arab and other Muslim societies. Formal discourse continues to stress family as a central and significant bond.

The month of Ramadan binds Muslims everywhere. It is the month during which Muslims fast from sunrise to sunset. This pattern intersects structurally with the rhythmic pattern of prayer and integrates seamlessly the two experiential modes, praying and fasting. It is interesting that while the month of Ramadan is based on the lunar cycle, fasting is based on the solar cycle. Fasting in the Muslim world is becoming a little problematic in two ways: the different time zones affect the beginning and end of the fast and crescent sighting is not unified. It used to be that once sighting occurred in a central country, all other countries in the Arab world followed and accepted that as a sign for the beginning of a Muslim month. Today, much debate by religious scholars centers around this problem. The people long for a homogenized pattern, a unity among countries so that once a sighting is established and legitimized by the religious establishment it gets accepted and followed by all Muslims. But as Shaykh al-Qaradawy states, Muslims should follow their own countries until some such pattern is established. Even regional areas such as Khalij countries (Arab Gulf countries) do not share one clock. A power struggle may also have developed since the days when Cairo (the home and center of Al-Azhar) was unchallenged in its authority on Islamic issues. The *kiswa* (the dress of the *Ka'ba*) used to be made in Cairo and brought in procession to Makka by pilgrimage time (Young 1993). Now there is a subtle competition between Saudi Arabia, the center of Islam and the place of its birth, and Egypt, the center of Islamic scholarship. Each heads an orbit of countries that follows its sighting.

Annual Cycle: Ramadan, Two 'Eids, and Pilgrimage (the Hajj) The Islamic calendar contains one fasting month, Ramadan, and two major feasts. In addition, Shi'a Muslims commemorate the martyrdom of the sons of Ali, son-in-law and cousin of Prophet Muhammad, whom they believe to be legitimate successor after the Prophet's death. During the month of Ramadan, Muslims abstain from food, drink, tobacco, sex, and profanity. Breaking fast is at sunset. The end of Ramadan is marked by 'Eid al-Fitr (the feast of breaking the fast, called the small 'Eid in some places). It lasts for three days, or from the first through the third of the Islamic month of Shawwal. The other major feast is 'Eid al-Adha (the feast of sacrifice, called the big feast in some places) marking the pilgrimage. It is celebrated from the tenth through the thirteenth or fourteenth of the last month of the Islamic year, *Thu-l Hijjah* (see Table 5.7), lasting for five days. This feast commemorates Prophet Ibrahim's intent to sacrifice his son, Ismail.[4]

Ramadan and Hajj are about obedience, discipline, and cleansing. They follow an annual lunar rhythm. Hajj marks the last phase of an individual's religious maturity and completes the required pillars of Islam. The principal hajj is performed in Makka at the *Ka'ba*. The sacredness of the house of worship is confirmed in the Qur'an, Sura al-Ma'idah (The Table Spread) 5: 97:

> Allah made the Ka'ba, the Sacred House, an asylum of security for people, as also the Sacred Months, the animals for offerings, and the garlands that mark them: That ye may know that Allah hath knowledge of what is in the heavens and on earth and that Allah is well acquainted with all things.

Once pilgrimage is performed a Muslim man or woman attains an irreversible state of sacredness and social respect accompanied by the acquisition of the irreversible title of *Haj* (for males) or *Hajja* (for females). This cycle of celebrations and observances is diagrammatically represented in Figure 6.3.

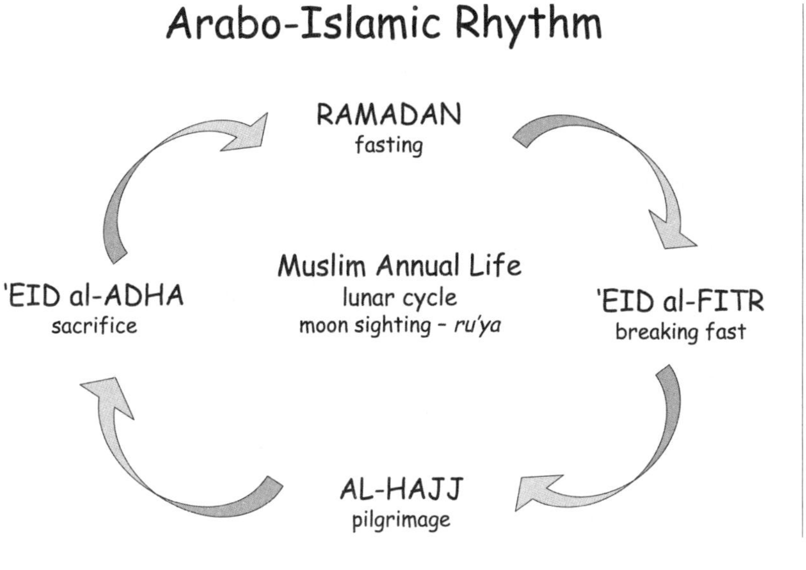

Figure 6.3 Annual cycle of Muslim observances – lunar. © El Nil Research

Space Conversion

Akoub finished his task just as evening prayers were coming to an end.
Abdel Rahman Munif, *Cities of Salt*, (Munif 1989 (1984, Arabic))

The imagery of Akoub finishing his "ordinary" task just as "sacred" time was about to end in the fictional prose of novelist Abdel Rahman Munif is part of a remarkably "ethnographic" account of a desert Khaliji (Arab Gulf) town environment. In very simple straightforward yet poetic language, Munif captures Islam's rhythm without missing a beat of Muslim life. Whether in Munif's *Cities of Salt*, in an international airport today (see Figure 6.4), or while teaching class or holding a meeting at the Khaliji (Arab Gulf) higher education institution, Qatar University, there is a marked rhythm that is followed daily – a rhythm that permeates all aspects of life and activities all the way up to the national level. A collage of photos, Figure 6.4 shows public spaces marked for Islamic prayer and for sacredness.

At prayer time, five times a day, a period begins within which a Muslim person moves temporarily out of ordinary time and space and into sacred time and space and back. Intermittently throughout the day a Muslim person briefly leaves what he or she is doing, irrespective of its nature or importance, and, if already cleansed, stands facing Makka and prays. This happens seamlessly. It could be anywhere – at home, at work, in a shop, in the aisle of an airplane, in the airport, or in the street. A Muslim prays in a spot that he or she marks out, perhaps by spreading a

Figure 6.4 Public spaces for praying. © El Nil Research

mat, rug, or newspaper. During business hours, a merchant in his store can simply mark the spot where he is standing, thus converting it into a sacred space for worship. A buyer waits for the merchant to end his prayer to resume transactions.

For praying singly, although desirable, Muslims do not necessarily have to interrupt their routine activity upon hearing the call for prayer, since there is a period of several hours during which a Muslim can perform each particular prayer. But even when engaged in ordinary conversation, a Muslim interacts with the call chant the instant it is heard: he/she recognizes the call by saying to oneself prescribed phrases as a response to different segments of the call, intermittently resuming ordinary conversation. For example, upon hearing "Allah-u Akbar" the person would say "Allah-u A'tham wal 'Izzatu lillah" (God is supreme, Glory be to him). This and other phrases are spoken intermittently throughout the call in normal speech style, but with a different demeanor. Another person present would recognize this as being individual talk in individual sacred space, not part of ordinary public conversational space. This kind of intermittent interaction with the call for prayer is visually demonstrated in the visual ethnography *Ghurbal* (El Guindi 1995 [film]) in which I was watching Hoksha, the rural Egyptian master craftsman, craft a ghurbal (traditional animal skin sieve) while interviewing him as he was being filmed. Hoksha smoothly and spontaneously flowed in and out of ordinary space and time and sacred space and time.

Any undesignated area, facing the direction of Makka, can be temporarily "designated" as sacred Muslim space by the act of the prayer itself. An area is marked as prayer area when a Muslim of either sex, in a cleansed purified state, performs any of the daily prayers. Ritual purification is achieved by Muslim women or men through dress code, cleansing by *wudu'* (an Arabic term for cleansing, not simply

Figure 6.5 Public praying. © El Nil Research

washing), facing Makka (the sacred center of Islam situated in Arabia), and performing prescribed rites of worship. This turns a public area into a private space. Figure 6.5 shows an ethnographic photo taken of a passenger turning sacred space out of the coat hanging and luggage storage room of the luxurious Business Lounge at Doha International airport in Qatar.

In the ethnographic photos we see how ordinary Muslims temporarily convert any worldly place (street, shop, aircraft aisle) into a sacred space set apart, simply by marking it and occupying it in a cleansed state facing Makka. An individual faithful turns any worldly place into individual sacred space by performing the daily prescribed five prayers.

During prayer a Muslim, stripped temporarily of worldly identity, is in a sacred state. While persons stand, bow, prostrate themselves, and sit, they recite verses from the Qur'an and the various ritual formulae.

Space conversion can be effected singly or collectively. The mosque during Friday noon prayer and the annual pilgrimage to Makka represent collective sacred spaces activated by groups of Muslims. Both collective spaces, one activated once a week, the other once a year, provide a temporal rhythm to routine life. In Qatar University almost every building on campus has a prayer room, additional to the university mosque. There are two mosques, one on the men's campus and one on the women's campus. From the mosque minaret the athan (call for prayer) is heard five times a day. Individuals, students, faculty, and staff either pray individually in the nearest space convenient or go to prayer rooms assigned in almost all the campus buildings to cleanse and pray or pray if already cleansed. At the time of noon prayer, faculty and staff slowly head toward the prayer room to pray collectively. Noon prayer is more likely to be a group prayer.

Interweaving Pattern: Sacred–Ordinary

Neither cyclical nor linear nor radial really captures the Muslim rhythmicity characterizing the Muslim day, which does not start or end but is continuous in its pattern of interweaving in and out, sacred and ordinary. Sura 2: 189 talks about start of month and end of month, when it refers to new moons:

> They ask thee concerning the new moons. Say, They are but signs to make fixed periods of time in (the affairs of) men, and for Pilgrimage

To derive meaning in this case, this ayah is examined against another qur'anic segment, that from Sura Fatir (The Originator of Creation) 35: 13, whereby we read how moon and sun, day and night, merge:

> He merges Night into Day, and he merges Day into Night, and he has subjected the sun and the moon (to his Law): each one runs its course for a term appointed. Such is Allah

> your Lord: to Him belongs all Dominion. And those whom ye invoke besides Him have not the least power.

This same trope of merging of time is again affirmed in Sura al-Anibya' (The Prophets) 21: 33:

> It is He Who created the Night and the Day, and the sun and the moon: all (the celestial bodies) swim along, each in its rounded course.

In other words, one can locate the rhythmicity of interweaving spatiality and temporality of Islam in scripture. When combined with Muslim life, as described in the various chapters, a Muslim web of life is revealed that has been developing out of a creative idea since the seventh century. Moving in and out of the five daily prayers (salat) establishes a particular quality to the pattern of the day. It creates a distinctive Muslim rhythm, which is established by this interweaving of daily prayers in daily life. More than any other daily practice or task, intermittently praying throughout the day weaves a rhythm of fluid, interwoven temporality and spatiality that makes daily life of and for a Muslim distinctive and unique. The public call for prayer chanted five times a day (athān) by human voice from the minarets of mosques reflects and establishes this rhythmic pattern (Dorsky 1986: 64–73). This pattern is graphically represented in Figure 6.6.

This interweaving pattern is recurrent, pervasive, and powerful. It is established by Muslims as they follow the fard (requirement) of daily prayer. Upon hearing the voice from atop a minaret nearby calling Muslims to prayer (athān), which could be

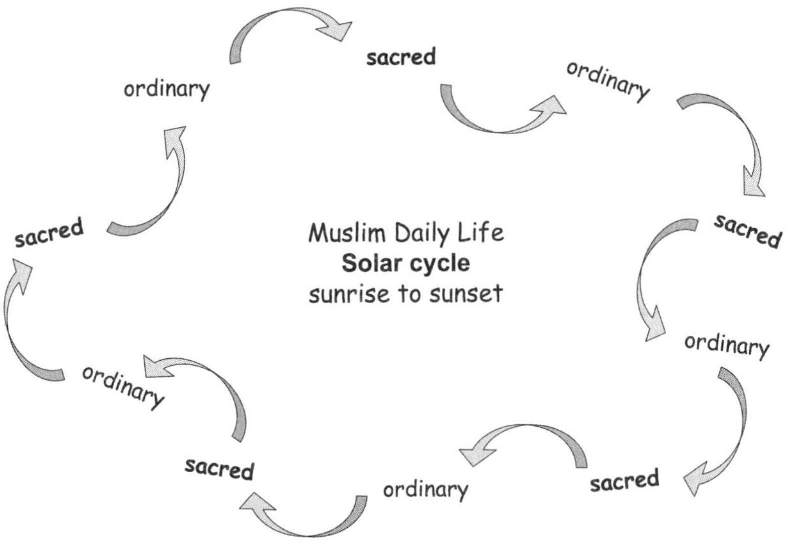

Figure 6.6 Muslim daily rhythm – Interweaving of sacred and ordinary. © El Nil Research

from the campus mosque at Qatar University, or through their watches or laptops, they respond by moving to pray in a designated or undesignated area. While it is only for a few minutes, if one is not in tune with the rhythm you might go all the way to a building to get some task done and not find anyone in their offices. Noon prayer is the one prayer that interweaves work time at the university, since most perform morning (or dawn) prayer at home before they go to work and the afternoon prayer at home after they leave work. Those who do stay on campus late, past noon prayer and through the afternoon prayer, might interrupt a meeting to perform their prayer and then resume the meeting. Arabic radio and television stations (except al-Jazeera Arabic Satellite television channel headquartered in Doha, Qatar) interrupt programming to broadcast a call for prayer in its exact local time. Arabic channels of satellite television directing their broadcasting to the United States interrupt programming for broadcasting prayer at US East Coast zone times.

Here we see how a rhythm of nature becomes a rhythm of culture. Through the interweaving effect of prayer there is a distinctive quality of the Islamic construction of space as it turns a public area into a private space, without entry of a stranger. Interweaving of space and time, as individuals move in and out during the course of the day between worldly and sacred spheres is distinctly, perhaps uniquely, Islamic. What Ardener might call "spaces within spaces" or "overlapping universes" (1993: 3) is best described in the analysis of Arab culture as fluidity of space and rhythmic patterns of time. The two interweave throughout the ordinary day.

Altered Experience and Calm Serenity

It must be noted that this shift to perform prayer is not done with suddenness, abruptness, or a sense of urgency. Muslims move to prayer smoothly, calmly, and gently. The effect of having to pray at prayer time is not at all like the effect of a factory worker, indoctrinated by the "time is money" ideology, stressfully looking at his watch. The pace of the Muslim believer is remarkably calm. It is as if Muslims are carrying internal prayer clocks, as it were, clocks that activate intermittently, guiding the faithful to prayer and then out of prayer to function between prayer times productively[5] in ordinary space and time, only to shift again to sacred time and space when prayer time comes.

This pattern creates a moment-by-moment awareness of one's place in both worldly and otherworldly space and time. It seamlessly moves the Muslim in and out, in and out, neither spatiality or temporality interrupting the other, instilling, as a systematic observation reveals, in the praying Muslim a sense of calm, serenity, and contentment. I was inspired to adopt the vocabulary of "altered experience" to describe this state after William Young's characterization of the praying experience among the Rashaayda. Young (1996) notes how the Rashaayda's experience of the prayer is integrated with their experience of time and space. Standing to pray facing the *gibla* (Makka) "creates an altered experience of space" (1996: 74).

Particularly in modern "pressure-cooker" society (as some like to call modern fast-paced urban life) this pattern that every Muslim internalizes intermittently relieves the pressure, transcends the routineness, and breaks the monotony of daily demands on the individual. The appropriateness of doing each task in its own time and space is beautifully expressed in the popular Arabic folk expression evoking an aspect of Islamic activity that is focal for creating that rhythm, namely the athan. The folk expression says كل وقت وله اذانه (each temporal segment has its athan or call for prayer). It obscures cause and effect. It is not that athan determines time, but that each time has its distinctive athan. Athan in this folk usage does not seem to be confined literally to prayer. It becomes a metaphor for the rhythm that is the quality of Arabo-Islamic life.

The Theory of Rhythm

The French School of collective representations and rhythm was discussed at length. For Durkheim, society came first; sociological collectivity has primacy. The same thinking guided his view on formal calendars; he observed that "[t]he division into days, weeks, months, years, etc. correspond to the periodical recurrence of rites, feasts, and public ceremonies" (Durkheim 1961 [1912]: 23). To him, a calendar expresses the rhythm of the collective activities, while at the same time its function is to assure their regularity. Space is to be viewed in the same way: "It is the rhythm of social life which is the basis of the category of time: the territory occupied by the society furnished the material category of space" (Durkheim 1961 [1912]: 23, 490). The rhythm of collective life dominates time and space. Society becomes the model for time and space and reproduces them. Time and space are localized in sociality. It has been established that rhythm was the sign of collective activity. "If this is true, it is legitimate to suppose that the rhythm of time does not necessarily model itself on the natural periodicities established by experience, but that societies contain within themselves the need and the means of instituting it" (Durkheim 1961 [1912]: 71–2).

Henri Hubert (1999 [1905]) transcends "the chicken or the egg" trap and moves from the sacredness of the collectivity to the sacredness of the sacred itself. He observes that calendrical systems reflect the need for a specific rhythm to govern "the dispersal of religious acts in time" (49). We may never be able to answer a "which came first" question but if we follow Hubert's discussion of time we are led to think that it is not measurement that time gives, but rhythm. He states it emphatically: "The object of a calendar is not to measure time, but to endow it with rhythm" (49). Hubert sees two series of representations: "One is constant and periodic, that is, the calendar and chronology with their points of reference . . . the other is perpetually being constructed through the contribution of new representations. The mind works constantly to associate certain elements of these two series within the same tension" (65).

Calendars constitute ways of notating time through a sequence of dates and durations; but, according to Hubert, "the object of a calendar is not to measure time but to endow it with rhythm." "Units of time," he writes, "are not units of measurement but of a rhythm" (61). As demonstrated in the first few chapters, we determine and we experience time. It is generally believed that we experience the division of time through certain easily observable astronomic phenomena.

There are two ways, according to Hubert, of determining the divisions of time, which are used concurrently. "On the one hand, calendrical limits are made to coincide either with phenomena which indicate approximately the actual change of the seasons . . . or else with critical moments in the course of certain heavenly bodies, the moon, the sun, etc." (66). It is claimed that the generative numbers of calendrical periods are suggested by experimental knowledge of the actual length of certain astronomical periods. "[T]he two processes are combined [such that] in a complete system of dividing time, one always finds numerical indexes associated with phenomenal indexes" (67). "The use of astronomical indexes also leaves much room for the arbitrary. As regards the length of the lunar month, one initial source of uncertainty derives from the fact that it does not always begin at the same hour of the day, another from the fact that the sidereal and synodic revolutions of the moon differ by approximately two days" (67–8).

For Hubert the general rule is that "it is not events that fix dates." Dates are times marked by a rhythm, which divides an indefinite duration into finite durations. In the same way, a rhythm determines the repetition ad infinitum of established dates, whatever they may be. "The representation of time," he says, "is essentially rhythmic" (71). Scholars see implications of Hubert's theoretical ideas going beyond the particular domains he is discussing. While his formulations are considered mainly to be about time in religion and spheres of magic, it is clear that their relevance is much more general and they have important conceptual implications (see James and Mills 2005: 7).

I find Henri Hubert's theoretical formulations, and particularly his significant contribution of centering the notion of the sacred in analysis, to be valuable. It supports my own conceptualization of time and space in Arabo-Islamic culture. I concur with the idea that sacred is a category and sacralization of time, space, and activity operates on thought. I differ with Hubert in some ways. First, while I center the sacred in analysis, I do not confine the sacred to the realm of religion. I consider the sacred to be conceptually separable from the sphere of religion. Nor do I adopt the Durkheimian vocabulary of profane opposing sacred. Further, I do not consider the "sacred" to be a category positioned in structural or conceptual opposition to the category "secular," as is assumed by Hubert. Rather I consider "secular" to be in opposition to religion, and sacred to ordinary. These are conceptual orientations that are empirically derived during my anthropological research on Islam and the Islamic Movement. The sacred is a category of thought but one that constitutes a quality that interpenetrates both spheres, secular and religion. So Durkheim finds rhythm in society and social collectivity. Hubert sees rhythm in the sacred. My own observational path in the study of the Islamic notion of time and space empirically and conceptually gravitated to the idea of rhythm, in response to the factual reality of Muslim life and the feel by Muslims living Islam hourly, daily, monthly, annually, and throughout their Muslim lifetime. Figure 6.7 represents this rhythm in Islam in which a pattern alternates between ordinary and sacred.

The theory builds on some ideas discussed earlier but unites them with cultural correlates from Arabo-Islamic culture: thus incorporating elements of the collective, the sacred and privacy, the realms of nature and culture, and the premises of interweaving fluidity of time and space. That is, the sacred penetrates time and space and it is the specific mode of penetration that is of relevance to this study of Islam. It is that environment, as Isambert puts it, in which one enters and emerges from, that is to say the attribute of fluidity, along with the notion of rhythm and cultural elements of the sacred, privacy, and collectivity, linking the spheres of nature and culture, that this study of Islam sets out to put together as a coherent paradigm.

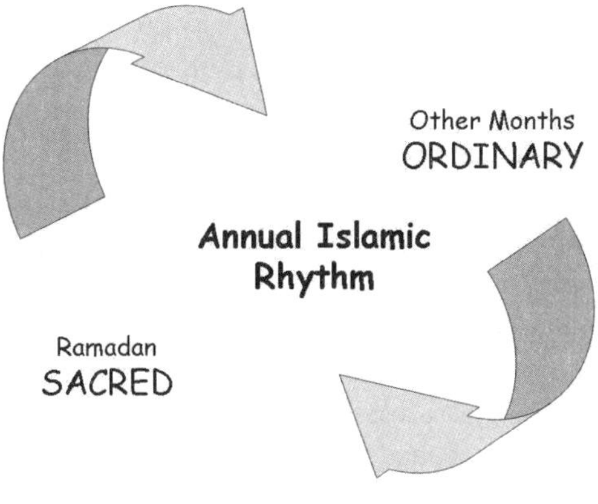

Figure 6.7 Annual pattern of alternations between sacred and ordinary. © El Nil Research

Elements of a New Paradigm

*The Sacred (*Al-Qudsiyya*)* *Harām* derives from the root *h-r-m*, considered "among the most important Arabic roots in the vocabulary of Islamic practice" (Reinhart 1995: 101); for expanded discussion see El Guindi (2003 [1999]:

82–96). It is a word widely used in the Arabic vocabulary to mean forbidden, taboo, prohibited, unlawful, and sacred, which evokes constraint and heightened sanctity. It further refers to all that is prohibited by divine authority. *Muharramat* (plural) denotes all that is forbidden for Muslims to eat or do. In legal thought an act deemed haram is one forbidden. Usually the term is synonymous with "proscribed," but it is sometimes used to denote the negative side of the legal scale of value, incorporating both the proscribed and the "reprehensible" (*makruh*). The continuum lies between what is *harām* (forbidden) and what is *halāl* (permissible). Words in Arabic that derive from the same root refer to women and sacred taboo (*hūrma*), to women's quarters (*harīm*), and to house of worship (*hāram*) and for home.

Reinhart expands on the taboos surrounding places of worship for which the term is used to refer to the area around the three holy cities of Islam: Makka, Madina, and al-Quds (Jerusalem). "[C]ertain restrictions apply that both reflect and define their sanctity. Hunting is forbidden, as is uprooting any tree or harvesting grain. Violence toward humans is proscribed. . . . The sanctity of the place is protected, and it protects those who flee to it" (1995: 101). The term used for this sanctuary in which violence and bloodshed is prohibited is *al-hāram al-sharīf* (the noble sanctuary). Other usages include *al-māsjid al-harām* (the holy mosque) or *al-bayt al-harām* (the holy house) or *bayt-allah al-harām* (the holy house of God), which are used interchangeably to refer to Macca's Grand Mosque (El Guindi 1985). A variant on mosques is the reference to al-Haram al-Qudsi, for the al-Aqsa mosque in Jerusalem, itself called al-Quds. *Al-Shahr al-Harām* (the holy month) refers to Ramadan, the month of fasting.

The same root also yields the word *ihrām*, which means the state of ritual purity for pilgrims on the hajj (pilgrimage) (Reinhart 1995: 101), which involves "a special dress consisting of two seamless wrappers, one passed round the loins, the other over the shoulders, leaving the head uncovered" (Crawley 1931: 159) and ritual ablution and other prohibitions, and which can only be undone by *fakk-il-ihrām* (untying or breaking from the state), or the oppositional but equivalent phrase *ihlal* (making halal or lawful). In the context of gender, men in a relationship to a woman defined and bound by the incest taboo are her *maharim* (pl. for *māhram*).

"Hāram so-and-so" means wife of so-and-so. *Harīm* becomes the part of the Arab home in which Arab women are both privileged and protected from encounters with non-mahram men (Graham-Brown 1988: 71–2). Women are the center of the family and its sanctity, and hence the term extends to the family in general, as commonly used in verbal greetings and inquiries about health. Hūrma is best translated as "sanctity" in English. Hurma refers to woman or wife, and is used as well to refer to the sanctity of the home as in "*al-bayt lahu-ohurma*" (a home has its sanctity). As mentioned earlier other derivatives refer to religious sanctuaries, such as mosques and pilgrimage sites. Antoun (1968) adds one other meaning of hurma – respectable woman, a connotation supported by the fact that the variant *ihtiram* (respect) is another derivative, connecting "respect" with haram. Respect, achieved by behavior and personal qualities and acquired by social or kinship status, is a key factor in the reputation of an individual and the group. Reputation is a carefully cultivated cultural investment. The quality hurma (which centers womanhood and home in the culture) embodies a pervasive complex of values that identifies primary social and religious spheres as sanctuaries – sacred and inviolable.

Sacred Code A cluster of Arab concepts, represented in English as sanctity–reserve–respect, together constitute in my analysis a code summing up the key notion of haram. Drawing upon various bodies of knowledge and diverse ethnographic accounts on Arab and Islamic culture I identify and group the following term-concepts: *hurma* (*h-r-m*), *hishma* (*h-sh-m*), *satr* (*s-t-r*),[6] *tahashshud* (*h-sh-d*), and *haya'* (*h-y-y*). As a group these constitute a cultural code of *sanctity–reserve–respect*. It is common in traditional circles for a man, upon entering a home, to "yihamhim" (a clearing throat sound), clap, or call out "*ya sattar*" (*s-t-r*) (O Protector of Privacy, an attribute of God) to announce his imminent entry upon women's, or a home's, privacy. Words like *bayt*, *dar*, and *haram* represent core conceptualizations related to the fundamental code of sanctity–reserve–respect. The interdependence between the sexes in building and guarding the group's reputation is supported in most reliable ethnographies such as those of Michael Gilsenan, William Lancaster, William Young, and Ahmad Abu-Zaid among others.

Al-Qudsiyya vs. al-Shar'iyya

Qudsīyya and *shar'īyya* are different notions of legitimacy in Arabo-Islamic culture. To clarify the difference, these two will be discussed in the context of a subject that does not seem to go away in the West, namely the *hijab* (or veil for simplification). The hijab continues to be a hysterical obsession of politics and media and has become increasingly the focus of European politics and controversy. The phrase *shar'iyya(t) al-hijab* means legal legitimacy for wearing the hijab. The word *shār'iyya* is rooted in *sh-r-'*, from which also derives the term *Sharī'a* (Islamic law). Shar'iyya can only be established by Islamic scholars (*'ūlama*) of religion who explore all the evidence available in the wide range of Islamic sources.

Stern observes that

> [t]he only ordinance that could possibly have any bearing on this subject is Sura 33, 59, which was addressed to his wives, his daughters, and the women of the believers enjoining that they should cover themselves with their *jilbabs* . . . [L]egists have never

> tried to support their theories of veiling on this verse, . . . [but] commentators such as al-Tabari, al-Baidawi, and as Suyuti do refer to veiling in their *Tafsir* [Interpretation] on this verse145 . Al-Tabari includes in his commentary on this verse the tradition on Muhammad's wives going out at night, which is amongst those given as being the origin of Sura 33, 53. (Stern 1939: 111)

Likewise, the tafsir of Sura 24: 31 "merely prescribes modesty in comportment and dress" (111). This does not directly relate to the actual content of the Sura, nor does it discuss how much of her person is to be covered. Plausibly these commentaries were written long after the first days of Islam after the custom had already established itself among Muslims.

What does the Qur'an say about the hijab? The Qur'an contains a number of references to hijab, only one of which concerns women's clothing. As Islam gradually established itself in the Madina community, what has come to be interpreted as "seclusion" for Muhammad's wives came from a reading of a qur'anic verse (33: 53). Evidence suggests that this sura concerning the hijab was revealed possibly before AH 5. During that time, many people from the growing Islamic community were going to the homestead of the Prophet for queries, favors, and requests. His wives resided in quarters surrounding the courtyard that became the first mosque the Prophet Muhammad founded for Muslims. This was in Madina. Stern describes the wives' quarters as huts "situated on one side of the *masjid* [mosque] with their entrances possibly on to its court . . . Aisha's hut had an entrance to the *masjid* . . . while Umm Salamah built some type of screen to her hut, in order to form a barrier between her and the people" (Stern 1939: 119, n.2). Sura 33: 53 is ultimately about privacy of the Prophet's home and family and the special status of his wives in two ways – as the Prophet's wives and as leaders with access to Islamic information and wisdom who are increasingly sought by community members. There was need to protect women's right to privacy by regulating the flow of visitors and the comportment of men who enter upon the women's quarters. It is not about women's clothing. Men entering the wives' quarters are required to ask permission or enter only when invited and, even then, to talk to the Prophet's wives from behind a partition or curtain.

The reference to women's dress is confined to *jilbab,* the long, loose garment. The terms hijab and *niqab* are not mentioned. The text uses *khimar* (head cover) and jilbab (body dress or cloak), and the focus of both verses on restrained behavior and reserve in comportment, starting with men who are enjoined to cover their genitals, as well as on the special status of the Prophet's wives, and the special status of relations who are outside the pool of sexual and marital access for women. Other references stress the separating aspect of hijab. For example, *al-hijab* is mentioned in non-gendered contexts separating deity from mortals (42: 51), wrongdoers from the righteous (7: 46, 41–5), believers from unbelievers (17: 45), light from darkness and day from night (38: 32).

In terms of *shar'iyyat al-hijab*, Stern examines the Hadith which was said to have been the grounds for arguing for the institution of the hijab and finds credence to the notion that certain Hadith did have influence in the development of this institution. In the above Sura (33: 53) she gives two clarifications with regard to the ordinance addressed to men to talk to Prophet Muhammad's wives from behind the curtain: the first being that Muhammad had no definite plan for the seclusion of his wives at the time of this revelation, but it was connected with annoying intrusions occurring during Zainab's wedding feast and a few other incidents.

In sum, none of the passages presented above mentioned the word hijab itself. When mentioned it conveys more the sense of separation than veiling. The three Arabic terms khimar, jilbab, and tabarruj are the ones used in the context of women's dress to stress privacy, general comportment, and the special status of the Prophet's wives. Shar'iyya, however, is not based on the literal presence of the word but rather on the general meaning from related contexts. But French law, as discussed below, challenges or ignores the hijab's shar'iyya altogether, yet women who have adopted the hijab since the mid 1970s have no doubt about its shar'iyya. q*udsiyyat al-hijab* (sacredness of hijab) is born out of the conviction of the faithful that wearing the hijab at all time in public space is what their faith demands. *Qudsiyya* derives from *q-d-s*, from which many Arabic words derive, ranging in meaning from worship, to sacred, to holy. *Al-Quds al-Sharif* refers to the Arab holy mosque of Jerusalem. As an Arabic word it is not Islam specific. Christians use word derivatives from the same root to refer to holy practices and objects. *Al-Kitab al-Muqaddas* is what the Holy Bible is referred to in Arabic. The Qur'an is referred to as *Al-Qur'an al-Karim*. My use of the term qudsiyya is intended to convey an attribute of sacredness. In this historical, sociopolitical moment, in which we live, the hijab acquired the attribute of qudsiyya to Muslims wearing and advocating it. Those secularists who are adamantly against it and argue that expedient reasons are behind wearing the hijab are simply wrong.

In a two-hour interview (2005), which was aired on a prestigious talk show called *Yohka Anna* (As the Story Goes) on Lebanese television channel NBN,[7] the interviewer (Su'ad al-'Ish) stated that the conclusion from my study on the veil suggested removing the qudsiyya from the veil. I was surprised and unprepared for this interpretation. My study traced historical and textual (Islamic) contexts in which the practice of veiling (anywhere, anytime) and the notion of the veil were considered. I discovered heterogeneous usages for hijab that are not confined to the connotation of head or face cover. I distinguished veiling that is customary from veiling that is religious, veiling by men and veiling by women, veiling by Christians and veiling by Muslims.

I had in an earlier publication (El Guindi 1981), the first to challenge the usage of the term hijab in the Qur'an as an article of dress, identified the multiple uses of that term employed in the Qur'an. It is safe to say that the primary connotation was conceptual rather than literal, and the references to hijab were about separateness not about the actual material cover used by Muslim women. In my analysis, however, I did make explicit that there is in fact in the Qur'an and in contemporary cultural conceptualizations evidence for a generalized principle or premise that supports a public comportment of reserve and respect for men and women, popularly referred to as modesty, and that the interpretation and translation of this imperative among Muslim women takes the form of wearing the hijab in public at all times. I do not equate the religious (*dini* in Arabic) and the sacred (*muqaddas* in Arabic), nor do I conceptualize the sacred as confined to the religious realm. Within my conceptual framework the cultural importance given to the hijab by a large segment of the Muslim population worldwide, whether with legal justification, shar'iyya, or not, would still make the hijab sacred.

That is why I was taken off guard by the interviewer's comment. Probably Ms Su'ad, like most people, equates the sacred and the religious. I distinguish between sacred and ordinary, but do not pose sacred versus secular. Secularists are not detached observers or objective analysts of religion. Scholarship on religion by secularists must be subjected to the anthropological *instruments of objectification* (to use Bourdieu's phrase). They need to go through anthropological training to internalize a particular "relation to the world".[8] It must become a relation of observation, analysis, and discovery rather than a relation of disguised judgment and hidden condemnation toward the subject of religion.[9] Religion is a sphere that must continue to be subjected to anthropological analysis, and not be left to the approaches of area, religious, or cultural studies, and most importantly not to be monopolized by biases of secularist ideology.

The Headscarf Affair Does secularism have the right to impose itself on the right to choose and the right of religious believers to exercise their freedom in public space? If it does, then it is a selective democracy that is being exercised in Europe. No subject is a better test for this question than what has become referred to as "the headscarf affair." While this issue is not new, it is now a matter of newsworthy international headlines because of serious measures taken against it in Europe. Olson (1985) described the headscarf crisis as it developed decades ago in Turkey, and Norton (1997) and Quataert (1997) traced sartorial rules in the Ottoman Empire.

Is the headscarf worn by Muslim women, or what is termed veil in general, seen simply as an item of clothing, like panties worn by American women? When does a material clothing item become a symbol around which social, political, and moral campaigns are mobilized? The "bra affair" of the early 1970s in the United States comes to mind, in which wearing or removing the bra became a symbol of belonging or not belonging to women's lib (a term with derogatory connotations and invoking antagonistic reprisals). While the analogy between the veil worn by Muslim women and underwear worn by American women might seem far-fetched and sound provocative, I think there is something to it. It can provide perspective and clarity to what seems to be an irrational focus on the headscarf.

Some hate-opponents of the hijab, who, in addition to politically motivated groups, include secularists of all ethnicities and cultural backgrounds, tend to resort to hygienic, health, and sight reasons in expressing the negative impact of wearing the veil by Muslim women. It is often suggested that wearing face veils has a bad health effect on sight. This, it is argued, should be sufficient reason to abandon the custom.[10]

The hijab worn by Muslim women in Arab, Muslim, European, or US society is about identity and privacy of space and body. Veiling "proxemics" communicates exclusivity of rank and nuances in kinship status and behavior. A simple headscarf can be a symbol of power and autonomy and functions as a vehicle for resistance. Hijab becomes ideologized as a symbol of resistance. The issue of the hijab and its ban in France (and elsewhere in Europe) was discussed in some detail earlier as issues of *laïcité* and *culte* that intersect with the headscarf affair.[11]

Hijab embodies an Islamic morality of reserve and an act of resistance against imposed measures, local non-participatory politics, hegemonic secularism, colonial occupation and legacy, namely, Israeli occupation of Palestine, current global economic dominance, US invasions of Muslim and Arab countries. The hijab is increasingly at the center of a field of operation. It is perceived as a threat to secularism and a symbol of militancy in France, Denmark, England, Germany, and in the United States. It is politically charged in most of Europe, where measures have been passed to ban it, some purportedly for maintaining the integrity of secularism. The issue is considered to be fraught with anti-Islamic implications. Preceding the invasion of Afghanistan, the Feminist Majority in the United States, an extremist feminist group, took a fanatic posture toward the Afghan *burqu'*. An awareness of the difference between burqu' and hijab is just beginning. The racist bias against both, however, is not disappearing. To many, the hijab represents an identity of choice and a freedom of expression they hope they would not lose. France, and other European countries seeking to ban the hijab, are defying its shar'iyya and its qudsiyya. Muslims, rightly, are not happy about this. Put in a larger apolitical context, hijab connects the sphere of dress to sacred space and the latter to privacy. Dress in general, but particularly veiling, is privacy's visual metaphor. Privacy constitutes another element in the theory of Islamic rhythm. It is to be discussed next.

*Privacy (*khususiyya*)* In a recent publication (El Guindi 2007: 172–3) I made the point that conceptually a private–public polarity refers to a division of space that has become reified into a heuristic paradigm used to describe gendered social and cultural activities. In the 1970s the anthropology of women – which grew out of feminist concerns that sexist bias in anthropological studies of earlier decades resulted in neglect of women's roles, activities, and concerns in studies of society and culture – set out to compensate and correct this neglect by adopting the division of space and spheres into public and private and converting it into a paradigm for description and analysis. Although applied universally, it tended to be used mostly to describe Mediterranean European and Arabo-Islamic cultures. A link was made between the public–private and gender. A valuation was attached to the duality: the public domain was described as a highly valued sphere in which men were active, and the private sphere of women was used interchangeably with domestic sphere, a private domain of women less valued universally.

Circularity in this set of claims is obvious. Men's work is highly valued because it is public, and public work is valued because it is men's domain. In this framework men and their work are universally considered superior. This was ethnocentrically extended to describe men's universal superiority as stemming from their being perceived as closer to culture, whereas women are closer to nature. This whole line of argument and its underlying assumptions were strongly and successfully challenged on ethnographic and conceptual grounds.

However, women's studies and culture studies were not as critical of these assumptions and continued to apply the public–private duality to Arab and Muslim women. The Arabo-Islamic East is the cultural region best suited to challenge the rigidity and universality of the gendered pair of spheres. Two spheres considered private in the Middle East are women and family. Here I find the notion of privacy closer to cultural understanding; it reflects better culture conceptualization than the rigidly imposed private–public polarity.[12]

After a visit around the campus of Qatar University, for example, one questions not only the universality of the division but also its accuracy. It becomes evident that assumptions of domesticity, separation from the public, and inferior valuation of the private are distortions of the ethnographic reality. A private sphere of female students on campus is neither seen by women, men, faculty, or administrators as an imposition on women, nor is their private space, whether by dress or in the physical layout of the campus, seclusion from the public. In dress and appearance, privacy is active in public. In Qatar, female university students walk around campus in long, elegant black *'abayas* and head covers, regally worn. Tails trailing behind them and chiffon scarves layered softly to cover their hair, women glide from building to building and from classroom to classroom at a measured pace, with straight postures, holding their heads high in dignity and with pride in their gender and identity. There is no sense of inferiority or secondary status. These are women who are both veiled and very self-assured in the public realm. It is worthwhile to add that at Qatar University, which is a mixed-gender public institution, the university president is a Qatari woman, the vice president is a Qatari woman, the dean of the College of Arts and Sciences is a woman, and many other deans, department and program chairs, and students majoring in professional fields are women. This pattern is not unusual in Khaliji society. In a chapter I wrote in the 1980s, using data from Bahrain and with predictive implications for the Khaliji

(Gulf) Region, I predicted a significant increase in professional women (El Guindi 1985: 79–95).

The notion of privacy is much more adequate conceptually and ethnographically to describe the cultural reality that focuses on the centrality of family and women. Instead of secluding, domesticating, or devaluing, privacy guards women's place and participation in public. It is a privacy without domesticity and without secrecy. In Qatar, as in other Arab and Islamic societies, there is a culture that cultivates and guards privacy in such a way that family remains a core foundation of the culture, and women can simultaneously be most private and most public.

Based on English common-law traditions (which had legal recognition in the United States as early as 1890) the term privacy is used with reference to an individual's right to be left alone and in contexts of trespassing private property. So the Western usage of the term is linked to the Western notion of individualism and individual rights to property (El Guindi 1985: 90–1). It is commonly presumed that privacy is a universal notion tied to individuated space or to seclusion.

Previously I indicated how in my search I found that the English word "privacy" has no single adequate equivalent in Arabic. The Arabic–English dictionary translates privacy in terms that correspond with the Western notion, such as "personal," "secluded," "secrecy," and "solitary." The relatively recent Arabic term applied to connote privacy is *khususiyya*. While still evolving into a more adequate usage, it remains at an embryonic phase of development and often mixes the two notions: the Arab concept of a valued right over body and space for women and over space for family, and the Western application referring to an individuated experience of space. I will nevertheless adopt the Arabic term khususiyya for convenience and with the hope of contributing to its more culturally based formulation, rather than a mix of inherently contradictory, cross-cultural elements. On the basis of studying Arabo-Islamic culture I propose a use of khususiyya that is not only of analytic value but is itself culturally derived. Arab privacy is not personal but collective, not secret but sacred. It is carefully guarded and concerns primarily the two core cultural spheres of women and family. Arab privacy is neither about individualism nor seclusion. It is relational and public.

In this study privacy goes further. In its transformational fluid form, privacy embraces Arab cultural constructions of space as it intersects, not only with gender, but primarily with time and space. In an Arab cultural context, space is nuanced and dynamic. It is characterized by the spatial and temporal interweaving pattern – the moving between sacred space and time to ordinary worldly space and time throughout the day every day. It also accommodates privacy in public. This is seen in dress and behavior of Muslims. Sacred space and rhythmic time are both public and private (on this point see El Guindi 2007).

Space, rather than materially fixed, is a relationship in which open (undefined) spaces are rare. The terminology deriving from *h-r-m* and, relating the notion of haram to other similar concepts, links various aspects of Arab-Islamic culture which these usages underlie. The concept of sanctuary, which connects sacred places, like mosque and pilgrimage center, house of worship and house of learning, also applies to women, women's quarters, and family – a connection that brings out the significance of the idea of sanctity in these contexts. Veil, veiling patterns, and veiling behavior are therefore, according to my analysis of Arab culture about sacred privacy, sanctity, and the rhythmic interweaving patterns of worldly and sacred life, linking women as guardians of family sanctuaries and the realm of the sacred in this world. I argue for the centrality of the cultural notion of privacy, as one that embodies the qualities of reserve, respect, and restraint, as these are played out in fluid transformational bi-rhythmic space.

Qatari Wedding We know that in Arab social systems in which public life is marked by gender segregation, it is the women who "choose" a groom or bride. In a recent upscale wedding in Doha, Qatar, the daughter of a colleague of mine was married to an affine – a young man getting higher education in the United States and whom she had never laid eyes on. It was his sister in Doha (already married into the family of the young woman) who promised to marry her to her brother. The bride was sent a photo of the groom. They were escorted to dinner a few times in Doha and arrangement for the wedding began. They both approved and liked each other. But it was the sister of the groom who saw a good union between the two. She wanted that pretty young woman for her brother.

Often the Arab male seeking a bride finds himself to be the one being looked at and scrutinized – invisibly gazed at for approval or rejection. While not apparent, as in the case when women relatives of bride or groom are choosing and matching spouses, often the bride is choosing a groom while he is unaware. An Egyptian taxi driver in Doha, Qatar was eager to leave during his summer vacation to Cairo to present his bride with the *shabka* and ring for betrothal. How did he meet her? "I never saw her. I asked my mother to choose a bride for me. My mother knows me the best and would choose the bride who would make me happy and get along with her. I sent the bride a picture. But I never saw her" (personal communication, 2007).

The Qatari wedding is particularly interesting since it creatively maintains the gender separation as it centers women in power and decision-making in the social structure. As earlier mentioned, this is by no means unique to Qatar (see El Guindi 1985). The main wedding party is a women's event. Men hold separate secondary gatherings on that night, at which the groom and his male relatives would be present. I will describe one particular elite wedding held recently (January, 2007) in a five-star hotel in Doha, Qatar in which I was participant-observer.

> Invitation cards for the henna night (a few days prior to the wedding night) go out in the bride's mother's name to female guests and on the main wedding night in the grooms' mother's name to female guests. Guests do not go to the wedding as hetero-

sexual couples. All the hotel personnel receiving, serving, and waiting on the female guests are women. Photography by guests is strictly forbidden, but the wedding is filmed and photographed in detail entirely by hired crews of women. In the case of the wedding being described the groom's family had decided they wanted a particular singer/band and it was male. The solution was for them to perform from behind a curtain where they would be in a space apart from women guests and they could not see the guests at all. This did pose some logistical problems, as music had to mark certain wedding events. The room would be organized with a long rectangular platform, the end of which would be the bride's ornamented seat. The guests arrive, are seated, and served coffee, juices, and water. No alcohol is served. The band plays festive Qatari pieces to which guests who are dressed in the most revealing, gorgeous evening gowns (that match in opulence Academy Awards celebrity gowns) get up singly or as doubles to dance rhythmically and sensuously to the music and singing, slowly moving from one end of the platform to the other, round and back. Women relatives and particularly the mother of the bride who would be holding enormous amounts of paper money would begin to throw this over the heads of the dancing women. Paper money would be flying all over the dance floor like confetti. Women working for the band immediately appear on the stage and begin to collect the cash. These nogut (money gifts) go to the band. More dancers and more nogut (money gifts). Then some commotion occurs near the closed doors of the wedding hall suggests something is about to happen. Guests murmur that the bride brought by her mother arrived. The music changes, the gates open, and the gorgeous bride in wedding dress enters alongside her mother (regal in dress and posture). Several women would be helping the bride with her bridal gown train, up the platform at a measured pace all the way to her bridal seat. Photographs are taken. The bride is then helped to sit down and the bride's mother returns and begins to receive congratulations from the guests. Dancing resumes. Money gifts are showered over women who get up to dance. Suddenly the dancing stops. All the women guests, while at their seats, don the traditional black abayah, which they brought with them – signs of anticipation of some major shift in the environment of women's privacy. I am told the groom and his father and brothers have arrived and are outside the door. They would be the only males in the entire wedding hall. The music changes, the doors open, and the groom dressed in traditional clothing and accompanied by his father and brothers begin in procession toward the platform. They walk up to the platform and in step with the music walk slowly toward the bride who is on a platform at the end of and somewhat higher than the dancing platform. When they arrive, the bride would be standing up to receive her groom. He stands by her surrounded by his male relatives who are then joined by the female relatives of the groom: the mother and sisters. Picture taking intensifies. When the photo taking session is over, the bride and groom sit on the bridal seat. The only women in the hall who would be bare headed and without abaya at this time are the groom's mother and sisters. The groom stays, but his father and brothers walk in procession back along the platform and out the doors. The guests remain headcovered but get up to bring the food from the buffets. They eat and drink and have dessert. Dancing resumes. A while later, the bride and groom stand up and at measured pace in time to the music walk down their platform, across the dance platform, and down to the hall

> floor. As relatives stand on both sides of the door, led by the bride's mother, the doors are pushed open and the bride and groom leave. Guests remove their headcovers then, as no men are in the wedding hall. The music resumes, sensual dancing resumes, and more money gifts are showered on friends and relatives. Guests begin to leave.

The entire wedding ceremony is a female event and female run – from food making and catering to flower arranging, music, photography, ushering, and serving. Without men they dress lavishly and move around freely, showing off their revealing evening gowns. Once the groom enters their private space, the guests cover. After he leaves, they remove their covers again. This dynamic is done smoothly without effort. To the guests at that wedding, this is routine. When women's space is intruded into by men, they will cover.

For Arab women in general, privacy is both a right and an exclusive privilege and is reflected in dress, space, architecture, and proxemic behavior, as we have seen in the wedding. A woman is guardian of the sanctity that is fundamental to the community. Upon marriage, the Arab woman becomes *sitt el-bait* or the lady of the home – a term that stresses, not domesticity as in the West, but an autonomous managerial role (El Guindi 1985, 1986b).

The traditional architectural feature of *mashrabiyya* represents the essence of traditional notions of Arab privacy – who has the "*right to see whom*," who has the "*right not to be seen by whom*," and "*who chooses not to 'see' whom*." Veiling resembles *mashrabiyya*, but whereas *mashrabiyya* is stationary veiling is mobile carrying women's privacy to public spaces. A woman carries "her" privacy and sanctity with her much the same as when a Muslim worships in any public space, converting it albeit temporarily to one that is sacred and private. Otherwise, as in the case of the Qatari wedding, the entire public space becomes a woman's space for the duration of the gendered event.

Collectivity: al-Jama'iyya Al-Jama'iyya comprises the third element (along with al-Qudsiyya and al-Khususiyya) in the theory of Islamic rhythm. It has been conceptually established by Ibn Khaldun, as solidarity, and by the Durkheimian philosophy which gave primacy to the sociological collectivity. *Al-Jama'iyya*, is a term I selected to use to denote that. It is Arabic, a derivative of the root *j-m-'*. Other derivatives include *jāma'a* (verb meaning to gather), *jamā'a* (noun meaning group and also a reference to family or wife), *jam'īyya* (association), *jāmi'* (mosque), *jām'a* (university), *jūm'a* (Friday). It is a clearly rich lexical referent with a rich corpus of derivatives. They all have one thing in common: a meaning relating to group or collectivity. What connects group, association, mosque, university? What these terms and concepts have in common is their reference to "collectivity of people." The culture that weaves richness of expression around the notion of collectivity stands in stark contrast with ideologies that emphasize individualism.

Arab culture does give primary significance to the group, from family, to larger kin forms, to community. We discussed earlier how the realm of the sacred includes constructs of home, house of worship, womanhood. In other words, the realm of the sacred intersects the realm of collectivity and both intersect the realm of privacy. In earlier discussion it was demonstrated that privacy in Arab culture is not about the individual, the personal, or the secret. Again it is about the realms of home, house of worship, body, and dress, all contextualized in the collectivity of community. Individuals in Arabo-Islamic culture experience privacy when they are with their sex group and when with family. It was earlier argued how the notion of the sacred, *haram*, covers homes (bayt), houses of worship (mosque), and houses of knowledge (university), intersecting realms of family, religion, and knowledge.

The one day of the Islamic week that is not named according to consecutive numbers is the day of collective public worship, which its distinctive name, al-Jum'a, denotes. Muslims consider Friday to be special because of that moment of public collective prayer. 'Eid prayers early in the morning are also public collective prayers. Entire communities go out at dawn for these prayers. In general, collective concerns, group activity, community support, family, and kin are highly valued. The latter is reported to be changing gradually, but in contrast to societies in which it is almost entirely absent it remains very visible, strong, and binding. Observations otherwise seem to be made at a superficial level.

It is proposed here that the conceptual element of al-Jama'iyya in relationship with the other two identified earlier, al-Khususiyya and al-Qudsiyya, make up the necessary components of an Arabo-Islamic theory of rhythm.

Theory of Arabo-Islamic Rhythm

This theory consists of a new conceptual framework for a more systematic understanding of Muslim life. It builds on notions of relationality and the idea that living systems span a broad range of spheres of knowledge. There is an alternate temporality and spatiality that brings together the calendrical, the cosmological, the astronomical, and the sociocultural constructions of sacredness, privacy, and temporal-spatiality into a unified understanding. Rhythm is the construct that best describes this unity. It is also culturally derived. Muslims follow a rhythm in all spheres of their life – private and public, ordinary and sacred, work and recreation. Rhythm is not only a unifying idea, it integrates spheres of lived experience and brings thought processes and categorization of thought into it. It takes understanding beyond the common cliché of religion versus state, or the overused separation of church and state. It brings forth the contradictions and inherent biases in the regulations enforced in France, themselves steeped in historical Christian Western notions about individual, society, and religion, yet unfairly, undemocratically, and hegemonically imposed on Muslims in Western Europe in the name of secularism.

Arab privacy is not about individualism or secularism. Arab privacy is based on a specific cultural construction of space and time central to the functioning of Islamic society in general, in the dynamics of Arab gender identity, and for direct unmediated individual or collective communication with God. Space in this construction is one of complementarities. It is relational, active, charged, and fluid. According to Ardener, "[s]pace . . . is not a simple concept" (1993: 3–4). It is connected to social life and is interdependent with people's action. It is people living in a particular space who determine its nature. This line of thinking is not very different from that of Durkheim and Mauss (1963 [1903]), who considered social life as one given shape in correspondence with the physical world, which becomes its "social reality." "Cosmic space and tribal space are thus only very imperfectly distinguished and the mind passes from one to the other without difficulty, almost without being aware of doing so" (Durkheim and Mauss 1963 [1903]: 65). There is the sacred in privacy, the sacred in worship, in knowledge, in collectivity, and in learning. As discussed above, the Arabic words deriving from the root *j-m-'* cover community, mosque, and university. The category and notion of the sacred goes beyond religion to cover the space and time of both worldly and non-worldly life. A unified theory of Muslim life that brings together these elements is shown diagrammatically in Figure 6.8.

Aveni (1989: 338) wrongly asserts that modern secular time transcends both nation and religion, both environment and demography. He views time as becoming more objective, less spiritual, and unemotional. He suggests that the World calendar proposed by the United States may have failed on its last go-around, but like the metric system, it will ultimately triumph. Today's world, however, has experienced the failure of a coercively imposed ideological para-

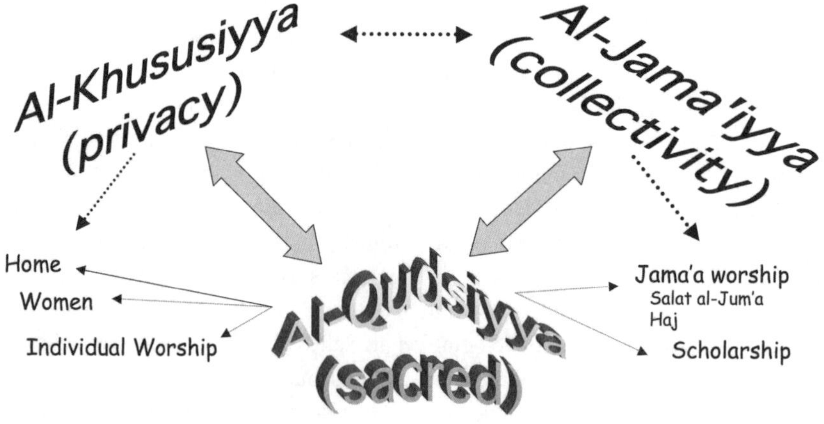

Figure 6.8 Arabo-Islamic temporality and spirituality. Time and space merge in a unified temporal-spatiality of Muslim life. Concept and graphics are by F. El Guindi, © El Nil Research 2007.

digm. Resistance is growing against American feminism, American democracy, and a universal secularism. Earlier studies have described alternatives to American feminism. This study shows an alternative to modern secular time. It remains to be seen whether, as Aveni predicts, the World calendar (conceptualized by the United States) will ever prevail.

Islam has already triumphed in producing a non-secular working alternative temporality that characterizes the most economically successful nations today. The Arabo-Islamic rhythm described in this study is marked by a temporal and spatial continuity that has proven to be successful for its people, and seems to be spreading numerically around the world. It is a viable alternative "deep ecology" model, perhaps better adapted to the contemporary global environment.

–7–

Conclusion

قمت بتغسيله وتكفينه ولما حان موعد صلاة

الظهر صلينا عليه صلاة الجنازة

Anonymous

In Islam the kin closest to a deceased person (usually a daughter for her mother and a son for his father) cleanse and shroud them in preparation for Muslim burial of the body, which is put in the ground facing Makka. It is interesting that according to ethnographic accounts of rural Arab communities, the nephew is obligated to participate in the *taghsil* of his maternal uncle's body. In Kafr al-Ma' (studied by Richard Antoun when the village was part of Transjordan) matrilaterality is highly significant. There is a reciprocal relationship known as *makhwal* (mother's brothership), which is central to the cohesion of the community in which local inhabitants formally organize their kinship relationship in terms of patrilineality. In this regard Antoun writes: "the sister's son is expected to help wash the body of his mother's brother before burial" (1972: 115). The kinship chart (Figure 7.1), clarifies these kin relations in *taghsil* obligations.

In general, bodies of males and females in the family are buried in the same

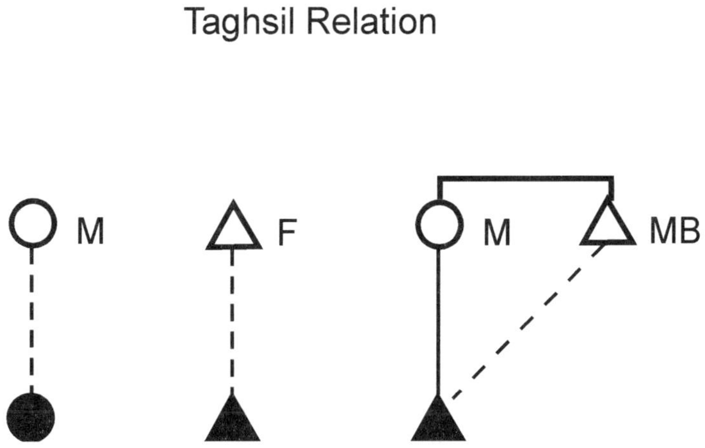

Figure 7.1 Taghsil chart. © El Nil Research

burial ground, in close but separate corners. The sphere of death and burial patterns in Arabo-Islamic culture are areas rich in insights about kin relations and core values. One can examine kin breakups during life and kin rebonding after death and vice versa. At the time of the death of an individual, the closest kin "receive *'aza*" (condolences). Giving and receiving *'aza* is ceremonially interactive and relational. Reception areas in homes, guest buildings in villages, mosques in cities, or closed public places are all possible spaces for receiving *'aza* from friends and acquaintances. Obligations are met, old relations are renewed, animosities are dissolved or reinforced, new bonds are forged. One is obligated to give *'aza*, as it represents a serious family and community obligation within the realm of Muslim practices, but such *'aza* has to be properly *received* by appropriately linked kin and within a particular time frame.

This interactive relationality in Muslim practices applies also to fasting. A Muslim may fast but he/she has first to declare intent to fast and God has to accept or receive his/her fasting. A common expression addressed to persons fasting Ramadan is to wish that their fast would be "maqbul" (received or accepted) by God. Also fasting is not simply abstention from food, drink, or sex. In a situation in which an individual has no access to food or chance to eat during the legitimate fasting hours of the day, the person cannot convert that lack of eating into a fast; it has to be preceded by the intent to fast. There is an appropriate time for the person to express their intent to fast, namely before dawn on the fasting day.

Death does not disrupt life. It is a natural continuation of the cycle. Many premises and practices are observed after death. For example, the privacy of females is extended to their death as well, where the space in which their bodies are buried would be in the same burial ground but, if feasible, beyond that of the men, so that men burying bodies of kinsmen would not "pass by" the bodies of females buried there. The reverse is permissible. That is, men burying women can pass by the space when men are buried. This[1] way the sanctity of women's privacy (El Guindi 2003 [1999]) continues after their death. In ideal situations respect for women's privacy is not violated after their death.

Another aspect that continues after the death of the individual and is reaffirmed in times of death is bonding among kin. There are mutual duties and obligations. The young are obligated to take care of the elderly and the living of the dead. The obligation of *taghsil* and *takfin* of a parent's body, mentioned above in a quote by an anonymous writer, is a strong aspect of family bonding in Arabo-Islamic culture. This practice leaves no room for denial of death. It gives closure and finality to it. Death is confronted upfront. The practice of *taghsil* and *takfin* allows sons and daughters to meet their obligations when they give their parents the most rewarding, the warmest, and most personal care in preparing them for the afterlife when their lives end. This reaffirms generational ties, regenerates bonding, and renders investment in children as most worthwhile. Death continues the journey of life for individuals into the afterlife where they are judged by the divine for their deeds during their life on earth. There is continuity from birth to death and beyond in the spatiality and temporality of Muslim life.

As we have seen in earlier chapters of this book, ideas and concepts that relate to the notions of time and space in Arabo-Islamic culture have been in processual development for millennia. Within the creation narrative of Egyptians, the sun is born out of the sky-goddess, then passes over her body until reaching her mouth, into which the sun disappears, journeying through the inside of her body (which is nighttime) until it is re-born the following morning to fill the world with its rays (daytime). The daily cycle of the sun is marked by the theme of cyclical rebirth from inside the body of the fertile reproductive woman who embodies the sky.

Beings personify nature and embody a cosmic universe, such that a corporeality of representation includes a genealogy of kinship generation and regeneration and rebirth by passage through a female body. An astrological universe is mapped onto the human body and the sacred world is mapped onto the animal world. Different sacred beings take the attributes of and transform into different animals. Beings of nature and of the animal world are described in sacred vocabulary as gods and goddesses. Human institutions, such as primogeniture, heterosexual marriage, and cross-gender sex and fertility, are moralized by a spiritual world, and life is immortalized in afterlife.

Time and space are not only eternal and universal but also controversial. We have seen how local populations, as exemplified by the Kodi people of Indonesia, protested intervention in their calendrical affairs. In the case of the Kodi, the foreign district administrator claimed he could do what the local priest does. The people rejected that claim. The local priest "holds on to the year" and commands the knowledge because he has been watching the stars and the seasons. By imposing Western calendrical premises on the traditional ceremonial season, the district administrator was seeking an exact correspondence that was not, in fact, possible. The local people and the local priests knew that. The foreign administrator did not. The Roman months did not begin with a new moon. Disempowered by the foreign power but in command of local knowledge, the local priest felt outsiders could not tell local people how to count the moons.

The evidence shows that keeping time is a practice that may go back more than 20,000 years, when hunters of the ice age notched holes in sticks or bones, to track the days between phases of the moon. The unceasing rotating of the heavens, the regular changing of the seasons, and other cyclicities are why humans measure all activities in terms of suns, moons, and climatic seasons. Early Egyptian observances were based on the flood, as well as around solar and lunar motions, whereas farther across the Red Sea and the Arabian Gulf astronomical observations and calculations were being made. In Egypt observation of the sun was a useful way of telling time and it was in Egypt that the earliest known solar clock was invented, a fragment of which discovered dating from about 1500 BC.[4]

A dance of interacting parts, to use Bateson's words, is what scientific observation is all about. It is also what time and space are about. It is my argument in this study that the fluid nature of space and time, the dance of parts as it were, is well illustrated in Arabo-Islamic culture. As discussed in earlier chapters, notions about space and time and constructions of calendar and cosmology span millennia. Thinkers and scholars have raised queries about whether there ever could be humans without time or humans who manage their lives without a concept of time. Humans measured time on the basis of nature (climate, plant and animal life) and celestial movement based on astronomical observations. The moon, in its waxing and waning, has always been used as a temporal measurement between the day and the year. The beginning of the month is determined by the new moon and the month would be based on lunations, while the sun determines seasons and the related rhythm of life. It is indeed in the interweaving of moon and sun that the Arabo-Islamic rhythm choreographs the dance of its parts.

There is a core element in any historically deep tradition that underlies and shapes culture, and in turn defines the pulse of a people – a quality that would have been developing over a period of perhaps as much as thousands of years. This quality is referred to in this work as rhythm. In a study carried out in the town of Kumming in China, which was in process of modernizing its urban centers, Zhang (2006: 471–2) describes the problems resulting from these changes. It invokes the folk Chinese concept *renqi*, a notion rooted in the Daoist idea of harmony with nature and physical surroundings. Renqi denotes a kind of energy, vitality, and dynamism that derives from human presence and, therefore, is relevant to urban landscaping. Zhang points out how traditional cityscapes in Kumming produced intense face-to-face human interactions, a condition which generates vigorous renqi. By contrast, according to Zhang, the newly installed modern avenues, malls, and other city designs with features to accommodate modern lifestyles with cars and other vehicles, "tend to 'kill' crowds and are unable to generate or maintain renqi" (471).

Interestingly in this regard, Zhang observes how a neighborhood of Muslim families of the Hui minority lived in an area that still had lively traditional street life and distinctive Islamic food. This area continues to have the energy of renqi. This is so, according to Zhang, because that kind of energy derives not only from the density of people in a given place but also "from a state of being at ease in a space that is capable of mingling everyday living experiences with commercial activities" (472). These "spaces within spaces" or "overlapping universes," as Ardener (1993: 3) calls them, energize people's engagement in them and generate renqi, whereas the urban forms produced by new planning and modernizing development tends to overpower renqi.

Renqi in China is conceptually relevant to understanding Chinese culture and is significant for dealing with the change that this Chinese town is undergoing. That this quality has a clear linguistic reference makes it more easily identifiable in analysis. As argued in this book, however, we often find that some core cultural qualities have no obvious single referent and can only become identifiable when analysis breaks down and recoheres cultural notions into embedded clusters of concepts. This was the challenge facing the study of privacy and veiling for example (see El Guindi 2003 [1999]).

This book hopes to reveal Islam's renqi, as it were. It seeks to shed light on temporality and spatiality in Muslim life. To do this, the notions of time and space are contextualized in theory as well as in the analysis of cross-cultural ancient cosmologies, history of calendars and time-reckoning, ethnology, poetry, field-based ethnography, and Islamic text. It argues that central to the understanding of time and space is the notion of rhythm, which in this study is empirically derived in analysis as the core expression that defines the pulse of Muslim life, its renqi as it were.

How did this whole project on space and time in Islam begin with noon prayer and end in rhythm? As an anthropologist carrying out ethnographic study on Islam and living for a lifetime and observing Muslims over decades, my analysis uncovered something unique and special embracing the culture that the religion of Islam (perhaps particularly as it mixes with Arab culture) produces. This "special something" cannot be revealed through the traditional approaches focusing on the "Five Pillars" or through the Islam-As-Way-of-Life notion. Further, it is more than a superficial pattern.[2] Rather, it is a quality that goes deep and thus eludes many works and even anthropological analyses of Islam or Islam-related aspects.

To locate this "special something" one cannot be confined to individual Muslim behavior, a specific Islamic institution, or one historical moment. One needs to go beneath and beyond these and other interventions. Interventions were generated through the climate of recent global politics, as special interest public intellectuals and career politicians distracted understanding by trapping discourse in superficial labels such as clash, jihadist, Islamist, terrorist, veil, headscarf, honor killing, female genital mutilation, suicide bombing, and much more. Where in all of this "noise" is that special quality of Islam? When such attention is out of focus, as it has become in globalized politics, how can one reach any adequate level of understanding? There was concern that Islam was being reduced in public discourse to hijab, burqu', and headscarf, thus shifting Islam's core emblem from crescent to veil. Who is responsible for this blurring of reality? Who is doing the discourse framing? We are kept from reaching the core by being distracted by the margins and by distortions framed by ideological politics, by inaccuracies from uninformed media and dehumanizing vocabulary framed as national security issues. Beyond current events (such as the headscarves' controversy in Europe) and beneath reduction to single phenomena (such as the polemics on women's mosque activity in Egypt or the new veiling), this study transcends superficial polarities imposed by secularist, political, or ideological orientations posing a political Islam vs. an Islam of worship, jihadist vs. moderate, or the related fragmentary orientations that overly focus on divisions: Shi'a Islam vs. Sunni Islam, women against men, and so on. This study rejects approaches that distort, mislead, or misdirect understanding.

It was necessary to transcend these intrusions in order to reach that quality of Islam that visibly has such a strong hold on its adherents and which makes Islam quite unique. Systematically and empirically this study uses tools of analysis and discovery to examine cross-cultural and cross-disciplinary data. By drawing upon comparative data, original, primary, and secondary, historical materials, scripture, text, poetry, ethnography, and the visual medium, this book re-centers Islam and its powerful hold on a continually expanding population that numerically far exceeds the Roman Catholic world population today. David Smith, a schoolteacher, wrote an interesting publication that asks us to imagine the whole world, which has a population of six billion people, as a global village of only 100 inhabitants (Smith 2002). By examining the proportional equivalents of populations it became evident that there is a large disparity between power, access to food and wealth, and population size. What would be the relative size of religious populations in this imaginary village? In proportion, this global village of 100 inhabitants would have 19 Muslims, 16 Roman Catholic Christians, 6 Protestant Christians, and 1 Jew. I ask: How are access to power and control of the flow of wealth distributed among these religious populations? I also ask: Despite the campaigns to dehumanize Muslims and deform the image of Islam, what is the "secret" behind the rapid and continuing growth of the Muslim population worldwide?

To answer the last question, it was necessary to re-examine the Islam that is felt and lived by Muslims. A framework to analyze the central rhythm of Islam was formulated, drawing upon several thinkers and analysts in the social sciences: Emile Durkheim's societal collectivity, the sacred in religion of Henri Hubert, Ibn Khaldun's concept of social/cultural *asabiyya* (solidarity), Leroi-Gourhan's concept of rhythm. Their different conceptualizations become elements in a theory of Islam constructed from data, ideas, and process. Rhythm, writes Leroi-Gourhan, creates time and space. Time, writes Hubert, gives rhythm not measurement. Egyptians imagined the sun entering the mouth of the sky, traveling through its womb in a night journey to be born and reborn daily to shine on the world at sunrise until it sets back into the womb of the sky. Arabs look at their moon every night for clues for worship and Muslims interweave daily, weekly, and yearly moments, moving out of ordinary space into sacred time and from sacred space into ordinary time.

Rhythm in this analysis is not merely a superficial pattern; it captures the very core of Islam. A theory is formulated of Arabo-Islamic rhythm that links the Arabic notions of *khususiyya* (privacy), *qudsiyya* (the sacred) and *jama'iyya* (collectivity) to form an inner triadic relational structure. The three (khususiyya, jama'iyya, and qudsiyya) are qualities empirically derived from the culture and social practices of Muslims. They interweave in time and space in a way that defines Islamic thought and underlies its inner workings. In this way *By Noon*

Prayer goes to the heart of Islam to touch the pulse of Muslim life (its renqi, as it were).

Can humans manage without time? In ordinary life many Arabic terms are used for time, such as *sa'ah*, *waqt*, *zaman*, *hin*, and many expressions, such *kan zaman* (before or long time ago) or *kan yama kan* (translating as "once upon a time"). But translation from one language to another can dilute rich meanings embedded in wording. *Kan* denotes past, *yama* denotes quantity in both space and time. In storytelling one begins the event by saying *Kan yama kan, ya sadah ya kiram, ma yihla al-kalam illa bi-thikr al-nabi 'alayhi as-salat was-salam* (Arabic for "once upon a time, generous gentlefolk, speaking is sweet only after mentioning the prophet peace be upon him"). So any story for children or adults, of religious or ordinary content, is Islamized in character by the introduction. The expression of unlimited temporality in folk terms *fil mishmish* (meaning "in apricot season") or the expression *insha'allah* (meaning "God willing") are not about procrastination, postponement, submission, or fatalism. They are about the present with a future, about hope, and about faith. Repeatedly I complained to the technician at the telephone company in Doha, Qatar that the telephone had no dial tone. Repeatedly his answer was "insha'allah, there is a dial tone."

There is hope and denial of submission to negative outcomes in a phrase like that. In bedtime interactions with children in Egypt an adult telling the child a bedtime story would end it thus: *tuta, tuta firghit il-hadouta, hilwa walla maltouta* (in rhyming Arabic it says "mulberry, mulberry, the little story is over," then the child is asked, "was it nice or maltouta [nicely rhyming, but eluding my search for its meaning]"). If the child says "hilwa" (nice) then the adult answers "you owe me a song," which of course rhymes, and if the child answers "maltouta," the adult would say "you owe me a little story," which also rhymes in Arabic. This whole interactive event keeps going until the child falls asleep.

André Leroi-Gourhan points out how

> [h]uman time is and remains an ambiguous measure because natural rhythms are shared by all living matter. The measurement of lived time refers to phenomena unrelated to measurement as such . . . in all agricultural-pastoral civilizations, the complex movements of the stars have engendered astronomic reference systems that tend, whether it be among the Maya, the Chinese, the Egyptians, or the Romans, to order the passage of the seasons geometrically within a grid established by the periodically recurrent position in space of some of the main celestial bodies. Endeavors to ensure regularity of the calendrical grid are inseparable from advances in computing space and quantities. (1993: 316)

We know humans have for millennia gazed at the stars and the cosmos for models for culture, seeking answers to mystery, or in response to processes of thought. It is through the sky, as the Egyptians eloquently told us, that journeys of death are part of the journey of life (not, as some scholars claim, in order to deny death's finality[3]), but to embrace it in a sacred terrain of spatiality and temporality that gives rich meaning and logical order to everyday experience in which present is future and future is not only faith but hope, as the notion of insha'allah (God willing) truly connotes.

The rhythm of Islam evokes a concept that is of increasing significance in the psychological and cognitive sciences, namely the notion of mindfulness. In the last twenty years mindfulness has become the focus of considerable attention (Bishop et al. 2004). Building on a concept originally developed by Langer (Langer and Moldoveanu 2000), Bishop et al. described it as a process of bringing a certain quality of attention to moment-by-moment experience. Mindfulness in contemporary psychology has been adopted as an approach for increasing awareness. In this context, mindfulness can be considered "a metacognitive skill (cognition about one's cognition)" (2004: 233).

Metacognition is thought to consist of two related processes – monitoring and control. The notion of mindfulness as a metacognitive process evokes both control of cognitive processes (attention self-regulation) and monitoring the stream of consciousness. It is a "a mode of awareness that is evoked when attention is regulated . . . a psychological process" (Bishop et al. 2004: 234). It is a mode (state) rather than a trait which develops with practice. Its evocation and maintenance is dependent on the regulation of attention while cultivating an open orientation to experience. Langer and Moldoveanu (2000) observe that mindfulness is not a cold cognitive process. It is more of a heightened state of involvement and wakefulness or being in the present. Its essence is change but it keeps one situated in the present. The whole individual is involved.

A question of interest in this regard is whether the rhythm of Islam, intermittent prayer throughout the day, one whole month every year of strict fasting, a strict adherence to ritual requirements throughout pilgrimage, is instrumental in producing a state of mindfulness. Asked how and why he converted to Islam, an Asian worker in Doha, Qatar said: "it all started when I expressed admiration to a co-worker about the calmness and even temper of Muslims. I asked about the reason and source of this state. My co-worker said, 'it is from Islam. You are in a state of rida.' Wanting to be in that state I found out more about Islam and converted." If this is true, then how does one explain that state and its connection with Islam?

Mindfulness embodies a number of qualities or components that can be considered most relevant to Muslim rhythm – such as patience (allowing things to unfold in their own time), trust (confidence in the ability to stay in contact with private experience), nonreactivity (calmness), wisdom (self-knowledge), and compassion (empathy for oneself) (Bishop et al. 2004: 235). The concept has been invoked in the context of Buddhism – the capacity to evoke mindfulness using various meditation techniques that originate from Buddhist spiritual practices. In Buddhist traditions, mindfulness occupies a central role in a system that was developed as a path leading to the cessation of personal suffering. It has never been invoked in the context of Islam. Observing the rhythm of Islam, one can propose that mindfulness practice over a long period of time.

In the Islamic case, mindfulness works on an entire community not only on individuals. The Durkheimian rhythm of social life is the basis of the category of time and the space occupied by society and provides the material for the category of space. It is a different trajectory in the West. Aveni reminds us that: "*We* have framed it [time] in tiny blocs and hung it on a wall . . . linearized and circularized it, endowed it with a quality of irreversibility, even artificialized it by wrapping it around *our* wrists, and exalted it in the turrets of our religious buildings" (Aveni 1989:135). Expanding on this materialist thread, Whitrow writes: "All the elaborate mathematization of time comes down to the desire to put time to work. Once a new technology has been invented, it tends to proceed with its own relentless logic and thus may have a lasting effect on a whole civilization" (1989:181).

Despite all this mechanization and with all the scrutiny on Islam, Islamic time eluded many. Yet while smoothly globalizing it continues to march to its own drummer. Augustine remarked (Augustine 1961, Book X, chapter 14) "If one asks me, I know what it is. If I wish to explain it to him who asks me, I do not know." It is hoped that this study, and the new paradigm of "deep ecology" has revealed and explained the rhythm that underlies the lived temporal-spatiality in Muslim life.

Notes

Preface

1. True, making images of the Prophet Muhammad is not new. It is to be noted that despite the Islamic prohibition against depicting the Prophet Muhammad, for fear of "image worship" and idolatry, paintings, drawings, and other images have been created over the eras. However, the controversy that turned into international furor during which there was a successful boycott of Danish products by Muslim nations was undermined in Denmark and Europe by discussions of freedom of expression. Whose freedom and at whose expense? Seen also in the context of a historical moment in which assault on Muslims comes from all directions, it is hard to locate freedom in such selective actions.
2. Globalism is shaping itself in accordance with superpower globalist politics; it finds difference inconvenient for commercial corporate consumerist behaviors. It finds homogenization more compatible with its agenda. On the difference between globalism, globality, and globalization, see Steger 2003. In brief, globalization refers to "a multidimensional set of social processes that create, multiply, stretch, and intensify worldwide social interdependencies and exchanges while at the same time fostering in people a growing awareness of deepening connections between the local and the distant" (13). Globality is a social condition. "Globalism is an ideology that endows the concept of globalization with neoliberal values and meanings" (94). Some argue against the trend toward sameness resulting from globalization. American social theorist Francis Fukuyama explicitly welcomes globalism of Anglo-American values and lifestyles, a position equating Americanization of the world with the expansion of democracy and free markets. Hillary Rodham Clinton, US New York Senator, is cited by Steger (2003: 110): "The emergence of new businesses and shopping centers in former communist countries should be seen as the backbone of democracy."
3. A political economy approach or an area studies approach would tend to look at Islam dichotomously. The shift in paradigm and to a new scholarship insists on the receding of mechanism and moving to holism, from substance to pattern, from quantity to quality from static configurations of components to the perspective of phenomena as a whole.
4. Translation and transliteration: When using Arabic words and names I am guided by the style of the *International Journal of Middle East Studies*. Much of the translation from Arabic is mine. For practical reasons, the only diacritical marks used are the 'ayn (') and hamza ('). On occasion, the stressed syllable in a word has been indi-

cated by a macron). The Qur'an and Tafsir used here are in their original Arabic derive primarily from The Holy Qur'an (9.01), Harf Information Technology, 1997–2005.

5. Fritjof Capra (1996) invokes the term "ecological," which he draws from both a philosophical school and a global grass-roots movement, which is rapidly gaining prominence, known as "deep ecology."

Chapter 1 Conceptual Overview

1. Terms such as "civilizations" (as in Clash of Civilizations) or "cultures" are avoided here because anthropology respects the integrity of these notions, which it has itself empirically and conceptually developed. These particular terms are being distorted by certain writers, perhaps for political expedience.
2. It is thus puzzling to read Zerubavel (1981: ix) claiming sociology of time as a "new area of investigation" in which his work introduces temporality to sociologists (in this regard, see some of the sociological works: Engel-Frisch 1943; Sorokin 1943; Rosengren and DeVault 1963). Zerubavel writes: "the way authors define their work and the way it is perceived by others are two entirely different things" and seemed surprised that his work on hospital and temporality is categorized as study of hospitals (1981: x). The task of general conceptualization of time had already been significantly done starting with Henri Hubert (discussed in Chapter 4 in this book) and culminating in the brilliant analysis by Edmund Leach (discussed in Chapter 2).
3. Prominent is the tripartite public discourse kit, adopted and embraced as primary reading and study materials in prestigious academic institutions subjecting students to such ideological works. The three authors are: Samuel P. Huntington, Francis Fukuyama (1993, 1996), and Thomas Friedman (1992). Their three works: *The Clash of Civilizations* (article in *Foreign Affairs* in 1993, a book in 1996), *The End of History*, and *The World is Flat* are intended to influence or serve US policy – they are not scientific works marked by accuracy and reliable knowledge – in fact they linguistically challenge empirically derived anthropological knowledge.

   Huntington cleverly dismisses the entire anthropology project as one obsessed with primitives and proceeds to appropriate profound anthropological contributions twisting established theories and anthropological knowledge to fit his proposed paradigm of fault lines between religious traditions which he calls civilizations, making, as do the other two authors, ridiculous claims that challenge the core of anthropological scientific conclusions and concerns. These works dumb down world affairs for the public (and politicians) to understand.
4. Zamit (2002) in a pre-Contents page has ayah 21 of this sura but mistakenly gives the reference as 30: 22 instead of the correct reference 60: 21.
5. I am happy to have come across the following comment on one of these two essays made by Stanley Tambiah (2002: 351) just as I was beginning to wonder about anthropology's indifference to these two nuggets of creativity and imagination. Tambiah describes "Time and False Noses" as: "an early condensed jewel of an essay."
6. The two essays are "Cronus and Chronos" and "Time and False Noses." Leach writes that the two short essays had originally "appeared in the Toronto University publica-

tion *Exploration*" (Leach 1961: 124). He mentions amendments made to the text of "Cronus and Chronos" for republication and acknowledges that they "are largely due to the very helpful suggestions of Mr. M. I. Finley of Jesus College, Cambridge."

7. The quote comes from Rigby (1983: 435–6) who uses these references (Lenin 1962:177ff; Engels 1940: 327; 1975).
8. For a background on the life and lifestyle of Leach and the kind of family background he comes from, see Tambiah 2002. It is evident that Leach was absorbed with the class and environment he grew up into in England, yet a "rebellious" side of him steered him to anthropology and a comparativist stance in analysis.
9. A strong orientation in anthropology has been one that sets understanding one's own culture as the ultimate goal of the inquiry. Studying other cultures was for the purpose of understanding one's own. Alternatively, the goal of anthropological cross-cultural projects should be to understand humankind. Other cultures are not a tapestry against which we locate perspective on Western culture. The latter is only one among many and should not be assumed as the point of reference.
10. One common error in analysis of other cultures is when the analyst imposes constructs from his/her cultural or personal ideological orientation thus biasing local cultural concepts. This error is committed by Western feminists when exploring non-Western conditions of women, by secularists attempting to explain away religious phenomena, by individualists who impose individual-centered orientations on cultures and religions otherwise formed around ideas of collectivity, and so on. Another error is to dismiss a cultural notion for lack of a single or simple verbal or linguistic referent for it. Both errors detract from understanding local knowledge. The most productive constructs are ones that develop in the course of exploration of cross-cultural phenomena and instead of challenging local cultural realities further contributing to their understanding. In many earlier works, I repeatedly critiqued the imposition of Western models, assumptions, and claims, presumed to be universal, on the study of women in Arabo-Islamic culture. Works from women's and cultural studies by Nadje al-Ali (2000) and Saba Mahmoud (2005) are examples of this. Pakistani secularist scholar Saba Mahmoud writes: "cemented in the minds of *progressive feminists like myself* . . . an unflinching stance *against the Islamization* of Pakistani society. If there was any shred of doubt in our minds that Islamic forms of patriarchy were responsible for our problems, this doubt was firmly removed. . . . feminist politics came to require a *resolute and uncompromising secular stance*" (2005, Preface, p. x, emphasis added). It is difficult to conceive how someone can do anthropology of Islamic topics who so passionately carries a combination of extremist ideologies – feminist, secularist, anti-Islamic – and carries out fieldwork in an Arabic-speaking setting working through translation, without being in command of the Arabic language.
11. It is privacy that best describes Arabo-Islamic culture whereby separation of the sexes in private or public is not accompanied by seclusion of women or an ideology of asexuality as is the case in Christianity, particularly of the cultural tradition of cloisters and seclusion for Catholic nuns. In his recent book, Bowen (2007) takes the discourse back prior to 1999 when he uncritically repeats the old analogy of the early 1900s (Crawley 1912, 1931) between hijab in Islam and the Catholic wimple (for elaboration on the fundamental difference between Catholic veiling and seclusion and Muslim veiling and non-seclusion, see El Guindi 2003 [1999]).

12. As a noun in English, "privacy" has no parallel in Latin or neo-Latin languages. Sciama (1993) points out that Latin has no word equivalent to privacy in English. The term privacy derives from the Latin verb *privare*. It is interesting that in the course of the development of the word in English the noun form "privacy" was formed. It became widely used in literary contexts, eventually becoming noun form, without equivalent verb and adjectival forms.
13. The Maya calendar is significant but is beyond the scope and space limit of this work.
14. Recently the Center for Contemporary Arab Studies at Georgetown University, USA organized a conference entitled Complexity of Islamism. Here complexity is used as an English word not as a scientific construct.
15. Al-Biruni's full name is Muhammad Bin Ahmad al-Biruni, known as Abil-1 Riyhan al-Biruni, originally from Khawarizm, west of Uzbekistan, today known as Khiwa Khawarizm became Muslim under Qutaiba Bin Muslim in AD 711 (AH 93). Al-Biruni died in AD 1048 (AH 440). His contribution is described as being in comparative religion. He pioneered ethnological cross-cultural comparison, seven centuries before ethnology was instituted in the West. Ibn Khaldun, the fourteenth-century Arab social philosopher from Tunis, was the first to conceptualize culture on the basis of empirical observations. He introduced a cyclical theory of the development and evolution of culture based on the notion *asabiyya* (solidarity).

Chapter 2 The Anthropology of Time and Space

1. Unfortunately for the analysis, he did not seem able to distance himself from the contradictory framework of psychological explanations (see his discussion 1961: 130).
2. Leach describes what he calls the "primitive, unsophisticated" people who most likely would experience metaphors of repetition in a "homely nature" such as vomiting (126). Countering mentalities of imagined superiority is the sophisticated analysis of Zapotec farmers as scientists by Roberto González in *Zapotec Science* (2001).
3. San Francisco Lachigoló is a farming town whose inhabitants are Valley Zapotec, predominantly bilingual in Spanish and Valley Zapotec, with an overwhelming majority following the Roman Catholic faith. Few individuals have been converted to evangelical Protestantism. The town is situated bout nine miles southeast of Oaxaca City in the State of Oaxaca, Mexico. During my study the population of the town ranged between 900 and 1,200 native residents.
4. Zerubavel expands on the idea by stating that it was the pervasive "daily rhythm of liturgical activity . . . which by far exceeded that of any other services, at particular hours [at which time] monastery bells rang . . . as 'landmarks' punctuating the daily cycle of the monastery"(1981: 35).
5. On this he cites John Beckmann (1846: 349), Sebastian de Grazia (1964: 40), H. Alan Lloyd (1966: 389–91), J. D. North (1975: 382–3), and others.
6. The dates given here are probably approximate. The original Arabic text of Ibn al-Haytham's *Optics* (*Kitab al-Manathir*) survives in five copies, only one of which is complete. As to the first three books, the text is extant in three copies all preserved in libraries in Istanbul. The oldest and best copy consists of three volumes, part of a

set, purportedly transcribed by a relative of Ibn al-Haytham's at Basra in 1083–4, which is about forty-four years after the author died. The *Optics* consists of seven maqalas, books, divided into two main parts. One consists of three books on a theory of direct radiation and direct vision, and the second consisting of the last four books, dealing with optical reflection and refraction.

7. Whitrow (1989: 71) observes how by then "learning in western Europe was confined to Ireland and the coast of Northumbria. The only centres of learning were the monasteries in those remote areas, and it is in one of these, founded in 682 at Jarrow by a wealthy Northumbrian nobleman turned monk, Benedict Biscop, that we find 'the first scientific intellect produced by the Germanic peoples of Europe.'"
8. Of course, religion is one matter, Church altogether another. Political ideas about separating church from state or religion from politics are themselves not neutral or value free. The call for secularism stems from an ideological posture that is not different from religious postures. Also Church is a notion and institution that is irrelevant in the study of Islam since Islam is an organized universal religion without Church. It is the Christian Church that found itself in conflict and political struggle, particularly in the West, leading to the formation of godless ideologies ranging from communism to secularism. Neither of these latter ones is neutral or objective about religion. Nor are they necessarily compatible with democracy if the latter means freedom of choice and expression and equal access to opportunity. Both privilege select sectors that are compatible with its ideological premises. Ironically we might find that it is Western Christianity that is incompatible with Western notions of democracy and science. Islam carved a different path that is compatible with knowledge, science, and democratic consent. And it is for a better understanding of Islam and Muslim life that the notion of rhythm becomes useful.
9. To paraphrase Islamic historian of Georgetown University (USA) John Fowl who cites Rodney Stark who writes that we must declare the end of secularism as a viable or inevitable idea. We are witnessing a world that has excised the idea that modernity is necessarily accompanied by the elimination of religion, and are moving to an epoch in which we recognize the failure of the idea that the secularist ideology is an aspect of the process of modernity. He calls for the field of sociology to drop its faith in secularism as inherent to modernity. Many human societies around the world have been modernizing without secularizing and without eliminating religion from the lives of their people.
10. Maimonides (1135–1204) was an Arab philosopher, physician, and scholar of Arab ethnic roots and the Jewish faith. It might not be obvious to readers who equate faith with ethnicity, but there is no contradiction between being of Arab origin and a Jewish faith. The name Maimonides is a Greek rendition of his original Arabic name, which is Musa ibn Maimun ibn Abdullah al-Qortobi (with reference to the fact that he was from Qurtuba (Cordoba) where he was born and lived during the golden age of the Islamic civilization). He fully participated in the dynamic scientific and scholarly life of the Arabs in Spain at that time. His main work written in Arabic is called *Dalalat al-Ha'erin* (*A Guide for the Perplexed*), which begins with a challenge to an anthropomorphized view of God. The Islamic influence was clear when he opposed any Jewish expressions describing God in corporeal or human terms. Ibn Maimun was instrumental in making an important and original contribution to the scholarly conceptualization of time when he brought forth the Arab theory of discontinuous or

atomistic time. There was much rewriting of Maimun's Arabic contributions and frequent translations which were distorted in attempts to infuse a political revisionism that would minimize his Arab roots in an effort to "Israelize" his record.

11. D. B. MacDonald (1927) has speculated on the difficult question of the origin of this view in Islam and has suggested that it arose from a Muslim heresy "in that dark but intense period of theological and intellectual development which stretched from the death of Muhammad for at least two and half centuries" (341). Whitrow states (1989: 80) that the atomistic theory of Epicurus, the methods of the Greek skeptics, and Zeno's paradoxes concerning time and space may all have influenced the heretics concerned, but MacDonald could find no trace of any Greek theory combining material and temporal atomism and sought instead to attribute the occurrence of the latter in Islamic thought to Indian influence.
12. As earlier mentioned, Ibn al-Maimun was from Qurtuba (Cordoba). He fully participated in the dynamic scientific and scholarly Arab life in Spain during the golden age of the Islamic civilization. After the Castilian invasion Maimun's family left Spain to live in Fez, Morocco where he went to the University of Fez and received a formal Arabic education. He later settled in Fustat (Old Cairo), Egypt. In Egypt he served as the physician of the Grand Vizier Al-Fadil and other known leaders. Being of the Jewish faith, he also held the office of Nagid (head of the Egyptian Jewish community). In addition he was the court physician. It was in Egypt that he wrote his important Arabic works. His main work in its original Arabic, handwritten in AD 1190, is called *Dalalat al-Ha'erin* (translated into English as *A Guide for the Perplexed* (trans. Friedlander, 1885). In Dalalat he challenges an anthropomorphized view of God and opposed expressions that describe God in human terms. He wanted to correct the Jewish view that assumed God to be corporeal. In this as well as in his overall logical and scientific approach Maimun was clearly a product of the Arabo-Islamic climate of thought prevalent at the time of al-Andalus. An Arabic copy of the original work exists in Turkey (see Maimonides 1974). Although according to the web link http://en.wikisource.org/wiki/The_Guide_for_the_Perplexed_(Friedlander)/Translator's_Introduction "[T]he library of the British Museum possesses two copies of the Arabic text; the one Or. 5423 is complete, beautifully written, with explanatory notes in the margin and between the lines."
13. It is suggested that the closure by Justinian of the Neoplatonic Academy at Athens in 529 pushed non-Arab scholars to join Arab scholars and, with the advent of Islam, the region was emerging as the innovator of learning and scholarship.
14. A good English account of it was given by the poet Chaucer in the second half of the fourteenth century. It consisted of a circular metal plate (usually brass) graduated in degrees around its rim. It was marked with a datum line (or diameter) and hinged to its centre was a rotating line (or pointer). Portable models could be hung from a ring on the rim so that the datum line was horizontal. By directing the pointer at a particular star, its altitude could be read off against the scale on the rim to an accuracy of about one degree. For any given latitude the Pole star has effectively a constant altitude and the other stars appear to revolve around it owing to the Earth's diurnal rotation. On the front of the astrolabe there was a thin plate (the tympan) on which was engraved a stereographic projection of the lines of attitude and azimuth (angular distance along the horizon) as they would be for an observer at a given latitude. An open-work star map in stereographic projection (known as the rete) was in front of

the tympan, and could be rotated by hand over the lines of altitude and azimuth (Whitrow 1989,78).

15. On this, see de Solla Price 1964.
16. Whitrow notes that this has recently been edited and translated into English by Dr. R. Hill 1976, who points out that "horologically, it provides an important link between the water-clocks of the Hellenistic world and those of Islam." Detailed discussion of some other Islamic clocks will be found in a book written in Baghdad about AD 850 (Hill 1974; 1976: 9).
17. Many have suggested possible influence on Durkheimian conceptualization from medieval Arab scholarship, particularly that by Abdul Rahman Ibn Khaldun who contributed a cyclical theory of culture change centering the concept of solidarity (*'asabiyya*) as its core element and whose works were available in French translation during Durkheim's lifetime.
18. Henrí Hubert (1872–1927) was a core member of the Émile Durkheim group in Paris.

    His seminal pioneering work on time has now been translated for the first time into English (by Robert Parkin and Jacqueline Redding) and appears in a publication (see Hubert 1999) by Durkheim Press, which includes an English translation of a valuable essay by François-André Isambert, French sociologist and specialist in religion, here used as Introduction to the book (3–42). Isambert's Introduction serves to introduce readers to the life and work and depth of thought of Henri Hubert, and in the process can shed some light on the confusion in the collaborative nature of references by Hubert, Mauss, and Durkheim. It was quite confusing to sort out collaborative works in which the same citation mentions Hubert as primary author and elsewhere mentions Mauss as primary author. The Introduction makes clear how intellectual influences permeated the works of all three, but also suggests that perhaps other factors intervened that produced such confusion. Other than the Introduction, the publications contains the English translation (with minor editing) of Hubert's original Essay on Time (43–91), and concludes with a chapter that is a review that had been written by Mauss which is critical of Hubert's essay. Later the same work appeared in the names of both. The book also includes three Bibliographies: works by Hubert, works on Hubert, and a general bibliography.
19. This is its first translation into English. It is introduced by François-André Isambert and is edited by Robert Parkin, both leading scholars in *Durkheimian Studies*. Isambert is author of *Le Sens Du Sacré: Fête et Réligion Populaire* (1982, French) and Parkin is author of *The Dark Side of Humanity: Work of Robert Hertz and Its Legacy* (1996).
20. Seeds for the ideas developed here were planted over a decade ago and developed in earlier works, particularly in my book *Veil: Modesty, Privacy and Resistance* (2003 [1999]).

Chapter 3 Order and Creative Beginning

1. Note the adjectives used for the different holy places in Islam: Al-Azhar al-Sharif, al-Quds al-Sharif, al-Haram al-Sharif and al-Madina al-Munawwara, Makka al-Mukarrama.

2. It is worth noting here that the Arabic word *madrasah* simply means school.
3. Mubaraka proposes that Aramaic, the mother tongue throughout today's Arabic-speaking region, had an Eastern and a Western dialect and that gradually the merging of the two developed into the Arabic known today (Mubaraka 1998: x).
4. Contemporary Baghdad housed a research institute called *Bayt al-Hikma* which was named and modeled after the Abbasid-era learning center. The original one, along with all the other libraries of Baghdad, was destroyed during the Mongol invasion in 1258. Ironically, modern-day Mongols have caused similar destruction: the Anglo-American invasion of 2003 led to the looting and destruction of the contemporary *Bayt al-Hikma*, which was a complex that included a thirteenth-century madrasah. The Baghdad museum, which housed immeasurably valuable treasures and artifacts of knowledge, also saw much destruction and looting. Looted materials have been illegally bought and sold around the world.
5. Actually the Arabic word *'ilm* is quite interesting. It means science, also knowledge. *'Alim* (male) and *'Alima* (female) refer to male and female scholars of Islam both actively present in Islamic history. A distortion of the original meaning of the feminine referent led to its popular and derogatory use *'alma*, for female performing artists. In modern times the same words are used for science in general not just the science of Islam. From the same foundational root *'-l-m* derives the term *'ilmaniyya.* It translates in contemporary English usage as secularism, which stands for an ideology that is opposed to religiousness. The Qur'an makes reference to two different words *al-'alamayn* which means worlds or universes over which God is supreme, and *al-'alimin*, which means "the learned." Some scholars confuse these two and both with another two terms that are the subject of debate on secularism. The terms *'ilmaniyya* or *'almaniyya*, which are the subject of debate, are not in the Qur'an. Dr. Yusuf al-Qaradawy (2005 [2000]) points out the error of using the word *'almaniyya*, since it has no base in the correct Arabic language but has become widely used. Al-Ali, among others uses in her study (2000) the word *'almaniyya* as Arabic for secularism (which could be attributed to inability to distinguish the two due to lack of mastery of the Arabic language). Al-Qaradawy critiques the translation of secularism to *'ilmaniyya* on different grounds. "Secularism means the separation of religion from society and life" (58). On that basis, this uncritical borrowing of vocabulary from the West includes the uncritical borrowing of ideas that are alien to Arab and Muslim culture. He goes on to say that in Arabic the term *al-'ilmaniyya* shares derivation with *al-'ilm* (science and knowledge) which is an unfortunate translation of secularism, because it puts science against religion – an idea that comes from the West and distorts Islamic conceptualization. In her apologia for Western thought and secularism, Al-Ali dismisses the association between secularism and the West as essentialist (2000: 130–1). The ideological character of secularism for secularists is obvious here. Of relevance to this point are the recent developments in Europe where secularism is given as the reason behind increasing crackdowns on headscarves worn by Muslim women, cartoons defaming the Prophet of Islam, and verbal abuses by fundamentalist Protestant leaders in the United States against Islam, its women, its prophet, and its people. This reasoning (and on this, see Bowen 2007) – that secularism is behind a ban on headscarves or the license for defamation through cartoons – is not universally accepted, of course, as many see Western politics and attitudes of prejudice against Islam.

6. This should be contrasted with the period of Christian Inquisition in which Christianity saw itself opposed, not only to any other religion or any other form of Christianity, but to science and scientific knowledge.
7. It is noteworthy to remember that during medieval times while Europe was in the Dark Ages the Arabs and Muslims were, despite political upheavals, enjoying their Golden Age of art, architecture, science, and knowledge.
8. The physical copy of the Bible used here belongs to my husband mathematician-anthropologist, Dwight W. Read. It was a gift from his deceased mother, my mother-in-law, whom I have never seen except in black and white still photos. It is a special Bible, being a Christmas gift from a Christian Protestant mother who in her hand-written words (see Figure 3.1, p. 44) wished it to be a "guiding light to living" for her son. I had a gift of the Qur'an from my father, which I cannot locate, with a cover made of mother-of-pearl, which he had obtained in Jerusalem when he performed the Muslim pilgrimage there at the Dome of the Rock when I was a child. Interestingly, an olivewood memento from Jerusalem sits in our sitting room today, which was acquired by my husband's mother on her visit to Jerusalem. These are important material witnesses of lives lived, religious roots, identities, and contemporary beliefs strongly held. Had my mother-in-law, Wilma Webster, been alive as I go through the analysis in this book I believe she would have agreed with my analysis. From memories shared by her children, siblings and in-laws, I formed the image in my head of an enlightened woman who used her Christian Protestant upbringing to guide her life morally but not to challenge scientific contributions. She raised her children to obtain doctorates in mathematics, physics, psychology, and marine biology.
9. Note the sequence in the creation narrative of ancient Egypt: "The self-existent God . . . created: 1. The light. 2. The firmament, or home of moisture, i.e. clouds and rain. 3. Mankind. 4. The second Eye i.e. the Moon. 5. Plants, and herbs, and reptiles, and creeping things. 6. Seven deities, four being male and three female" (Budge 1969 [1904] I: 300).
10. There is confusion when exploring the roots and developmental history of the Arabic language, because language has been used sometimes to refer to script and sometimes to spoken dialects. Another source of confusion, I speculate, comes from the mistaken use of the name of a group (Akkadian, Babylonian, Chaldean, Hebrew) as if it is also the name of a separate language. This kind of confusion is not uncommon among scholars trying to sort out contradictory data. Often while carrying out fieldwork in Nubia (1963) (on a major Nubian project sponsored by the Social Research Center of the American University in Cairo during the directorship of Dr. Laila El Hamamsy) researchers kept confusing name of group with name of language. The Nubians tried to straighten this out for us when we used the word *Kenuz* to refer to the people and their language. The name of the language the Kenuz spoke was Mettoki. Often, to this day in the United States, I am asked whether Egyptians spoke Egyptian. Such mistaken extensions of group name to languages and a closer look at linguistic data from historical lexical studies on the linguistic region of Arabic-speakers make me skeptical about conventional classifications of language families. In some cases languages (or dialects) are classified as separate languages that share a common ancestry, or are classified as belonging to the same family of languages. Such classification is static and implies rigidity and fixity, whereas we know from

historical/ethnographic studies and from recent linguistic studies of the presence of fluidity of languages through natural developmental change, historical adaptation, hybridity through contact, and transformation that are not dissimilar from what we know occur in other spheres of human activity. Were there in fact languages called Akkadian, Babylonian, Hebrew, Phoenician, Nabataean? Or do these labels stand for dialectical variants of a mother tongue for the entire Semitic-speaking region? Do some "languages" refer to script forms and others to spoken dialects? I will venture that Aramaic (which itself evolved over millennia) existed as a script in written form (with variants) throughout the region that is today Arabic-speaking. Recent archaeological research discovering Semitic alphabet inscription on rocks in southern Egypt attests to the widespread existence of a Semitic script. Semitic roots are based on what is called a "semantic nucleus," a semantic element intrinsically embedded within the consonantal root (a feature noticed by medieval Arab grammarians) (Zammit 2002: 20). Medieval linguistic scholarship, as in science scholarship, flourished in a stimulating scholarly milieu characterizing civilizational centers in the Islamic empire, such as al-Andalus, Baghdad, Cairo, and Damascus. Kaltner (1996: 11; cited by Zammit 2002: 19–20, n.11) noted that studies of lexicography in Europe by Jews were not marked by such vitality and creativity as that demonstrated by Arabic-speaking Jewish philologists living in the Islamic region (including al-Andalus) because Europeans were distant from access to Arabic sources and outside the vibrant intellectual milieu Arabs created.

In his quantitative analysis of a corpus of the Arabic lexicon from primary sources, searching for lexical relationship and patterns of correspondences between Arabic and the major Semitic "dialects" and from research by other scholars, Zammit (2002: 20) concludes that Arabic is the true representative of the most ancient form of Semitic. Calculations by researchers using the lexicostatistical method reveal that Arabic might have separated (I would say evolved) from Syriac around 1650 BC. Classifications obscure relations, as in the case of Syriac and Aramaic. Some observers point to the fact that Hellenic colonizing of parts of the region, as at any historical era, was accompanied by processes of Hellenization of culture and vocabulary. Syriac, a Greek word, is the term used for the language of Damascus and the surrounding region, which was according to evidence Aramaic. The closeness of Arabic to Aramaic is supported by the fact that Arabic and "Syriac" shared 54% of a common vocabulary (2002: 25). All three languages (or versions of the same language) are spoken and written. Evidence of spoken Aramaic (Syriac) is found today among Syrians in towns such as Ma'loula and the community north of Damascus studied by Mubaraka, called Sadad, which is the source of his lexical corpus. Aramaic is also used for worship in some communities in Iraq and as a valuable systematic exploration demonstrates in the vocabulary of Egyptian Arabic, Bedouin Arabic, and in much of spoken Arabic today (Mubaraka 1998). The next chapter, on calendars, further confirms the affinity when it demonstrates the continuing daily use by Arabs today of Aramaic month names. Evidence shows a high rate of and a wide-ranging lexical retention of Aramaic in today's Arabic. All this evidence builds a strong foundation of evidence upon which one can propose that today's Arabic language represents a transformational continuity developing out of Aramaic.

11. The *th* would have become the Arabic ع. Arabic sābi' means "seventh." The word is numerical and has no other intrinsic connotation.

12. In the publication "Genesis as Myth," Edmund Leach performs a structural analysis on a number of biblical stories and their variants. Taking the first four chapters of Genesis, which contain three separate stories of creation, he breaks down the stories into elements and then puts together these elements in the form of a meaningful structure. For the full analysis, see Leach 1967: 5–13. The diagrams, on pages 7 and 11, represent his analysis and are most interesting. He notes that stories recur as different versions. "Man is created in Genesis (chapter I, verse 27) and then he is created all over again (II, 7). And, as if two first men were not enough, we also have Noah in chapter VIII. Likewise in the New Testament, why must there be four gospels each telling 'the same; story yet sometimes flatly contradictory on details of fact?" (1–2). "The whole of Christendom shares a single corpus of mythology," he observes, yet in a remarkable way "the members of each particular Christian sect are able to convince themselves that they alone possess the secret of revealed truth" (3).
13. In the United States the rejection is obviously manifested where the teaching of the theory of evolution in schools and universities has become a major political issue. Some view evolutionary theory as equal in weight and evidence to what they consider to be a counter "theory" labeled *creation theory* and *intelligent design*.
14. To read the report in its entirety, go to the website (NCSE 2007). It is to be noted how evangelical Protestants tend to be more supportive of biblical renderings than other groups. The second question asked in the poll is: "Do you think the scientific theory of evolution is well-supported by evidence and widely accepted within the scientific community?" Forty-eight percent of respondents in general said that it was well supported; 39% said that it was not well supported; 13% didn't know. But when we break down respondents by group we find that among evangelical Protestants, 63% said that it was not well supported, while 57% of non-evangelical Protestants, 58% of Catholics, and 73% of agnostics/atheists said that it was well supported. It must be stressed that this issue is not new to Americans or the United States. It has recurrently popped up in different forms and contexts for many decades (see El Guindi 2004: for a discussion about Congress and public reaction to the introduction of an anthropology curriculum in US school education). It is now seriously affecting the teaching of science in schools around the United States and even at the university level. It has become extraordinarily politicized by the 1990s. There is now effective campaigning using forums of media, politics, and electronic communication aimed at removing the teaching of the scientific fact of evolution from classrooms and textbooks and replacing it or at least co-teaching it along with a proposed alternative – the biblical "theory" of creation as an equally valid theory to that of science.
15. A controversy surrounded the well-known film produced by the late Mustafa Akkad (who was killed in 2006 while attending a wedding in Jordan) about the birth of Islam. The controversy concerned the title of the film, which was originally *Muhammad: The Messenger of God*. Objections were made against its implications centralizing the figure of Muhammad. Islam centralizes the message, which is revealed from God through Muhammad to the people. It is the message that is holy and of divine origins, not Muhammad. In response, the name of the movie was changed to *The Message*. Islam considers the message of Islam, not the messenger, as the center of emphasis.
16. This was evident in the outpouring of emotion and intense protest and outcry by

Muslims the world over in response to the insult to them by the Danish cartoons, which they perceived as an act of defaming their Prophet.

17. See Ruel 1982 on the relation of the vast history of development of the Christian Church to Christian identity. There was first "the critical, initial phase in which Christians, the Nazarene sect, emerged as a distinctive religious movement" (Ruel 1982: 10), which Ruel refers to as "a community of believers." Then "the immediately succeeding period leading to the Council of Nicaea (325) that witnessed both the developing formal organization of the Church and the establishment of orthodox creeds, sanctioned by the Church councils" (10). My usage of church is confined to the formal organization that became differentiated throughout history until the present into churches and smaller churches within churches. Note Ruel's observation (1982) that "From the time of the early church . . . baptism came to be used to mark the transition to membership that is so characteristic of Christianity" which is about boundary-marking (14). Contemporary transformations on baptism are interesting. A South Los Angeles Pentecostal congregation was reported in the *Los Angeles Times*, February 9, 2008, B2, to announce holding its "second annual street baptism by fire hose" expecting several hundred people to attend. This is part of the denomination's eighty-first annual Holy Convocation, which draws 500 church representatives from across the United States.

    Common usage of the notion of church with reference to Christianity alternates between physical structures of worship and the many congregational groups. This phenomenon of congregational divisions has no exact parallel in Islam. The Christian church was not in fact founded until after the death of Jesus, whereas the Umma, the newly founded Islamic community of believers, was founded by Prophet Muhammad as a major accomplishment in his lifetime. The very notion of belief is different in both: the Christian notion of belief is about "commitment to Christ" (see Ruel 1982: 27).
18. There are no marked widespread extremist rejections of science in Islam resembling those in Christianity. One example of an ideologue in the name of Islam who explicitly challenges the process of evolution of humankind is Harun Yahya whose website is http://www.harunyahya.com/.
19. Other European nations followed: Toeger Odegaard, head of Oslo education department, reported that the council wanted to ban the burqa' and niqab, that is face covers, so that teachers can do their jobs better. The Belgian town of Maaseik has forbidden them. This must be seen in the context of attacks on Islam, the Qur'an, and Muhammad. Recently the Dutch right wing Freedom Party is reported to have said: if Muslims want to live among us they should tear half of the Qur'an which is just awful, and that Islam is a violent religion and its Prophet extremist.
20. Bowen writes how Sevaistre asked The State Council for an explanation of *culte* and of having seen the handwritten notes on that. The State Council is called the *Conseil d'Etat*, which was originally created as an advisory body to the king and now serves as the highest administrative tribunal in France, hearing appeals from schools and other state institutions, including being the ultimate arbiter in headscarf disputes (Bowen 2007: 16). It is an interesting twist on the subject of headscarves and secularism that quite recently (2008) Turkey voted to allow the wearing of headscarves in educational institutions.
21. Clearly Abraham Marcus is wrong and ethnocentrically biased when he states that

by "denying the finality of death and integrating it into a sacred order that transcended everyday experience, Islam . . . legitimizes death" (1992 [1989]: 274). First, Islam does not legitimize death nor is it accurate to claim that it denies the finality of death. The reality is much more sophisticated and nuanced than that. Second, integrating death in a sacred order as a continuation of life is a pervasive idea in world cosmologies. Third, Marcus misses the uniqueness of Islam's view of life and death that creates a sense of "contentment" for its faithful and which is seen by many as the strength of Islam's popular acceptance and rapid spread and continued growth. The latter observation is supported by data from interviewing voluntary converts to Islam from other faiths who are part of the expatriate labor force in the Khalij (Arab Gulf) region today. A sense of *rida* (contentment and calm) on the part of Muslims was mentioned as a virtue that attracted many of the converts who could not achieve this state in their own faiths. In a sense, this study is an anthropological exploration of the factors that together create a culture of rida.

22. Given that Islam was born in Arabia surrounded by developments out of two major civilizational cultures, the Egyptian and the Mesopotamian, it would make sense in our context here to explore Mesopotamian imagery as well. But this significant and big project has to await another publication. It is beyond the scope of this work.
23. In the original Egyptological sources, cosmological beings are presented as gods and goddesses. Instantly meaning is imbued to such terminology suggesting shared understanding. The notion of deity in our contemporary understanding is automatically attached to the usage. I suggest that ancient Egyptian usage of a vocabulary of sacredness was probably differently nuanced than current usages. I therefore refrain in this publication from uncritically adopting this terminology of gods and goddesses, because I question that assumption of equivalence in meaning. In fact, I boldly propose that the English translation to gods and goddesses of the ancient Egyptian usage denoting the different beings populating the cosmological universe is misleading and over-simplifying.
24. Griaule and Dieterlen (1954: 86) describe the beginning of time among the Dogon of the Sudan also in terms of the Egg of the world, which divides into twin placenta, along with seven vibrations of the universe.
25. For the notion of visual ethnography, see El Guindi (2003 [1999]); for extended discussion on continuity of aspects of Egyptian thought in this contemporary form, see El Guindi (2004).
26. This kind of representation will bring to mind the impressive Lévi-Straussian works containing analyses of mythology in which he performed structural-mathematical analyses. Unfortunately, this paradigm gets reduced in some works to superficial oppositions. Sherry Ortner is associated with the equation male, female, culture, nature (Ortner 1974: 67, 71, 72, 77, 78; for a critique of such claims, see Moore 1988: 13–21, n.8, 201) Paradigms of cultural dualities and equations of correspondences are not sufficient to make such paradigms Lévi-Straussian. For analysis to be Lévi-Straussian there should be an analytic theory that consists of a systematic set of ideas that are primarily generative, and reveal not only binary oppositions, but mediations, transformations, and triadic interrelationships (El Guindi 2004: 114–16).
27. It is interesting that Egyptological sources most often use sky rather than heaven as the translated notion. In equivalent Judaic-biblical translations, heaven is most often used when sky should have been.

28. This opening scene is much more complex than the biblical rendering of creative beginnings. It is perhaps too complex to represent the entire Egyptian story in a dramatized play mode as I have done earlier for the biblical version. As more knowledge about creation unfolds, a complex generative series of processes of embeddedness and transformationality reveal themselves. By the time we see the whole picture of Egyptian creation, imagining it (or re-creating it as it were) in dramatic form becomes a formidable task, too much of a challenge to attempt. This is because it is not a simple linear chronology of events nor can it be reproduced as one act. It would need an expert or even a genius. I retreat from the challenge into theater, but will continue with anthropological analysis of the materials in the papyri and Egyptological documentation. The analysis presented here might inspire a genius of theater.
29. This story left a strong imprint on popular culture when Marcel Khalifa, the well-known singer/artist sang the story in the words of Mahmoud Darwish, the well-known Palestinian poet. It proved to be a controversial development for Marcel, as some conservative Islamic religious elements were suspicious of turning qur'anic text into popular song. Marcel was legally cleared, but it was difficult for a while.
30. In his exploration of time, Leach (1961: 128–9) invokes Greek mythology which is of contrastive interest to the picture drawn by the ancient Egyptians. Cronus is father of Zeus. In *de Mundo* chapter seven, Aristotle claimed that Kronos (Cronus) was a symbolic representation of Chronos, Eternal Time. Leach observes that etymologically Kronos and Chronos are not closely connected, yet such a presumed connection formed a basis for a major issue of theology surrounding a Cronus cult in a period in which Cronus was regarded as a symbol of Time. It is not clear why Cronus seemed appropriate to personify Time. It certainly is not clear from the stories relating to him as summarized briefly by Leach (1961: 128–9). The story about Cronus is summarized this way: "Cronus, King of the Titans, was the son of Uranus (sky) and Ge (earth). As the children of Uranus were born, Uranus pushed them back again into the body of Ge. Ge to escape this prolonged pregnancy armed Cronus with a sickle with which he castrated his father. The blood from the bleeding phallus fell into the sea and from the foam was born Aphrodite (universal fecundity)." Leach goes on: "Cronus begat children by his sister Rhea. As they were born he swallowed them. When the youngest, Zeus, was born, Rhea deceived Cronus by giving him a stone wrapped in a cloth instead of the new-born infant. Cronus swallowed the stone instead of the child. Zeus thus grew up. When Zeus was adult, Cronus vomited up his swallowed children . . . Zeus now rebelled against King Cronus and overthrew him; according to one version he castrated him. Placed in restraint, Cronus became nevertheless the beneficent ruler of the Elysian Fields, home of the blessed dead." Leach relates how when King Cronus ruled there were only men and no women. Pandora, the first woman, was created on Zeus' instructions. It was a golden age of bliss and plenty. Since there were no women, there was no strife. The era of Zeus will one day come to an end and Cronus will resume his reign. Men will cease to grow older. They will be born from their graves. Women will once more cease to be necessary, and strife will disappear from the world.

    My inclination in interpreting these chronologies with themes of antagonisms, of husband against wife, of wife against husband, of son against father, of father against children, of men against women, and violations of family and taboo is not to reduce this narrative to structural oscillations and reversals. In fact I tend to disagree with Leach's analysis of this story as a good example of oscillation versus circularity or cyclicity. It is interesting that Greek culture serves as an ideological archetype for Western culture, leaving a strong impact on psychoanalysis and psychological orientations focused on phallus, castration, and antagonism within the family. From the narrative above, we find no orderly universe emerging out of conflictful relationships and no complementarities of polarity. Polarity is linked to antagonism, a pattern that ought to be looked at in direct contrast with the Egyptian imagery.

31. It would be interesting to explore the point at which and the context in which the historical chronology of stories and scripts shifted to an ethos of revenge known as "an eye for an eye," or evil as in "evil eye." It is interesting to note how there is no apparent evidence, as far as my exploration goes, of connotations of revenge or evil in connection with the human eye in ancient Egypt.
32. My research in the Oaxaca Valley of Mexico was supported by NIMH Fellowship and Research Grant MH 48273-01. UCLA Academic Senate supplied a grant for analysis of field data. UCLA Latin American Center provided a grant to write up the analysis. Research and analysis of the Zapotec data benefited significantly from collaborations and scholarly discussions with linguist Dr. Harvey Rosenbaum and mathematician-anthropologist Professor Dwight W. Read.
33. I conducted intensive fieldwork among the Nubians of Egypt (1962–5) and in rural Egypt prior to my doctoral field research. The latter I carried out among the Valley Zapotec of Oaxaca, Mexico with NIMH support. I spent more than thirty-two months engaged in intensive fieldwork among the Zapotec in the village of San Francisco Lachigoló, Oaxaca, over a period of twelve years of study between 1967 and 1979.
34. I could not verify a hypothesized absence of a reference to sky as "the house of Nut" or references to a house of Isis or a house for the moon. I propose a conceptual reason behind the absence of such equivalence.
35. Further exploration of Egyptological materials (a project beyond the scope of this work) might reveal such usage,
36. I will refrain from offering further analysis of why sky is not considered the house for Nut at this time, until a more thorough reading of Egyptological materials is completed.
37. For my anthropological analysis, Budge was a good source of materials that are as close to the primary Egyptological data as one gets. I kept away from sources that constituted Egyptological analysis, although analysis cannot be completely avoided since any descriptive material involves some level of analysis.
38. It is interesting in this regard to mention a story published on June 26, 2006 by Reuter news agency regarding Spain's move to recognize the rights of great apes. "Spain's parliament is to declare its support for rights to life and freedom for great apes. In what will apparently be the first time any national legislature has recognized such rights for non-humans." However some controversy ensued. The nature discourse surrounding the controversy is worth noting. At first, Spanish media quoted the Catholic Archbishop of Pamplona as saying it was ludicrous to grant apes rights not enjoyed by unborn children, in a reference to Spanish abortion laws (reported on Aljazeera's English website, see http:englishaljazeera.net). The report goes on to say that a spokesman for Archbishop Fernando Sebastian said that the words of the

Archbishop had been taken out of context and that he now supported the resolution. However, of relevance here is the remark reported as made by Father Santos Villanueva, the spokesman for the Archbishop of Pamplona: "We are in favour of defending animals, but people come first." This hierarchy among beings finds support in the Bible.

Chapter 4 Science, Religion, and Business of Temporality

1. There is inconclusive evidence about the calendar that is sometimes referred to as the Jewish calendar and sometimes as the Hebrew calendar (see Parise 2002: 12). I contend that it is more appropriate to refer to a Judaic calendar (rather than Jewish or Hebrew) because there is more certainty about its religious and Arabic basis irrespective of where Jews lived prior to the formation of Israel (e.g. eastern Europe, Western Europe, etc.). The present Judaic calendar is presumed to date from the year of *the Creation*, or Anno Mundi, which would be at 378 BC by Gregorian calendar calculation. The year AD 1980 corresponds to the Judaic years of 5740–1 AM. It borrows elements from Aramaic, which is an early form of Arabic, such that the names of months used in the Judaic calendar today are very close if not identical to the Arabic names of the Arab calendar centuries before Islam. The religious component consists of about fifteen holy days specific to Jews today.
2. Converting dates: the following equations convert roughly from Gregorian to *hijri* and vice versa. However, the results can be slightly misleading: they tell you only the year in which the other calendar's year began. For example, 2006 Gregorian spans both 1426 and 1427 *hijri*, but the equation tell you that 2006 equals 1427, when in fact 1427 merely began during 2006.

   Gregorian year = [(32 x *hijri* year) / 33] + 622

   Hijri year = [Gregorian year – 622) X 33] / 32

   Alternatively, there are more precise calculators available on the internet, see www.rabia.com/convert; www.ori.unizh.ch/hegira.html.
3. This whole section on Egyptian calendars and clocks is largely based on the account by Whitrow 1989: 25–9.
4. Unfortunately, it is housed in a museum in Berlin. It should be returned to Egypt.
5. It would be worthwhile for Egypt to officially request from England the return of this object, the Merkhet, to its original homeland, Egypt.
6. Following http://en.wikipedia.org/wiki/Epiphany_%28holiday%29, we note that "Epiphany (Greek for 'appearance' or 'revelation'), is a Christian feast day which celebrates the 'shining forth' or revelation of God in human form in the person of Jesus Christ. The feast falls on January 6. Western Christians commemorate the visitation of the Magi to the child Jesus on this day, i.e., his manifestation to the Gentiles. Eastern Christians commemorate the baptism of Jesus in the Jordan River, his manifestation as the Son of God to the world. It is also called Theophany ('manifestation of God'), especially by Eastern Christians. However, in the majority of Christian churches, January 6 commemorates the Nativity of Christ."
7. Aveni's idea that the calendar being countered was Hebrew is not acceptable, as the language of the region at the time was Aramaic, eventually evolving into present-day

Arabic. The month name that he uses, Nisan, is the Arabic name that is used to this day in the Arab calendar (see Aveni 1989: 115).

8. Poole writes about such reactions, as for example, when English writers saw the riots as: "popular ignorance in the age of Enlightenment and in more recent ones as an example of the gulf between elite and plebeian perceptions" (1995: 98–105).
9. It is interesting that the two English words *time* and *tide* are derived from the same Anglo-Saxon root word *tid*, which means "season," "hour" (Aveni 1989: 17).
10. I am grateful to Khalid Rosenbaum for bringing this to my attention not simply as a relevant story to my exploration of time, but after he made the connection between the implication of abolishing the siesta, an age-old tradition of Mediterranean, Latin, and other cultures, and the English workers' protest reaction to the state's manipulation of clocks and calendars also for purposes of business and profit.
11. For studies of time from different perspectives: philosophy, poetry, music, biology, aging etc. see Fraser and Lawrence (1975), an edited volume of chapters of different studies using various approaches.

Chapter 5 Marking Time, Carving Space

1. Soueif (2000 [1999]).
2. Sachau describes his task as a difficult task facing a philologist working with Arabic due to the ambiguity of the Arabic writing – *proh dolor!* – which is the reason why a manuscript expresses only three-quarters of the author's meaning, whilst the editor is compelled to supply the fourth quarter from his own knowledge and discernment (vi). In this regard, it should be mentioned that Sachau reacted to text by al-Biruni which stated that "The Hebrews, Jews, and all the Israelites, the Sabians and Harranians, used an intermediate system" (13) with reference to reckoning time combining lunar and solar cycles. Here al-Biruni demonstrates objectivity and detachment in his scholarship, since people did differentiate between faith, ethnicity, and language group. Sachau, on the other hand, says in an ideological note/comment regarding al-Biruni's original wording: "It is difficult to explain what differences the author [al-Biruni] meant to express by these three words [Hebrew, Jews and Israelites], which *to us* mean all the same" (370, emphasis added). I ask: Who is "us"? It is curious that Sachau does not see any differences between reference to a nomadic tribe, a settled clan, and a group adhering to a particular faith makes one doubt the validity of other parts of the translated/edited work. Sachau describes, in the Preface, how attention was first drawn to the works of al-Biruni when "Sir Henry Rawlinson [wrote] . . . the celebrated article on Central Asia in the 'Quarterly Review' for 1866, in which he gave some valuable information derived from his own manuscript copy, now the property of the British Museum."
3. Arabic poetry provides a rich source of ethnographic information, which I have drawn upon in my earlier work. See El Guindi (2003 [1999]).
4. Ishmaelites, using the distortion of the Arabic name Ismail, refers to Arabs who are considered descendants of Ismail the son of Ibrahim. In other words, Ismail is considered a remote ancestor of the Arabs.
5. In Sura 91: 11 the Qur'an refers to the Thamud as people engaged in wrongdoing and who rejected their prophet.

6. According to Yusuf Ali in his Qur'an commentary, footnote 1295, on Sura 9: 36: it may be noted that the Arab year was roughly lunisolar like the Hindu year, the months being lunar and the intercalation of a month every three years brought the year nearly but not accurately up to the solar reckoning. Months are calculated by the actual appearance of the moon.
7. What is sometimes called the Jewish or Judaic calendar consists mostly of Arabic months, and as Parise (2002: 27) writes is fundamentally based on the Arabic calendar.
8. I draw on Wikipedia and related sources for the spelling and certain information on the topic of the Coptic months.
9. Thout can also be Tout, which is the first month of the Coptic calendar, corresponding to the period between September 11 and October 10 of the Gregorian calendar. The month of Thout is also the first month of the Season of "Akhet" (Inundation) in Ancient Egypt, when the Nile floods, covering the land of Egypt. The name of the month of Thout comes from Thot, the Ancient Egyptian God of Wisdom.
10. Another name for it is Baba, the second month of the Coptic calendar, falling between October 11 and November 10 in the Gregorian calendar. It is also the second month of the Season of "Akhat" (Inundation) in Ancient Egypt. The name of the month of Paopi comes from Hapy, the Nile god.
11. Hathor is also Hatur, the third month in the Coptic calendar, falling between November 11 and December 9 in the Gregorian calendar. It is the third month of the Season of "Akhet" (Inundation), and it relates to the goddess Hathor.
12. It is also known as Kiahk, the fourth Coptic month, between December 10 and January 8 in the Gregorian calendar.
13. I would be skeptical about this interpretation.
14. It also shares the root for derivatives such as mubadra (initiative), bādara (verb with stress on first syllable) (initiate, begin), etc.
15. Bamyeh seems not to understand kinship at all, let alone Bedouin kinship. He considers breaking up larger kin units into small ones in literal terms, and sees it as the only way to manage a nomadic lifestyle and ecology (44), hence shifting of solidarities ('asabiyyahs) (44), and citing (perhaps not understanding) Khazanov (127) that Bedouin kinship units are more nuclear than extended, and that Bedouins borrowed the idea of the family from sedentary groups (50).
16. Forbidden is the term mostly used by Bamyeh as the translation of haram. A more accurate term would be sacred, which he used more infrequently.
17. Zammit includes *nasi'* in his lexical corpus as an Aramaic word that meant both intercalation and usury (Zammit 2002).
18. Sachau asserts that kalammas signifies a full-flowing sea. It is more likely that the term derives from the root that means word or speech, perhaps speakers.
19. Sachau in his translation of al-Biruni uses the word profane instead of ordinary. I consider ordinary to be more accurate and appropriate.
20. See Zammit 2002: 399.
21. Ayah 4 in Arabic:

إِذْ قَالَ يُوسُفُ لِأَبِيهِ يَٰٓأَبَتِ إِنِّي رَأَيْتُ أَحَدَ عَشَرَ كَوْكَبًا
وَٱلشَّمْسَ وَٱلْقَمَرَ رَأَيْتُهُمْ لِي سَٰجِدِينَ ﴿٤﴾

Readers should also try to listen to this verse sung in Marcel Khalifa's superb rendering "Oh, My Father, I am Yusuf," from his album *Arabic Coffeepot.*

22. An exception to this is the superstitious association made even by college-educated folk between the moon in its full phase and odd happenings.
23. To read more about female circumcision as a ritual for sexualizing females see El Guindi (2006a).
24. This whole section benefits from the publication by Paul Lunde who specializes in Islamic history and literature. His most recent book is *Islam: Culture, Faith and History* (2001).
25. See home.pacific.net.sg/~makhdoom/calend2.html.
26. According to Burnaby (1901: 387, n.2), in accordance with the qur'anic Sura 57, the name of the sixth day of the week was changed from its former Arabian word al-'Aruba to al-Jum'a.
27. Of course, there has been (since 1948 and again in 1990 until today 2007) a renewed Euro-Israel-US military-forced colonial occupation of Arab and Muslim lands (Palestine, Iraq, Afghanistan). Other forms of colonial dominance prevail around the Arabo-Islamic East.
28. In this regard, attention must be drawn to the baselessness of Zerubavel's statement that "two of the three days of the week that are *regarded by Islam as unfortunate and evil are none other than Saturday and Sunday*" (Zerubavel 1981: 73, emphasis added). Unfortunately, the situation is worse. Zerubavel cites Burnaby (1901: 387) by exact page as the source for his comment. Upon checking Burnaby, it was found that Zerubavel totally misrepresented what Burnaby wrote, which was: "Tuesday, Saturday and Sunday are unfortunate and evil days" (Burnaby 1901: 387). Burnaby does not give any source for this remark nor does he associate that with Islam. Rather it was in the context of existing superstitions of the time. It is irresponsible for Zerubavel to lift this passing remark and tweak it enough to make a false claim about Islam.
29. The *Ahkam* comprise a flexible range from primary to secondary, from personal to community, from individual to collectivity, from ordinary to emergency as follows: primary for ordinary situations in personal affairs, secondary for emergency situations in personal affairs, public affairs.
30. In the *New York Times* recently (Zoepf 2006), a story describes how Islamic revival among women in Syria is intensifying: "Though men across the Islamic world usually interpret Scripture and lead prayers, Syria . . . is seeing the resurrection of a centuries-old tradition of *sheikhas*" These are local female religious leaders. The author is wrong when she states that the situation is unique, new, or very different in Syria than other Muslim countries. These emergent trends have been observed and studied as having begun the intensification process in the mid 1970s (El Guindi 1981: as the earliest). Likewise, Mahmoud (2005) in her published dissertation, exaggerates the novelty of Egyptian women moving into piety by joining mosque discussion.

Chapter 6 Khususiyya, Qudsiyya, Jama'iyya

1. It is the last sermon of the Prophet before his death, reported to have been very long, important, and well-attended, and is mentioned in many books of Hadith, as in Sahih al-

Bukhari (see Hadith 1623, 1626, 6361), in Sahih Imam Muslim (Hadith 98), in Sahih Imam al-Tirmithi (Hadith 1628, 2046, 2058), in Masnud Imam Ahmad ibn Hanbal (Hadith 19774). The method of gathering its content is reported to have been through oral transmission by different listeners, subsequently compiled together as one *khutba*.

2. Aveni (1989: 105) invokes this nursery rhyme to make another point, namely that of the associative way of thinking – a way to recall perceived patterns in the universe. Aveni sees that as the principle embodied in the old nursery rhyme.
3. I would like to thank and recognize Egyptian architect Dr. Tarek Fathy (1991) co-founder of T.H.E. Architects, Planners and Civil Engineers Inc., Mohandseen, Cairo, Egypt, who upon hearing that I planned to write a book about Islam's rhythm casually remarked that "few people are aware that Islam follows both moon and sun." I started paying attention to this point and was led through my research exploration to the rich material used in this study. I also thank Dr. Tarek for donating the Arabic calligraphic artwork used on the cover of this book, which was designed and executed in his architectural office in Cairo.
4. Many scholars continue to Judeo-centrically focus on Isaac as the son Ibrahim was going to sacrifice (Parise 2002: 72). In Islam it is Ismail. Another Judeo-centric error is when it is assumed that Arab customs are based on Jewish customs. Arab customs with continuity from the long cultural tradition of the region are much older and are prior to the birth of Judaism. The Arabs who adopted the Judaic faith clearly share with the Arabs' customs and traditions. Similarities of names and linguistic terms stem from the fact, increasingly finding support among many scholars of language who are moving away from the old static classification, that Aramaic (the ancestral Arabic language) was the common language of the region, which had dialect differentiations (Mubaraka 1998; Zammit 2002).
5. It does create a problem when workers who are distraught from the "bureaucratic and government routine" of their jobs use this rhythm to skip work. It is becoming a serious problem in a place like Egypt. A customer has to leave his own work to go to the telephone services facility to pay his phone bill or face a brutal long interruption of landline service to his home. He stands in line for an extended period. He reaches the window and is told the employee he has to see is praying. After a 45-minute wait, as the closing time of the facility approaches, the customer finds himself wondering whether he has to take another day off work in order to pay his bill. The culprit here is not prayer. It is the abuse of the Islamic rhythm to resist a dysfunctional system. When taking measures to reform the system, the anomie of routine and bureaucratic irrationality should be examined and changed, rather than abolishing prayer during work. There is nothing new about the abuse of the rhythm to skip work. It has been around since the era of colonial occupation.
6. *Haya'* is embedded in the notion of life itself. It is repeatedly mentioned in the Hadith as a quality central to the faith. Hadith (1406) states that "each religion has its moral character and the moral character of Islam is *haya'*." It has been reported that the Prophet Muhammad said: "If you do not have *haya'*, what does it matter what you do" (1080, 1087). *Haya'* shares core connotations with *hishma*. For a wide range of referents see Lisan al-'Arab [under Ibn Manzur]; and Mawdudi (1959). They are very similar to referents given for the word *hishma*.
7. It was flattering to be told that the show is known to air interviews with heads of state and prominent Arab personalities.

8. This subject is discussed in more detail in *Visual Anthropology* (El Guindi 2004).
9. Examples abound in works of ideologically secularist scholars coming out of cultural studies regarding the study of Islamic issues (see Saba Mahmoud 2005).
10. Here is where the analogy of panties might point to the invalidity of this logic. It is widely known how women's underwear (a superfluous and publicly invisible item of clothing) has been the cause of pervasive yeast and related infections of women's genital areas leading to other complications. For decades, gynecologists warned women of the connection between underwear and these symptoms. This established harmful effect has neither stopped American women from wearing underwear nor the lavish underwear garment industry from producing diverse shapes, forms, colors, fabrics, etc.
11. Bowen notes that the 1989 incident was referred to as the *affaire des foulards* and that in the 2000s the singular term *le voile* (the veil) was used more pervasively in the media. On the subject of headcovers of Muslim women, Bowen (2007) oversimplifies what the Qur'an says or does not say about the subject (2007: 68–9; for a more nuanced discussion, see El Guindi 2003 [1999]). We can imagine a scenario established on the precedent set by the Feminist Majority militant campaign against the Afghan *burqu'* in which, out of concern for the health and freedom of American women, Afghan feminists might organize a campaign to ban underwear worn by American women to save and liberate them from a useless dress item that is also established by the medical profession to be harmful to their health. For perspective, the historical precedent is invoked whereby Middle East women viewed Western underwear as ridiculous, restraining, and confining. In her travel writing about the public bath of Turkish women (the original inspiration for the famous painting *Le Bain Turc* by French painter Jean August Dominique Ingrès), British Lady Montagu wrote: "I saw they believed I was so locked up in that machine [of undergarments] that it was not in my power to open it, which contrivance they attributed to my husband" (Halsband 1965: 314).
12. The strongest objections come out of ethnography-based observations. William Young (1996: 54) challenges the dichotomy using his Rashayda (Bedouin) ethnography. "It would be misleading to characterize the men's work as 'public' and the women's work as 'private' or 'domestic'." He points out that the decorated product of women's work – tent cloth, camel covers, and women's veils – are always displayed publicly, hence one could say that women's work is "public." An ethnographic study of traders in Aleppo Syria by Annika Rabo describes a shop in the *suq* as a private space that is also public. She points out that "[s]pace becomes infused with meaning through relations between people. The public-ness or the private-ness of place is relative to who inhabits it and for what purpose" (2005: 21). The "dichotomy between public and private has long been plagued by the association of gender segregation. It has also been common to link Middle Eastern women with enclosed space and men with open space" (2005: 179, n.5).

Chapter 7 Conclusion

1. Stories are recounted of daughters having dreams after their mothers' death in which they are alerted by the mother to remove intimate clothing the mother wore in her

lifetime and destroy them lest their privacy is violated after their death if these are "seen" by some "stranger." For identifying who is "mahram" and who is "stranger" see the Kinship Charts 8, p. 86 and 12, p. 99 in El Guindi 2003 [1999]. The dreams suggest a concern on the part of daughters to protect their mothers' privacy after their death and it is that worry that appears in dreams.

2. Rush Benedict in *Patterns of Culture* defines patterns in terms of a generalized configuration. F. Capra utilizes the term pattern but defines it closer to what I would define structure rather than pattern. In fact Capra reverses pattern and structure from how I would define them, and tends to equate form and structure. I distinguish form (superficial) and structure (internal) and consider pattern as a notion that can be deployed in different ways.
3. Marcus (1992 [1989]).

References

Al-Ali, N. 2000. *Secularism, Gender and the State in the Middle East: The Egyptian Women's Movement*. Cambridge: Cambridge University Press.

Al-Alusi, M. S. 1964. *Balugh al-arab fi ma'rifat ahwal al-'Arab* (3 volumes), Muhammad Bahja (ed.). Cairo: Maktabat Muhammad al-Tayyib.

al-Athir, I. 1965. *Al-Kamel fi al-Tarikh (Arabic)*. Beirut: Dar Sáder.

al-Biruni, A. R. M. i. A. 1879. *The Chronology of Ancient Nations (Tarikh al-Hind, Arabic)*. London: William H Allen.

al-Biruni, A. R. M. i. A. 1914. *Alberuni's India*. 2 volumes. London: K. Paul, Trench, Trubner.

al-Biruni, A. R. M. i. A. 1964. *Alberuni's India* Delhi: S. Chand.

al-Biruni, A. R. M. i. A. 1998 [1879]. *The Chronology of Ancient Nations. English Version of Al-Athar al-Baqiya 'an al-Qurun al-Baliya*. Vol. 31. *Islamic Mathematics and Astronomy*. London: W. H. Allen & Co.

al-Maimun, I. 1190. *Dalalat al-Hairin* (handwritten).

al-Mas'udi. 1965. *Muruj al-Dhahab wa Ma'aden al-Jawhar.* [Arabic] Yusuf Dagher (ed.). Beirut: Dar al-Andalus Press.

al-Qaradawy, Y. 2005 [2000]. *Thaqafatuna Bayna al-Infitah wal-Inghilaq*. [Our Culture Between Openness & Closedness] (Arabic). Cairo: Dar al-Shorouk.

Anderson, J. W. and J. Green. 2006. "Shaking Spain Out of its Siesta," *Washington Post*, p. A12.

Antoun, R. T. 1968. "On the Modesty of Women in Arab Muslim Villages: A Study in the Accommodation of Traditions," *American Anthropologist* 70: 671–97.

Antoun, R. T. 1972. *Arab Village: A Social Structural Study of Transjordanian Village*. Bloomington: Indiana University Press.

Antoun, R. T. 1989. *Muslim Preacher in the Modern World: A Jordanian Case Study in Comparative Perspective*. Princeton, NJ: Princeton University Press.

Ardener, S. (ed.) 1993. *Women and Space: Ground Rules and Social Maps*. Oxford, Providence: Berg.

Aswad, B. C. 1963. *Social and Ecological Aspects in the Origin of the Islamic State*. Ann Arbor, Michigan: Center for Near Eastern and North African Studies, University of Michigan.

Aswad, B. 1970. "Social and Ecological Aspects in the Formation of Islam," in L. Sweet (ed.), *Peoples and Cultures of the Middle East*, vol. 1. New York: Natural History Press, pp. 53–75.

Augustine, S. 1961. *The Confessions of St. Augustine* (trans. Edward B. Pusey). New York: Collier Books.

Austen, L. 1939. "The Seasonal Gardening Calendar of Kiriwina," *Oceania* 9: 237–53.

Aveni, A. 1989. *Empires of Time: Calendars, Clocks, and Cultures*. New York: Basic Books.

Bamyeh, M. A. 1999. *The Social Origins of Islam: Mind, Economy, Discourse*. Minneapolis: University of Minnesota Press.

Barnes, R. H. 1995. "Time and the Sense of History in an Indonesian Community: Oral Tradition in a Recently Literature Culture," in D. O. Hughes and T. R. Trautmann (eds), *Time: Histories and Ehnologies, The Comparative Studies in Society and History Book Series.* Ann Arbor: The University of Michigan Press, pp. 243–64.

Bateson, G. 1972. *Steps To An Ecology of Mind: Collected Essays in Anthropology, Psychiatry, Evolution, and Epistemology*. San Francisco: Chandler Publishing Company.

Bateson, G. 1979. *Mind and Nature: A Necessary Unity*. New York: E. P. Dutton.

Beckman, J. 1846. *A History of Inventions, Discoveries, and Origins*. Vol. 1. London: Henry G. Bohn.

Beidelman, T. O. 1963. "Kaguru Time Reckoning: An Aspect of the Cosmology of an East African People," *Southwestern Journal of Anthropology* 19: 9–20.

Bendix, R. 1962. *Max Weber*. Garden City: Anchor.

Benedict, R. 1934. *Patterns of Culture*. Boston: Houghton Mifflin Company.

Bergson, H. 1896. *Matière et Mémoire*. Paris: Alcan.

Bergson, H. 1904. *Essai sur les Données Immediates de la Conscience*. Paris: Alcan.

Bishop, S., M. Lau, S. Shapiro, L. Carlson, N. D. Anderson, J. Carmody, Z. V. Segal, S. Abbey, M. Speca, D. Velting, and G. Devins. 2004. "Mindfulness: A Proposed Operational Definition," *Clinical Psychology: Science and Practice* 7: 230–41.

Bloch, M. F. 1991. "Language, Anthropology, and Cognitive Science," *Man* 26: 183–98.

Bohannon, P. 1967. "Concepts of Time Among the Tiv of Nigeria," in J. Middleton (ed.), *Myth and Cosmos: Readings in Mythology and Symbolism*. New York: Natural History Press, pp. 315–30.

Bourdieu, P. 1990 [1970]. "The Kabyle House or the World Reversed," in P. Bourdieu (ed.), *The Logic of Practice*. Cambridge: Polity Press, pp. 271–83.

Bowen, J. R. 2007. *Why The French Don't Like Headscarves: Islam, the State, and Public Space*. Princeton and Oxford: Princeton University Press.

Budge, W. E. A. 1969 [1904] *The Gods of The Egyptians*. 2 volumes. New York: Dover Publications.

Burnaby, S. B. 1901. *Elements of the Jewish and Mohammedan Calendars*. London: George Bell.

Capra, F. 1996. *The Web of Life*. New York: Anchor.

Carsten, J. and S. Hugh-Jones (eds) 1995a. *About The House: Lévi-Strauss and Beyond*. Cambridge: Cambridge University Press.

Carsten, J. and S. Hugh-Jones 1995b. "Introduction: About the House – Lévi-Strauss and Beyond," in J. Carsten and S. Hugh-Jones (eds), *About the House: Lévi-Strauss and Beyond*. Cambridge: Cambridge University Press, pp. 1–46.

Cohen, A. P. 1985. "Symbolism and Social Change: Matters of Life and Death in Whalsay, Shetland", *Man* 20: 307–24.

Cornford, F. M. 1926. "Mystery Religions and Pre-Socratic Philosophy," *Cambridge History Magazine* 4: 549–50.

Crawley, E. 1912. "Dress," in J. Hastings and J. A. Selbie (eds), *Encyclopedia of Religion*, vol. 5. New York: Charles Scribner's Sons, pp. 40–72.

Crawley, E. 1931. *Dress, Drinks, and Drums: Further Studies of Savages and Sex*. London: Methuen and Co. Ltd.
Daragahi, B. 2007. "Austere Version of Islam Finding a Home in India," *Los Angeles Times* Sunday edition, pp. A1, A12.
Davis, J. (ed.) 1982. *Religious Organization and Religious Experience*. A.S.A. Monograph Vol. 21. London. New York: Academic Press.
Davis, J. 1982. "Introduction," in J. Davis (ed.), *Religious Organization and Religious Experience*. London. New York: Academic Press, pp. 1–8.
de Grazia, S. 1964. *Of Time, Work, and Leisure*. Garden City, NY: Anchor.
de Solla Price, D. J. 1964. "Mechanical Water Clocks of the 14th Century in Fez, Morocco," in *Proceedings of the Tenth International Congress of the History of Science (Ithaca, 1962),* pp. 599–602. Paris: Hermann.
Donsbach, M. 2006. "The Scholar's Supernova," in *Aramco Magazine*, 57: 38–43.
Dorsky, S. 1986. *Women of 'Amran: A Middle East Ethnographic Study*. Salt Lake City, Utah: University of Utah Press.
Durkheim, É. 1912. *Les Formes Élementaires de la Vie Religieuse*. Paris: Alcan.
Durkheim, É. 1961 [1912]. *The Elementary Forms of the Religious Life*. New York: Collier Books.
Durkheim, É. and M. Mauss. 1963 [1903]. *Primitive Classification*. London: Cohen & West.
Eickelman, D. 1977. "Time in a Complex Society: A Moroccan Example," *Ethnology* 16: 39–55.
El Guindi, F. 1973. "The Internal Structure of the Zapotec Conceptual System," *Journal of Symbolic Anthropology* 1: 15–34.
El Guindi, F. 1977a. "Lore and Structure: Todos Santos in the Zapotec System," *Journal of Latin American Lore* 3: 3–18.
El Guindi, F. 1977b. "The Structural Correlates of Power in Ritual," in R. Fogelson and R. N. Adams (eds.), *The Anthropology of Power*. New York: Academic Press, pp. 299–308.
El Guindi, F. 1981. "Veiling Infitah with Muslim Ethic: Egypt's Contemporary Islamic Movement," *Social Problems* 28: 465–85.
El Guindi, F. 1982. "Internal and External Constraints on Structure," in I. Rossi (ed.), *The Logic of Culture: Advances in Structural Theory and Methods*. New York: J. F. Bergin, Pubs. Inc., pp. 176–95.
El Guindi, F. 1983. "Some Methodological Considerations for Ethnography: Concrete Fieldwork Illustrations," in J. Oosten and A. de Ruijter (eds), *The Future of Structuralism*. Germany: Edition Herodot.
El Guindi, F. 1985. "The Status of Women in Bahrain: Social and Cultural Considerations," in J. Nugent and T. Thomas (eds), *Bahrain and the Gulf*. Sydney: Croom Helm, pp. 75–95.
El Guindi, F. 1986a. "El Sebou': Egyptian Birth Ritual," El Nil Research.
El Guindi, F. 1986b. "The Egyptian Woman: Trends Today, Alternatives Tomorrow," in L. b. Iglitzin and R. Ross (eds), *Women in the World – 1975–1985: The Women's Decade*. Santa Barbara, California: ABC-Clio, pp. 225–42.
El Guindi, F. 1986c. *The Myth of Ritual: Native Ethnography of Zapotec Life-Crisis Ritual*. Tucson: University of Arizona Press.
El Guindi, F. 1995. "Ghurbal," 30′: Documentary Educational Resources.
El Guindi, F. 1998. "From Pictorializing to Visual Anthropology," in B. H. Russell (ed.),

Handbook of Methods in Cultural Anthropology. Walnut Creek, California: Altamira Press, pp. 459–512.

El Guindi, F. 2003 [1999]. *Veil: Modesty, Privacy and Resistance*. Oxford and New York: Berg.

El Guindi, F. 2004. *Visual Anthropology: Essential Method and Theory*. Walnut Creek, California: Altamira Press.

El Guindi, F. 2006a. "Had It Been Your Face Would You Leave It As Is? Female Circumcision Among the Nubians of Egypt," in A. Rogaia (ed.), *Female Circumcision: Multicultural Perspectives*. Philadelphia: University of Pennsylvania Press, pp. 27–46.

El Guindi, F. 2006b. "Shared Knowledge, Embodied Structure, Mediated Process: The Case of the Zapotec of Oaxaca." CogSci2006, 28th Annual Conference of Cognitive Science Society, Vancouver, British Columbia, Canada.

El Guindi, F. 2007 "Private Reflections," *International Journal of Middle East Studies* 39: 172–3.

El Guindi, F. and D. Read. 1979a. "Mathematics in Structural Theory", *Current Anthropology* 20: 761–82.

El Guindi, F. and D. Read. 1979b. "Reply to Comments on Mathematics in Structural Theory," *Current Anthropology* 20: 782–90.

El Guindi, F. and D. Read. 1980. "Reply to 'On Mathematics in Structural Theory'," *Current Anthropology* 21: 389–91.

El Guindi, F. and H. A. Selby. 1976. "Dialectics in Zapotec Thinking," in K. Basso and H. A. Selby (eds), *Meaning in Anthropology*. Albuquerque: University of New Mexico Press, pp. 181–96.

Engel-Frisch, G. 1943. "Some Neglected Temporal Aspects of Human Ecology," *Social Forces* 22: 43–7.

Engels, F. 1940 [1878]. *Dialectics of Nature* (translated and edited by Clemens Dutt with a preface and notes by J. B. S. Haldane). London: Lawrencc and Wishart.

Engels, Frederick. 1975 [1924]. *Anti-Dühring*. Moscow: Progress Publishers.

Evans-Pritchard, E. E. 1937. *Witchcraft, Oracles and Magic among the Azande*. Oxford: Clarendon Press.

Evans-Pritchard, E. E. 1939. "Nuer Time-Reckoning," *Africa* 12: 189–216.

Evans-Pritchard, E. E. 1940. *The Nuer: A Description of the Mode of Livelihood and Political Institutions of a Nilotic People*. Oxford: Clarendon Press.

Evans-Pritchard, E. E. 1967. "Introduction," in *The Gift: Forms and Functions of Exchange in Archaic Societies*. New York: The Norton Library, W. W. Norton & Company, Inc., pp. v–x.

Fabian, J. 1983. *Time and the Other: How Anthropology Makes its Object*. New York: Columbia University Press.

Fathy, T. A. 1991. *Telecity: Information Technology and Its Impact on City Form*. New York: Praeger Publisher.

Frankel, H. 1955. *Wege und Formen Früh-Griechischen Denkens*. Munich: C. H. Beck.

Franklin, B. and D. Hall. 1748. "Advice to a Young Tradesman, Written by an Old One," in *The Writings of Benjamin Franklin, Volume II*: Philadelphia, 1726–1757. Philadelphia: New Printing Office. Available online at http://www.infomotions.com/etexts/literature/american/1700–1799/franklin-philadelphia-248.txt

Frazer, J. G. 1906. *The Golden Bough: A Study in Magic and Religion*. New York: MacMillan.

Fraser, J. T. 1975. *Of Time, Passion, and Knowledge: Reflections on the Stategy of Existence*. Princeton: Princeton University Press.
Fraser, J. T. and N. Lawrence (eds) 1975. *The Study of Time II: Proceedings of the Second Conference of the International Society for the Study of Time*. Berlin: Springer-Verlag.
Fukuyama, F. 1992. *The End of History and the Last Man*. London: : Hamish Hamilton.
Geertz, C. 1973 [1966]. "Person, Time and Conduct in Bali: An Essay in Cultural Analysis," in C. Geertz (ed.), *The Interpretation of Culture*. New York: Basic Books, pp. 360–411.
Gell, A. 1992. *The Anthropology of Time: Cultural Constructions of Temporal Maps and Images*. Oxford: Berg.
Gell, A. 1998. *Art and Agency*. Oxford: Oxford University Press.
González, R. J. 2001. *Zapotec Science: Farming and Food in the Northern Sierra of Oaxaca*. Austin, Texas: University of Texas Press.
Graham-Brown, S. 1988. *Images of Women: The Portrayal of Women in Photography of the Middle East (1860–1950)*. London: Quartet Books.
Griaule, M. and G. Dieterlen. 1954. "The Dogon," in D. E. Forde, *African Worlds*. London: Oxford University Press, pp. 83–110.
Halsband, R. 1965. *The Complete Letters of Lady Mary Wortley Montagu* (2 vols.). Oxford: Clarendon Press.
Heintz, M. 2005. "Time and the Work Ethic in Post-Socialist Romania," in W. James and D. Mills (eds), *The Qualities of Time: Anthropological Approaches*. Oxford: Berg, pp. 171–83.
Hill, D. R. e. 1974. *The Book of Ingenious Devices*. Dordrecht: Reidel.
Hill, D. R. e. 1976. *On the Construction of Water-Clocks*. London: Turner & Devereux.
Hoskins, J. 1993. *The Play of Time: Kodi Perspectives on Calendars, History, and Exchange*. Berkeley, CA: University of California Press.
Howells, W. 1948 [1962]. *The Heathens: Primitive Man and His Religions*. Garden City, NY: Doubleday Anchor.
Hsiao, K.-C. 1979. *History of Chinese Political Thought* (transl. fr. Chinese). Princeton, NJ: Princeton University Press.
Hubert, H. 1904. "Introduction to Manuel d'Histoire des Religions de Chantepie de la Saussaye," Paris: Colin, pp. v–xlvii.
Hubert, H. 1905. "Étude sommaire de la representation du temps dans la religion et dans la magie" (reprinted under the names of H. Hubert and M. Mauss in *Mélanges d'histoire des religions*, Paris 1909, pp. 189–229, editors H. Hubert & M. Mauss). *Annuaire de l'École Pratique des Hautes Études, Section des Sciences Religieuses*: 1–39.
Hubert, H. 1909. "Étude Sommaire de la Representation du Temps dans la Religion et al Magie," in H. Hubert and M. Mauss (eds), *Mélanges d'Histoire des Religions*. Paris: Felix Alcan, pp. 189–229.
Hubert, H. 1979. "Texte Autobiographique de Henrí Hubert," *Revue Française de Sociologie* 20: 205–7.
Hubert, H. 1999 [1905]. "Essay On Time: A Brief Study of the Representation of Time in Religion and Magic," in R. Parkin (ed.), *Essay On Time: A Brief Study of the Representation of Time in Religion and Magic*. Oxford: Durkheim Press Ltd., pp. 43–91.
Hubert, H., and M. Mauss. 1899. "Essai sur la nature et la fonction du sacrifice" (reprinted in Hubert and Mauss 1909). *L'Année Sociologique* 2: 29–138.

Hubert, H., and M. Mauss. 1902–1903. "Ésquisse d'une Théorie Générale de la Magie," *L'Année Sociologique* 7: 1–146.
Hubert, H., and M. Mauss. 1909. *Mélanges d'histoire des religions*. Paris: Alcan.
Huntington, S. P. 1993. "The Clash of Civilizations?" *Foreign Affairs* 72: 22–49.
Huntington, S. P. 1996. *The Clash of Civilizations and the Remaking of World Order.* New York: Simon & Schuster.
Ibn Khaldun, A. R. 1961. *Al-Muqaddimah*. Beirut: Dar Ihya' al-Turath al-'Arabi.
Isambert, F.-A. 1976. "L'Élaboration de la Notion de Sacre Dans L'École Durkheimienne," *Archives de Sciences Sociales des Religions* 42: 35–56.
Isambert, F.-A. 1979. "Henri Hubert et la Sociologie Du Temps," *Journal Revue Française de Sociologie* 20(1): 182–204.
Isambert, F.-A. 1982. *Le Sense du Sacré: Fête et Religion Populaire.* Paris: Les Editions de Minuit.
Isambert, F.-A. 1999. "Introduction," in R. Parkin (ed.), *Essay on Time by Henri Hubert.* Oxford: Durkheim Press, pp. 3–42.
James, W. and D. Mills (eds) 2005. *The Qualities of Time: Anthropological Approaches. ASA Monographs*. Oxford: Berg.
Jami'at al-Duwal, a.-A. 1980. *Ibn Khaldun and Contemporary Arabic Thought*. Tunis: al-Dar al-'Arabiyya lil Kitab.
Kaltner, J. 1996. *The Use of Arabic in Biblical Hebrew Lexicography*. Washington, DC: Catholic Bible Association of America.
Kendon, A. 1982. "The Study of Gesture: Some Observations on its History," *Recherches Semiotiques/Semiotic Inquiry* 2: 45–62.
Kendon, A. 1983. "Gesture and Speech: How They Interact," in J. M. Wiemann and R. P. Harrison (eds), *Nonverbal Interaction*. Beverly Hills, CA: Sage
Kendon, A. 1990a. *Conducting Interaction: Patterns of Behavior in Focused Encounters*. Cambridge: Cambridge University Press.
Kendon, A. 1990b. "Gesticulation, Quotable Gestures and Signs," in M. Moerman and N. Nomura (eds), *Culture Embodied*. Osaka, Japan: National Museum of Ethnology, pp. 53–77.
Kendon, A. 2000. "Language and Gesture: Unity or Duality?" in D. McNeill (ed.), *Language and Gesture*. Cambridge: Cambridge University Press, pp. 47–63.
Kendon, A. 2004. *Gesture: Visible Action as Utterance*. Cambridge: Cambridge University Press.
Kendon, A. and A. Ferber. 1973. "A Description of Some Human Greetings," in R. P. Michael and J. H. Crook (eds), *Comparative Ecology and Behavior of Primates*. London: Academic Press.
Lakoff, G. and M. Johnson. 1999. *Philosophy in the Flesh: The Embodied Mind and its Challenge to Western Thought*. New York: Basic Books.
Lancaster, W. 1981 [1997]. *The Rwala Bedouin Today*. Prospect Heights, Illinois: Waveland Press, Inc.
Langer, E. J. and M. Moldoveanu. 2000. "The Construct of Mindfulness," *Journal of Social Issues* 56: 1–9.
Leach, E. R. 1950. "Primitive Calendars," *Oceania* 20: 245–62.
Leach, E. R. 1961. *Rethinking Anthropology*. Vol. 22. London: University of London: The Athlone Press.
Leach, E. R. 1967 [1962]. "Genesis As Myth," in J. E. Middleton (ed.), *Myth and Cosmos:*

Readings in Mythology and Symbolism. Austin: University of Texas Press, pp. 1–13.
Lee, D. 1973. "Codifications of Reality: Lineal and Nonlineal," in R. E. Ornstein, *The Nature of Human Consciousness*. San Francisco, CA: Freeman, pp. 128–42.
Lenin, V. I. 1962 [1908]. *Materialism and Empirio-Criticism*. Moscow: Progress Publishers.
Leroi-Gourhan, A. 1993. *Gesture and Speech*. Cambridge, MA: MIT Press.
Lévi-Bruhl, L. 1938. *L'Éxperience Mystique et les Symboles Chèz Les Primitives*. Paris: Alcàn.
Lévi-Strauss, C. 1985. *The View From Afar* [Orig. French: *Le Regard Éloigne*]. Chicago: The University of Chicago Press.
Lévi-Strauss, C. 1987. *Anthropology and Myth: Lectures 1951–1982*. Oxford: Blackwell.
Lévi-Strauss, C. 1991, "Maison," in Pierre Bonte and Michel Izard (eds), *Dictionnaire d'ethnologie et d'anthropologie*, Paris, PUF, pp. 434–6.
Lloyd, H. A. 1966. "Timekeepers – An Historical Sketch," in J. T. Fraser (ed.), *The Voices of Time*. New York: Braziller, pp. 388–400.
Lunde, P. 2001. *Islam: Culture, Faith and History*. London: Dorling Kindersley.
Lunde, P. 2005. "Patterns of Moon, Patterns of Sun," in *Saudi Aramco World CalendarFlavors 2005*, p. 3.
MacDonald, D. B. 1927. "Continuous Re-Creation and Atomic Time in Muslim Scholastic Theology," *Isis* 9: 326–7.
Mahmoud, S. 2005. *Politics of Piety: The Islamic Revival and the Feminist Project*. Princeton and Oxford: Princeton University Press.
Maimonides, M. 1885. "The Guide of the Perplexed of Maimonides." London: Trubner & Co.
Maimonides, M. 1974. *Dalalat al-Hairin*. Ankara: Ankara Universitesi Besimevi.
Malinowski, B. 1927. "Lunar and Seasonal Calendar in the Trobriand Islands," *Journal of the Royal Anthropological Institute* 157: 203–15.
Malinowski, B. 1935. *Coral Gardens and Their Magic*. Bloomington: Indiana University Press.
Maltz, D. 1968. "Primitive Time Reckoning as a Symbolic System," *Cornell Journal of Social Relations* 3: 85–111.
Marcus, A. 1992 [1989]. *The Middle East on the Eve of Modernity: Aleppo in the Eighteenth Century*. New York: Columbia University Press.
Marshack, A. 1972. *The Roots of Civilization*. New York: McGraw-Hill.
Mauss, M. 1967 [1925]. *The Gift: Forms and Functions of Exchange in Archaic Societies* [Orig. French: *Essai sur le don, forme archaïque de l'Échange*]. New York: W.W. Norton.
Mauss, M. 1990. *The Gift: The Form and Reason For Exchange in Archaic Societies* [Orig. French: *Essai sur le don, forme archaique de l'Échange*]. New York: Norton.
Mauss, M. 2003 [1909, French]. *On Prayer*. New York and Oxford: Durkheim Press/Berghahn Books.
Mawdudi, A. A. 1959. *Tafsir Surat al-nur*. [Interpretation of Surat al-Nur] Beirut: Dar al-Fikr.
McCluskey, S. C. 1977. "The Astronomy of the Hopi Indians," *Journal for the History of Astronomy* 8: 174–95.
Mills, M. A. 2005. "Living in Time's Shadow: Pollution, Purification and Fractured

Temporalities in Buddhist Ladakh," in W. James and D. Mills (eds), *The Qualities of Time: Anthropological Approaches*. Oxford: Berg, pp. 349–66.

Moore, H. 1988. *Feminism and Anthropology*. Minneapolis: University of Minnesota Press

Morphy, H. 2003. "Some Concluding Anthropological Reflections," in W. S. F. Pickering (ed.), *On Prayer by Marcel Mauss*. New York and Oxford: Durkheim Press/Berghahn Books. pp. 139–54.

Mubaraka, F. M. 1998. *The Aramaic Influence in the Vernacular of Sadad. Syriac Patrimony*. Aleppo, Syria: Mardin Publishing House.

Mumford, L. 1963. *Technics and Civilization*. New York: Harbinger.

Munif, A. 1989 [1984, Arabic]. *Cities of Salt*. New York: Vintage International.

Munn, N. D. 1992. "The Cultural Anthropology of Time: A Critical Essay," *Annual Review of Anthropology* 21: 93–123.

NCSE (National Council for Science Education) 2007. *A new creationism/evolution poll, but few surprises*. Available online at www.ncseweb.org/default.asp.

Needham, J. 1969. *Science and Civilization in China*. Cambridge: Cambridge University Press.

Needham, J. and W. Ling. 1956. *Science and Civilisation in China 2. History of Scientific Thought*. Cambridge: Cambridge University Press.

Nilsson, M. 1920. *Primitive Time-Reckoning*. Lund: C.W.K. Gleerup.

North, J. D. 1975. "Monasticism and the First Mechanical Clocks," in Fraser, J. T. and N. Lawrence (eds), *The Study of Time II*. New York: Springer-Verlag, pp. 381–98.

Norton, J. 1997. "Faith and Fashion in Turkey," in N. Lindisfarne-Tapper and B. Ingham (eds), *Languages of Dress in the Middle East*. London: Curzon with The Centre of Near and Middle Eastern Studies, SOAS, pp. 149–177.

Núñez, R. and E. Sweetser. 2006. "With the Future Behind Them: Convergent Evidence From Aymara Language and Gesture in the Crosslinguistic Comparison of Spatial Construals of Time," *Cognitive Science* 30: 401–50.

Olson, E. A. 1985. "Muslim Identity and Secularism in Contemporary Turkey: The Headscarf Dispute," *Anthropological Quarterly* 58: 161–71.

Ortner, S. 1974. "Is Female to Male As Nature Is To Culture?" in M. Rosaldo and L. Lamphere (eds), *Woman, Culture and Society*. Stanford: Stanford University Press, pp. 67–88.

Pankenier, D. W. 2004. "Temporality and the Fabric of Space-Time in Early Chinese Thought," in R. M. Rosen (ed.), *Time and Temporality in the Ancient World*. Philadelphia: University of Pennsylvania Museum of Archeology and Anthropology, pp. 129–46.

Parise, F. (ed.) 2002. *The Book of Calendars*. Piscataway, NJ: Gorgias Press.

Pocock, D. 1967. "The Anthropology of Time Reckoning," in J. Middleton (ed.), *Myth and Cosmos: Readings in Mythology and Symbolism*. New York: Natural History Press, pp. 303–14.

Poole, R. 1995. "'Give Us Our Eleven Days!': Calendar Reform in Eighteenth-Century England," *Past and Present* 149: 95–139.

Quataert, D. 1997. "Clothing Laws, State, and Society in the Ottoman Empire, 1720–1829," *International Journal of Middle East Studies* 29: 403–25.

Rabo, A. 2005. *A Shop of One's Own: Independence and Reputation Among Traders in Aleppo*. London: Tauris.

Reinhart, A. K. 1995. “Haram,” in J. Esposito (ed.), *The Oxford Encyclopedia of the Modern Islamic World*. New York: Oxford University Press, p. 101.

Rigby, P. 1983. “Time and Historical Consciousness: The Case of Ilparakuyo Maasai,” *Comparative Studies in Society and History* 25: 428–56.

Rigby, P. 1995. “Time and Historical Consciousness: The Case of Ilparakuyo Maasai,” in D. O. Hughes and T. R. Trauttmann (eds), *Time: Histories and Ethnologies, The Comparative Studies in Society and History Book Series*. Ann Arbor: The University of Michigan Press, pp. 201–41.

Robbins, J. 2007. “Continuity Thinking and the Problem of Christian Culture: Belief, Time, and the Anthropology of Christianity,” *Current Anthropology* 48: 3–38.

Rocher, L. 2004. “Concepts of Time in Classical India,” in R. M. Rosen (ed.), *Time and Temporality in the Ancient World*. Philadelphia: University of Pennsylvania Museum of Archeology and Anthropology, pp. 91–110.

Rosen, R. M. (ed.) 2004. *Time and Temporality in the Ancient World*. Philadelphia: University of Pennsylvania Museum of Archeology and Anthropology.

Rosengren, W. R. and S. DeVault. 1963. “The Sociology of Time and Space in an Obstetrical Hospital,” in E. Freidson (ed.), *The Hospital in Modern Society*. New York: Free Press, pp. 266–92.

Rostovtzeff, M. I. 1966. *Social and Economic History of the Roman Empire*. Oxford: Clarendon Press.

Rubin, U. 1982. “The Great Pilgrimage of Muhammad: Some Notes on Sura IX,” *Journal of Semitic Studies* 27: 241–60.

Ruel, M. 1982. “Christians as Believers,” in J. Davis (ed.), *Religious Organization and Religious Experience*. London. New York: Academic Press, pp. 9 -31.

Salzman, M. R. 1990. *On Roman Time: The Codex-Calendar of 354 and the Rhythms of Urban Life in Late Antiquity*. Berkeley: University of California Press.

Salzman, M. R. 2004. “Pagan and Christian Notions of the Week in the 4th Century CE Western Roman Empire,” in R. M. Rosen (ed.), *Time and Temporality in the Ancient World*. Philadelphia: University of Pennsylvania Museum of Archeology and Anthropology, pp. 185–211.

Sciama, L. 1993. “The Problem of Privacy in Mediterranean Anthropology,” in S. Ardener (ed.), *Women and Space: Ground Rules and Social Maps*. Oxford/Providence: Berg, pp. 87–111.

Selby, H. A. 1974. *Zapotec Deviance: The Convergence of Folk and Modern Sociology*. Austin: University of Texas Press.

Smith, D. 2002. *If the World Were A Village: A Book About the World's People*. Toronto: Kids Can Press.

Sorokin, P. 1943. *Sociocultural Causality, Space, Time*. Durham, NC: Duke University Press.

Soueif, A. 2000 [1999]. *The Map of Love*. New York: Anchor Books.

Steger, M. B. 2003. *Globalization. A Very Short Introduction*. Oxford: Oxford University Press.

Stern, G. 1939. *Marriage in Early Islam*. London: Royal Asiatic Society.

Stix, G. 2006. “Introduction: Real Time,” *Scientific American, A Matter of Time (Special Edition)* 6: 2–5.

Stowasser, B. F. 2000. “A Time To Reap (1999 MESA Presidential Address),” *Middle East Studies Association Bulletin* 34.

Tambiah, S. J. 2002. *Edmund Leach: An Anthropological Life*. Cambridge: Cambridge University Press.

Thompson, E. P. 1967. "Time, Work-Discipline and Industrial Capitalism," *Past and Present* 38: 56–97.

Toda, M. 1975. "Time and the Structure of Human Cognition," in J. T. Fraser and N. Lawrence (eds), *The Study of Time II*. Berlin: Springer-Verlag, pp. 314–24.

Van Gennep, A. 1960 [1909]. *Rites of Passage*. Chicago: University of Chicago Press.

Weber, M. 1984 [1904]. *The Protestant Ethic and the Spirit of Capitalism*. London: Allen and Unwin.

Werner, L. 2006. "The Decorated Houses of Nubia," *Saudi Aramco World* 57: 2–7.

Whitehead, A. N. 1927. *Science and the Modern World*. Cambridge: Cambridge University Press.

Whitrow, G. T. 1972. *What is Time*. London: Thames & Hudson.

Whitrow, G. T. 1989. *Time in History: Views of Time from Prehistory to the Present Day*. Oxford: Oxford University Press.

Whorf, B. L. 1956. *Language, Thought and Reality*. Cambridge, MA: MIT Press.

Wilhelm, R. 1981. *The I Ching or Book of Changes*. Princeton, NJ: Princeton University Press.

Wilson, P. 1988. *The Domestication of the Human Species*. New Haven, CT: Yale University Press.

Wolf, E. R. 1951. "The Social Organization of Mecca and the Origins of Islam," *Southwestern Journal of Anthropology* 7: 329–56.

Yamamoto, M. 1975. "What Time is Not," in J. T. Fraser and N. Lawrence (eds), *The Study of Time II*. Berlin: Springer-Verlag, pp. 231–38.

Young, W. C. 1993. "The Ka'ba, Gender and the Rites of Pilgrimage," *International Journal of Middle East Studies* 25: 285–300.

Young, W. C. 1996. *The Rashaayda Bedouin: Arab Pastoralists of Eastern Sudan Case Studies in Cultural Anthropology*. Fort Worth, Texas: Harcourt Brace College Professors.

Zammit, M. R. 2002. *A Comparative Lexical Study of Qur'anic Arabic. Handbook of Oriental Studies Section One: The Near and Middle East*. Leiden, Boston, Koln: Brill.

Zerubavel, E. 1981. *Hidden Rhythms: Schedules and Calendars in Social Life*. Chicago: University of Chicago Press.

Zerubavel, E. 1985. *The Seven Day Circle: The History and Meaning of the Week*. New York: Free Press.

Zerubavel, E. 2003. *Time Maps: Collective Memory and the Social Shape of the Past*. Chicago: University of Chicago Press.

Zhang, L. 2006. "Contesting Spatial Modernity in Late-Socialist China," *Current Anthropology* 47: 461–84.

Zoepf, K. 2006. "Islamic Revival Led by Women Tests Syria's Secularism," *The New York Times*. (August 29, 2006).

Name Index

Subject Index